Union Public Library
1980 Morris Avenue
Union, N.J. 07083

P9-DBT-413

Homeschooling:

Take a Deep Breath, You Can Do This!

2nd Edition

Terrie Lynn Bittner

Mapletree Publishing Company • Silverton, Idaho

Union Public Library
1980 Morris Avenue
Union, N. J. 07083

To my family, who taught me everything I know (and how much I didn't know) about homeschooling.

Homeschooling: Take a Deep Breath, You Can Do This!

Second Edition Copyright © 2012 by Terrie Lynn Bittner

ISBN 978-1-60065-014-7
Library of Congress Control Number: 2012938289

All rights reserved. Neither this book nor any part thereof may be reproduced in any form whatsoever, whether by graphic, visual, electronic, filming, microfilming, tape recording or any other means, without the prior written permission of the Publisher except in the case of brief quotations embodied in critical articles and reviews.

Cover based on the first edition design by TLC Graphics
www.TLCGraphics.com

Mapletree Publishing, Mapletree Publishing Company, the Mapletree mark, and the Mapletree logo are trademarks of WindRiver Publishing, Inc.

10 9 8 7 6 5 4 3 2 1

Printed in the United States of America

Mapletree Publishing Company
an imprint of WindRiver Publishing, Inc.
72 N WindRiver Rd
Silverton ID 83867-0446

http://www.MapletreePublishing.com

Home a Little Longer
Teaching Your Preschooler and Kindergartner at Home
Available Now for the Amazon Kindle!
MapletreePublishing.com/Authors/Terrie_Bittner

Contents

One day, when my children were young, a new friend reported to me that my children had been talking to her children. One of mine said, "Oh, you go to public school? Well, we're sure your mother loves you anyway, and she'd homeschool you if she could."

—*Terrie Lynn Bittner*

Chapter 1

Homeschooling and the Super-Parent Syndrome

THERE ARE MANY NAMES for homeschooling, but I think the most accurate name would be *family schooling*. When homeschooling is done well, the entire family learns together. That's the reason parents don't have to know everything they're going to teach. It's the reason homeschooling builds closer families and creates better-educated children.

You don't have to be a professional teacher, a genius, or a structured person to homeschool well. Many people believe they can't homeschool because they're lacking some magical quality or skill successful homeschoolers have. But the truth is, homeschooling can be done—and done well—by most ordinary people.

Although homeschooling is wonderful, it isn't for every family. While the purpose of this book isn't to convince you to homeschool your children, the information given here may help you decide if it's right for you.

This is a book for ordinary people with ordinary concerns who just want to be sure they can do what they've decided to do and who want realistic help setting up their school and getting started. The following chapters will offer ideas, not mandates. Nonetheless, homeschooling offers the ultimate opportunity to personalize your child's education, and only you can really decide how it should be done.

You can't *major* in homeschooling. You can't become a "certified" homeschool teacher. Furthermore, being a credentialed school teacher with years of experience does not adequately prepare you to become a homeschooling parent because teaching your own child is different from teaching the children of others. The "experts" in this field are just ordinary people who taught their children successfully and now want to pass on what they have learned.

Since I wrote my first book on homeschooling in 2004, the homeschooling world has changed dramatically. Today, if your neighbors notice your children don't get on the big yellow bus, they presume you homeschool. If you tell them you homeschool, they don't ask what it is or if it's legal. Everyone knows about homeschooling and everyone knows people who do it. There are homeschool groups in every city, and the Internet is filled with useful information to help you. It's an exciting time to be homeschooling, but it's also a challenging time. With so much information available, it can be hard to know where to start.

Who are you and why are you telling me how to homeschool?

I'm a retired homeschooling mom and freelance writer. I was educated in public schools, but would have been homeschooled if I'd known it existed. However, I had a head start in understanding the power of learning in the home because my parents were what we today call *afterschoolers*.

Every day I went to school, alternating between boredom and frustration. I remember very little of what I learned in most of my classes except for those years I had truly astounding teachers. When I came home, I did my real learning. My parents filled our days with books, field trips, long conversations most people thought we were too young to understand, and service. We worked in campaign headquarters, circulated petitions, read books by the thousands, and talked . . . and talked . . . and talked. I remember nearly everything I learned at home.

My mother taught me to read as I curled up in her lap, and I taught mine to read the same way. I tried to duplicate the learning environment I had enjoyed as a child, but didn't think of myself as homeschooling—I was just parenting. It took many years of formal homeschooling before I understood that homeschooling is parenting at its most exciting level.

I played school with my oldest daughter because we couldn't afford preschool and we were both bored during a long snowy winter. At some point, what was an occasional game became a natural part of her day. I later preschooled her siblings, even though they went to preschool a few hours a week. When the children went off to school, I supplemented their educations at home. But homeschooling? I could never manage that.

I started my homeschooling career with lots of challenges standing in my path. I had several learning disabilities that had made school difficult for me. I wasn't organized. I loved to start things but tended not to finish them. I had a tremendously busy schedule, including a new writing career that was just beginning to see success. I thought those things would keep me from being able to do what I set out to do. What I learned was very little keeps a parent from homeschooling if she really wants to.

My children also had some learning disabilities, and when we talked about them, I made it clear they could do everything everyone else could do—they just might have to do it differently. I discovered this was true about everything that's hard, whether it stems from disabilities, personalities, or skills. It was certainly true of homeschooling.

The great thing about homeschooling is there's no specific way people are supposed to do it. Every family finds its own path and follows it, taking alternate routes and scenic side-tracks as it suits the family's needs. Whatever our talents or lack of talents, we can find a path that works for us.

When I wrote my first book, homeschooling was winding down in our home. Today, all my children are grown. Of the three, two are currently in college (yes, homeschoolers can go to college) and two are married (yes, homeschoolers get socialized and even marry). What you'll find in this book is a combination of what I did and what I wish I'd done—and a healthy dose of confessions about my big mistakes. I have the advantage of hindsight this time around. When we're busy homeschooling, we don't really know the long-term results of our choices. Today, I'm seeing them in action and can give you a little more perspective on the advice I'm offering.

One of my early frustrations with the homeschooling books I read when I started was the authors never confessed to getting anything wrong. I want you to know we all make mistakes—and our children turn out fine despite them. With all the mistakes I made, my children are intelligent, well-educated, and well-adjusted adults. I hope seeing that my mistakes weren't fatal will give you the confidence to accept your own mistakes.

What will this book teach me?
When I first started homeschooling, most homeschooling books were "rah-rah" books or "Harvard at Twelve" books. They usually insisted that homeschooling was easy, that anyone could do it with little or no effort, and that it always produced geniuses and perfect children. Maybe this was because the only people who could write homeschooling books were parents; and at a time when homeschooling was ridiculed, looked at as a subversive activity, or at best

questionable legally, those parents who chose to homeschool were cautious. They constantly had to defend their choice. It was risky to admit everything hadn't gone perfectly; it could mean the legal end of their homeschool if their admissions were used against them by a truancy officer.

Today, there is a growing group of parents who, like me, have "retired" from homeschooling. Their children are grown and they have nothing to lose by being honest. Homeschooling itself has enough success stories to make truthfulness less dangerous. That's why this book is not going to tell you homeschooling is always wonderful and perfect. As you'll see, there are days when you will hate your job and your kids would rather go to public school seven days a week than spend one more day with a tired and frazzled mother. But there will also be exciting days when none of you can imagine any other life and, over time, there will be more of those than of the other kind. It will never be perfect, but someday it will be natural and generally fun.

This book will not teach you how to get your child into Harvard at the age of twelve. Some homeschoolers are ahead of their peers because their education has been tailored to their needs and abilities and they have been able to progress as rapidly as they are capable of progressing. Homeschooling is efficient because the education is personalized. This means your children can be ahead of their peers, but it might also mean they just won't fall behind. Not all homeschoolers are advanced or even on schedule. It might mean a child with serious special needs will make more progress than he might have as a student in a large, diverse class, but he may still never catch up. Homeschooling can guarantee your child will learn as much as he can learn and as much as he is willing to learn, but it can't make him a genius or push him further than he chooses to go. No educational system can do that. It's okay for homeschoolers to be average or even behind.

Instead, this book will show you some of the ways home-schooling can work. We will explore the subjects children study and think about the ways they can be taught. We'll discuss lesson planning, problem solving, and scheduling. This book is just a starting place for your ideas. My methods aren't the only ones and may not be the best for you; however, they may spark ideas of your own or give you a method to start with. Most of us change our homeschooling methods regularly.

The additional resources at the end of each chapter will give you a few places to seek ideas and show you the range of possibilities. I don't necessarily agree with each resource, but I do find them interesting. Please keep in mind that Internet resources often change or disappear, so approach them with caution, although I've tried to select pages I suspect will stay online for a very long time.

Homeschooling isn't just about your children, however—it's also about you, the teacher. Teaching is hard work, whether you teach one child or forty, and your own needs must be addressed. We will spend time talking about you too. What are your fears about homeschooling? How can you overcome your own inadequacies in math and writing so you can teach these skills to your children? How can you take care of yourself when you're so busy? What will you do on the days you can't possibly teach?

Homeschooling is also about other people. As much as we'd sometimes love to conduct our school on a deserted island with no outside pressures, our world is filled with friends and relatives, and even spouses, who aren't too sure about this brilliant idea you've come up with. We'll talk about how to get them on our side, and what to do if we can't.

Over the years, as I've written about homeschooling on the

Internet and in print, I've received hundreds of e-mails from parents who homeschool, parents who are thinking about homeschooling, and parents who are worried because their spouse wants to homeschool. I've become aware of the range of concerns and hurdles these parents face as they take on an intense new way of life. I've tried to address these concerns in the chapters of this book. I've attempted to be as honest as I can, because I longed for someone to tell me the truth when I started out.

There are hundreds of books out there for Supermom and Superdad homeschoolers—this is a book for everyone else.

Chapter 2

Overcoming Your Lack of Self-Confidence

I NEVER INTENDED TO become a homeschooler. I'd met one once, but thought it was just another odd local custom. I had no idea homeschooling was being done all over, nor that it was legal where we now lived. My children started their educational careers in the local public school. However, I had been teaching them to read, write, and calculate at home during the preschool years, and I continued to supplement their schooling.

After a few years, school was no longer working for us. We tried changing schools, but that didn't help. Finally, when it seemed we were out of options, I read about the school district's new homeschooling program. The district provided the books and a teacher to oversee the work. Parents built the lesson plans and carried them out. Could I do it?

I felt inadequate. I didn't believe in myself. I tend to shy away from anything too hard; and this, I knew, would be hard. I didn't have credentials or even have a degree. I failed algebra three times. I had attention deficit disorder and learning disabilities. I could think of hundreds of reasons I shouldn't homeschool.

I was afraid, but I was also desperate to help my children. I started out homeschooling just the oldest. After a semester in the school district program, I learned that homeschooling without the district program was legal, so we decided to go solo. But I was still scared.

In retrospect, my fears seem ridiculous. Yes, homeschooling turned out to be the hardest and scariest thing I had ever done. Sometimes it gave me nightmares and sometimes it made me cry. Sometimes I made huge mistakes.

But I soon found we were having experiences that made me think maybe—just maybe—this was a good idea after all.

For instance, how many public school kids can say they had lunch with Thomas Edison? One day, we attended a presentation by an Edison scholar who portrayed the inventor. When we stopped at a fast food restaurant for lunch, he was there too, still in costume, and he joined us. We learned Edison had also been a homeschooler and had been learning disabled and gifted, just like my daughter. For the first time, because of "Thomas Edison's" encouragement, she was really proud of who she was and what she was accomplishing. As she bubbled over with excitement about her day, and then worked a little harder at her math, I stepped back and looked at our progress as objectively as possible.

My daughter was learning and having fun. The stress of her school days was a nearly forgotten memory. More importantly, she was rediscovering the thrill of learning. We'd certainly had our share of bad days and our personalities often clashed, but we were managing.

Over the years, I have become more familiar with the worries those of us who are timid have about homeschooling. If we take the time to identify our fears, we can overcome them and build our confidence. Following are some of the primary causes of insecurity in potential or new homeschoolers.

I'm not smart enough!

Homeschooling parents do not need to be overly smart or even well-educated to teach their children. They don't even need to be educated as teachers. Many public school teachers say the majority of their training is in discipline or multiculturalism, not education, and many teach outside their majors. Many of them also teach without a credential, although that's less common today. While it's probably best to be reasonably literate, you can teach your child even if you have no idea how to multiply fractions or use a microscope. So how do you teach what you don't know? You learn, or invite someone over who has the knowledge you lack.

For example, if you don't know how to use your new microscope, read the directions and figure it out. Better yet, let your children read the directions and figure it out for you. Or invite someone over who *does* know how to use a microscope and have them show you how.

Few of us remember much of what we learned in school. However, our counterparts employed by the public schools don't remember what they learned, either. Many professional teachers have scrambled to find a literary analysis of Shakespeare before they could teach it to their students, possibly because they were history majors who found themselves assigned to an English class. No one knows everything.

What happens when your child needs to know about the life of George Washington? There are a couple of possibilities. The first is you could go to the library, find some books on Washington, and spend your evenings reading about him so you could tell your child everything you've learned. This is how it usually works in traditional schools.

The other possibility is you could go to the library *with* your child and choose books about Washington. You could read them together, perhaps find a video on the man, and search out a few websites. By the end of the lesson, you and your child have both become better educated and your child has learned an essential life lesson: learning never ends. You've done it without a teacher and you've even proved that learning can be a fun way for two people to spend an afternoon. Can you think of a better lesson to teach your child? Your child might forget the facts he learns about Washington that day, but he will remember how to find the information when he needs it again and he will have discovered that learning is fun.

Stop worrying about what you don't know. If you and your child spend a few hours struggling over three different math books and a Web page until you both understand how to multiply fractions, you can count it as the best of quality time. My children still talk about some of those days, especially the times they were the ones who figured it out and explained it to me. They didn't think less of me because I didn't already know. They did, however, think more of themselves for discovering their own answers.

Intelligence isn't a factor in homeschooling and neither is knowledge. Are you willing to work hard? Then you are smart enough to homeschool. When the twelve or more years of homeschooling are over, you will know thousands of things you never knew before, including some things you wish you didn't know. Homeschooling is for parents too.

I have attention deficit disorder (ADD)

After the vision of the perfect homeschool (a vision in which my child would rush out of her room two hours early pleading to get started) faded away and reality set in, I worried I would fail at homeschooling because I have ADD. I was certain I would forget to hold school, or at the very least, forget to plan anything to teach. I would lose the materials, forget what 6 x 4 equals, and never keep track of the school records. I would get restless and bored and decide not to have school.

The truth? Sometimes I did do those things, but only

sometimes. I love to teach and I love learning. School was important to me, so I worked hard. I was determined to be good at this. Each summer, I devoted myself to planning and learning. I haunted school supply stores, memorized the location of every useful library book, and searched out used book sources. I even convinced NASA to send me a huge box of expensive materials usually reserved for schools. The more *stuff* I filled my closets with, the more secure I felt. *Stuff*, as those of us with ADD know, is a security blanket. We are collectors, clutterers, and mess-makers and so we need as much *stuff* as we can get our hands on.

This very compulsion to collect and over-collect actually works in our favor. It takes an amazing amount of *stuff* to make a good homeschooling program. The craft book says you'll need purple yarn, pipe cleaners, a pinecone, and a baby rattle. We have all of that tucked away somewhere—if we can remember where we put it.

We have the *stuff* we need and we'll hold school every day (well, okay, most days) because we love our kids and want them to be smart. We'll succeed because ADD moms make the very best lesson planners. Why? Because we can't sit still. We get restless, wiggly, and bored if things don't keep happening. For our own benefit, we plan lessons that have lots of action in them. We keep our kids moving around. At our house, we didn't sit quietly and label body parts in a worksheet. We traced the children's bodies and made life-size paper dolls and even life-size wardrobes for them. Then we made life-size models of our internal organs. Every few days, we learned about a new organ and glued it onto our dolls. This is the kind of teaching you do when you can't sit still. It's good teaching because it's hands-on, active, and loaded with sensory stimulation. Our children have fun in our schools.

Of course, we do have to cope with record keeping, schedules, and lesson plans. These are hard for us. But if you have lots of *stuff* and you've spent some time thinking about what to teach, most days you will be able to come up with something to do. You'll think of ways to keep track of the records, or you'll put someone else in charge that will do it for you. We'll work on that later. For now, put your overactive imagination to work and envision yourself having fun.

The public schools are better at this

You'll hear again and again that you need a teaching degree to homeschool properly and that reading and math are too hard for mere parents to teach. You will be told horror stories about homeschoolers who were failures and you will be subjected to fond tales of how wonderful school was for your detractor and her children. If you intend to make it past the first month of homeschooling, you will have to deal with this in your own heart, and arm yourself with knowledge. We'll learn how to explain your choice to others in a later chapter. For now, you need to be able to explain it to yourself.

The best explanation I've ever heard for this problem comes from Veronica Ugulano, a gifted and insightful homeschooling mother who has a very popular homeschooling website.[†]

"We are so conditioned to believe that 'the sun rises, the sun sets, and little kids go to public school.' A lot of it is not 'What Will Happen?' but the fear that public school has something we cannot offer. I think most people who contemplate homeschooling (except for the ones that have had to really wrestle with a school) believe that learning is a gradual, smoothly steady thing, that The Day Runs Smoothly in school."

Try to remember your own school days. You had some

---

† See Pontiac High School, http://homeschool.priswell.com/index.htm.

wonderful teachers and some delightful experiences. However, if you look back honestly, you will remember every day did not happen the way the teacher dreamed it would. There were sick children, playground fights, and outbursts of silliness. Some teachers were wonderful, some were awful, but most were average.

Did every child in your class learn? Did every child learn every minute of every day? Were your teachers unfailingly kind and cheerful? Of course not. Teachers are human, and kids have agency and varying abilities. I remember a terrific year when my daughter had a wonderfully gifted and wise teacher. I heard a few parents complain that she yelled at the children sometimes. I asked my daughter, who looked surprised and said, "It's not mean yelling; it's Mommy yelling. You know, when she says our classroom looks like a pigsty or we're all being fidgety-widgets. It's really funny. We like it." I was puzzled, but realized eventually that my daughter and her classmates understood their teacher loved and respected them. She treated them like her own children. They didn't expect perfection from their teacher, and our children don't expect it from us.

Professional teachers don't teach better than you do. The reason for this is one my daughter understood at the age of six: The best teaching is the teaching that results from love between teacher and student. You can give that love, and you can give it far better than the most loving of schoolteachers. Whatever failings you might have will be overcome by that love. The public schools can't do that better, so don't be afraid.

My schedule is already full—I don't have time!
This is a hard one. Stop and think for a moment, though, about what makes your schedule full. You have housework, chauffeuring, cooking, and . . . kids. Your children are the

main reason you are so busy. Now think about how they keep you busy and take note of everything that could be counted as schoolwork. If your children are currently in a public or private school, think about the things you will no longer have to do. Imagine life without PTA, getting to and from school, homework, selling candy bars, and the many other tasks required of a school child and his or her parents. Aha! You've found a few hours.

Your everyday life is full of education; you just haven't noticed it yet. Think for a moment about baking cookies. (This is a stereotyped homeschooling example, but it is also a very common homeschool experience.) What do children learn when they bake cookies? They have to read the recipe. That takes care of some language arts. They have to learn to read fractions and other measurements. They have to measure. If you make a double or triple batch, which you will in order to increase the learning and the cookies, they have to add or multiply fractions. They learn firsthand what one teaspoon or one tablespoon looks like. They haven't wasted dull hours at a worksheet, but they've learned math and reading. As an added bonus, they get to eat the cookies. (So do you!) What more can you ask of an educational experience?

Now, let's think about the laundry. More measuring of course, but laundry also involves sorting. Put your preschooler to work sorting socks and you have a pre-reading or pre-math lesson. You read to your children every day. You've always done it and called it good parenting. What will you call it now? You will call it language arts. And room cleaning? Home Economics.

In other words, you've been homeschooling all along. You only need the right vocabulary to describe what you are doing. All those educational activities can be listed on your time sheets as school because they do these things in school. Your formal school day might only be three hours while your children are young. By the time they need more hours than that, they will be expert learners, and they won't need much help.

You will still need to adjust your day. You can't put something into your day until you take something out. When I decided to become a writer while parenting three children— two of whom were preschoolers—I was sure there wasn't enough time. Only two things were even partly optional in my day and one was eliminated completely; the other was shortened. To become a writer I gave up television, but I didn't watch much anyway, so it wasn't enough. I decided to wake up a little earlier each morning and write before the children were awake.

Don't give up so much, however, that you lose yourself. We'll talk about that later. But for now, make sure you continue to reserve a little time for yourself and your spouse each day. You can't afford to lose that. Instead, look for meaningless moments to sacrifice. Simplify your life a bit. My friend Laura Betts only does one extra thing each day, and that allows her to stay sane no matter how busy her life is. I'm sure it takes juggling, but her life seems very balanced.

Make your children do housework. Delegation is an essential part of making time. Everyone works. In my house, there were no exceptions (except for the cat, and if I could have figured out how to make her do her share, I surely would have).

You are smart, creative, and determined. You will find the time. We always do when it really matters. You can't do everything, but you can do enough. If you don't know yet where the time is coming from, just start and figure it out later, as I did when I started writing this book. As I gradually increased the amount of time I spent on it, certain things didn't get done. I learned which of those things didn't really need to be done, and then I had the time.

What else?

I haven't begun to cover all the things you are probably afraid of, and many of them may be so vague that you can't define them except as a tightening in your heart and a queasy feeling in your stomach. What I have tried to show here is whatever your fears, everything will be okay. You don't have to know all the answers today. It's enough to want to homeschool and to love your children. Just begin. Work out the challenges as they arise. Deal with your fears one day at a time and with the understanding that you aren't expected to be perfect.

Surround yourself with people who help you believe in yourself. When you are afraid, present yourself to them for a dose of confidence and love. It's okay to say, "I'm scared." "I think I'm doing a terrible job." "I think this is too much for me." But it's only okay if you take those insecurities to the right person. Whether it's a spouse, a treasured friend, or a public school teacher who supports homeschooling, the person must be someone who cares about you and wants you to succeed. Choose your support network cautiously, then put it to work for you.

Finally, reach deep inside yourself. Find in your heart the reservoir of faith, courage, and self-confidence you may have forgotten you have. As you homeschool, write down all the things that go well—even if they are little and seemingly unimportant. Review them weekly, daily, or even hourly if you need to. Give yourself permission to brag a little, to say, "Hey, I did a good job today! We learned and we had fun. I can do this!"

You really *can* do this.

More Resources

➤ Attention Deficit Disorder Association
ADD.org
This organization began in 1989, primarily to serve adults and teens with ADD and ADHD. The site is extensive and includes interviews with professionals, lists of resources, and success stories.

➤ "You Can't Scare Me," by Debbie Harbeson
IHEN.org/content/articles/harbeson_021001.htm
Debbie Harbeson, a homeschooling mom, explains what she was afraid of when she started homeschooling and how she changed her way of thinking about her challenges.

➤ *So You're Thinking About Homeschooling: Fifteen Families Show How You Can Do It* by Lisa Whelchel
ISBN: 1590520858
Whelchel, a former child star, is homeschooling her three children. In this book, she introduces fifteen homeschooling families who use a variety of methods and who are not all perfect. Visit her website at LisaWhelchel.com for a preview of the book and some very good information about homeschooling.

➤ *Left Back: A Century of Battles Over School Reform* by Diane Ravitch
ISBN: 0743203267
An educational historian evaluates the various reforms schools have tested over the past one hundred years and analyzes what works and what doesn't. Are the schools really better at education than we are?

Chapter 3

Convincing Your Spouse, Grandparents, Kids, and Other Concerned People

TOO MANY HOMESCHOOLING BOOKS and websites share tales of a warm, supportive spouse who embraces homeschooling with all his heart. You'll hear of proud grandparents who brag about their homeschooled grandchildren. The writer will assure you her friends consider her the perfect parent. Within minutes, you will decide your marriage is in trouble and your parents and friends hate you. It seems like the entire homeschooling world, except for you, has a supportive network of family and friends.

Push for more information when you hear these stories. Ask them how it was at first when they announced their crazy decision to homeschool. Did everyone rush in with help and support, or did some people hesitate, or even loudly rebel? Of course, the speaker may not be honest, especially if the rebellious person is sitting there listening; but you might get a refreshing earful. Chances are the homeschooler's warm supportive network initially fretted or argued. The acceptance came later, when the children really were learning, or even when Mom started making money with her homeschooling books and lecture tours!

Today, most people know someone who homeschools. It's easier than it used to be simply because it's so common. Imagine the reaction when I announced homeschooling in 1992. There weren't all that many homeschoolers then. I'd only met one my entire life and I couldn't run to the Internet to find more of them. Most people said, "You're going to do *what*?" This was followed by questions of legality and even of my sanity.

Today, most people know about homeschooling, but they've also heard all the arguments on both sides. They've had more practice questioning your sanity. They all know the "S" word (socialization), which is asked about so often you'd think the government ran playgrounds instead of schools. So, one way or another, many who choose homeschooling are going to be challenged—but the most frightening, stressful, and hurtful challenges come from those you love, simply because their opinions are so important to you.

Convincing the nonteaching parent

When I started writing about homeschooling, I heard from many women who wanted to homeschool but whose husbands didn't feel comfortable with the idea. Today, I sometimes hear from men who want to homeschool but whose wives don't want them to. There are stay-at-home dads or dads who work from home or have family-friendly work schedules, and some of these men would love to teach their own children. Just to simplify the pronoun problem, I'm going to use an imaginary mother, not because fathers don't do this, but because it's still more common, even today, to find women doing most of the teaching.

Our imaginary mother is frustrated with her children's education. She has a few homeschooling friends and their lifestyle looks sort of fun. She starts reading about homeschooling on the Internet and it still looks sort of fun. Now all she has to do is approach her husband about it. Often, she doesn't anticipate problems simply because she doesn't realize he's had less exposure to the homeschooling movement than she has, and because she doesn't realize she's catching him off-guard.

First, the husband insists he doesn't want his wife to homeschool. Second, arguing, discussing, or other methods of resolution take place and the husband reluctantly agrees to a trial period. Third, the husband suspiciously watches the entire process, looking for signs of trouble. Fourth, people who hear what his family is doing start telling him good things about homeschooling or mention how much better behaved his children are now. Fifth, he thinks this isn't so bad after all. Sixth, he completely annoys his wife by acting like it was all his idea and by taking all the credit for the wonderful results she has produced! And yes, these days it seems to work the same way when it's the husband initiating the homeschooling request.

Later, you can be annoyed with your spouse for acting like he or she invented homeschooling; for now, you just want approval for your plan. How do you change a stubborn spouse's mind? You begin by figuring out what his or her objections are. The majority of parents who want me to talk their spouses out of homeschooling include three reasons for their objections:

#1   My spouse will have to give up his or her paid job
Parents are very worried about finances. This is natural. There are parents that work outside the home and homeschool their children. Usually they hire tutors, or give the lessons to the babysitter to teach, because someone needs to be with the children. By traditional definition (and by legal definition in some states), this is tutoring, not homeschooling, unless the tutor or sitter is a family member. Many states

have different rules for tutors than they do for parents. Be sure to find out who your state allows to homeschool your children. Some states allow someone else to oversee the work if the parent is still listed as being in charge and responsible for the results.

Homeschooling is usually done by a family member. Some grandparents do the homeschooling. Other parents take their children to work with them, especially if they own their own business and homeschool while they work. Some parents work at home and homeschool at the same time, often making the business part of the homeschool experience.

Traditional homeschooling, however, is done by a mother who is at home and less often by a father who is at home. (I realize it is not politically correct to treat the mother as the traditional at-home parent, but it is factual. In all my years of homeschooling, I have only met a few homeschooling fathers, but you will get to meet one later in the book.) The mother might work part-time and do the homeschooling when she is home. This is very challenging unless the parent buys a complete curriculum since there's little time for preparation in this arrangement. I tried this, unsuccessfully, but many do it quite well. Other parents work opposing shifts and take turns doing the homeschooling. Some parents run their own business from home and juggle effectively. More commonly, one parent gives up paid employment and stays at home. This is the simplest form of homeschooling and the most flexible for personalized teaching. It's also the hardest choice for spouses to accept because it means even more than the usual dramatic changes in lifestyle.

Before deciding to leave your employment, you need to make plans. You have to figure out how much money you currently spend and what you spend it on. Do this by putting an envelope in your purse or wallet and tossing all your receipts into it for a full month. Keep a small notepad and a pen with you as well. If you don't get a receipt, jot down the expense, including the date, the amount spent, and the item purchased. At the end of the month, add up your total expenses as well as your normal bills. Now create some charts that show you where the money went. Many software programs will do this for you. Once you know how you currently spend money, you can evaluate how to reduce the budget.

Remember, if you're not going to work every day, you will reduce some costs. You won't need childcare and you won't need to eat out as often. Your wardrobe will not need to be as extensive (sorry!). If the children are already in school, their expenses will also be reduced when you eliminate school wardrobes, PTA, fundraisers, expensive supplies, and school lunches.

When you've reduced your expenses as far as possible, take the plan to your spouse. Even if you haven't eliminated everything you paid for with your salary, you can show him what you have eliminated can make a significant difference. Together, the two of you can work out the other cuts.

Finally, prepare a list of benefits that will result from your return home. Paint a charming picture of home cooked meals, evenings without homework or paperwork, and children who have not been learning dirty jokes in daycare. Don't go overboard—you don't want to have to live up to a complicated fantasy—but share your vision of the future. If you know some nice homeschoolers, hold them up as examples. Make homeschooling sound so good your spouse will consider it more important than your income. (Okay, at least make it sound acceptable enough to take the risk.)

You may, once you are settled in, find ways to supplement your income. I did some freelance writing while I was a homeschooling mom. Many homeschool families run businesses from home. The business is often part of the curriculum, since children will learn small business administration from helping out. Just don't start the homeschool and the business the same day. You need time to settle into one before adding the other.

The challenges of income loss are likely to become your greatest trial. Work out the issues completely before beginning so money doesn't become a source of conflict later on. You may want to leave your job several months before you begin homeschooling to make sure you can survive before you've taken the children from school. You can also stop using the money you earn except for the expenses directly related to your employment. This money can be used to fund start-up costs for your homeschool or to build a safety-net.

#2   You aren't smart enough
This is the worst accusation to overcome because it hurts, especially if it comes from a spouse. It's important to realize that when one spouse says the other isn't smart enough, that person is usually referring to the amount of knowledge he or she thinks it takes to homeschool. People often confuse knowledge and intelligence. Chances are, the spouse doesn't think he or she knows enough, either. We talked about this issue in the previous chapter, but the pain is greater when our spouse is reinforcing the fear. He or she may ask you to explain how you plan to teach the children to read, how you will handle algebra (even if the children are only in preschool today), and how you will handle any disabilities. Your spouse probably believes you need special training to teach your children.

There are several solutions to this issue. Your choice depends on how you plan to homeschool, how determined your spouse is to believe you aren't qualified, and how confident you feel. You probably don't know yet how you plan to homeschool, so read through the ideas below and keep them in mind as you continue to prepare.

One solution is to use a prepared curriculum. These can be expensive, anywhere from two hundred dollars to a thousand dollars per child per year, so they aren't for everyone. The materials are often designed to be used directly from the box (causing them to be referred to as school-in-a-box) and come with complete instructions, so you don't have to know how to teach anything. Many homeschooling parents use them the first year of teaching while they are gaining confidence. Others use them throughout their homeschooling career. Some programs allow you to buy individual materials or subjects and others require you to buy a complete curricula. These usually have everything you need in order to teach (except for basic supplies such as crayons and paper). Today, many of these programs are online. Chapter 10 discusses curricula in more detail.

Another solution is to take your spouse to the school supply store. These are also called teacher supply stores and they are likely to become your favorite haunts when your children are young. In these little shops, you will find all sorts of workbooks, teaching supplies, and guidebooks. They're wonderful. If your spouse thinks you can't teach math, point out all the books there are to choose from. Show off the thematic unit books that contain worksheets, experiments, and information. Go to the library and explore the nonfiction materials available for children. Your spouse will be reassured you have access to information created by "experts." Later, as you make your own materials, you can gradually mingle them with these prepared items.

Finally, if your spouse is still concerned, go to a university and pick up a few teaching books. These books show you how public school teachers teach various subjects, and although some of the ideas have to be adapted, I have found them to be very helpful in areas I know little about.

If you know a public school teacher, ask her if she would be willing to advise you when you are insecure or uncertain. Before approaching her, be sure she is supportive of homeschooling. Surprisingly, many teachers are because they know better than any of us the limitations of public schools. Even if you don't have a friend who teaches, you may be able to approach someone in your church or neighborhood. If you had good relationships with any of your child's former teachers, they may be willing to help as well. Many former teachers become homeschoolers, and you may find some in your support group. Tell them you have chosen to teach your child at home, but you are a little nervous. You trust their wisdom and have been impressed by their teaching skills and would like to be able to call on them for ideas. Teachers, like anyone else, like to be treated as experts. You can make a fair trade by offering to help them with something, such as grading papers. When you teach your children to make cookies, send a plate to your mentor. I had two teachers helping me and they were both comforting and enlightening.

If your spouse isn't strongly involved in parenting, he or she may not even realize how much teaching goes on every day in your home. Point out all the things you have already taught your children. Teaching reading is no harder than teaching toilet training, the love of books, table manners, or shoe tying. If your children have learned their colors and shapes, you have even taught academics. If you have school-age children and help with homework, you're already homeschooling.

As the two of you discuss homeschooling, you'll be able to show what you're doing to research and plan. Enlist his or her help in putting together your school. When both parents participate in the educations of their children, they feel more secure that good things are happening in their home. Encourage your spouse to take over a part of the schooling, focusing in on a favorite subject or skill.

Remember, your hardest job isn't teaching your children, it's parenting them. If you have done a good job of parenting, teaching is already a part of your day. Any good parent is naturally a good teacher.

#3   How are you going to keep up with the housework?
You might be wondering that yourself, of course. Will your family continue to have a pleasant home, good meals, and your undivided attention on a regular basis; or will you spend all your time homeschooling to the neglect of everything else? Those of us who tend to get obsessed with things know there is a real possibility we will find planning lessons more fun than doing dishes. Once again, this requires a plan. If you are not used to planning so many things, consider it part of your training process for homeschooling. There are so many plans to be made at first, but by the time you get to the educational ones, you will have a lot of experience and many of the things you have to plan will already be done.

Chapter 6 discusses household management, so we don't want to go into detail here. This chapter is about talking people into things. For now, take inventory of what has to be done and who does it. Decide what can be eliminated. You did this when you were trying to decide if you had time to homeschool. If you think you have eliminated everything possible, look around your house. Consider a few options for simplifying your work. Can you sweep under the sofa less often? How often do you need to clean out cupboards, mop floors, or make beds? Revelation: Unmade beds are not a health hazard. They can be left undone if you and your spouse don't care. When choosing what to leave undone, think about the health issues first and then think about what matters most to you and your spouse. Once you've discovered your priorities, you can make changes that save time, but don't upset anyone.

This homemaking issue is actually a very tricky one. I feel homeschooling should be treated as a career for the parent doing it, just as if he or she had a job outside the home. This is particularly true for parents who create their own lesson plans. For this reason, the other parent should help more than if you were a stay-at-home parent whose children went to school all day. Don't make the process sound too easy or you'll get neither help nor sympathy, and there will be days when you need both. You'll have to find a balance that gives your spouse a little more to do, your children a lot more to do, and you less to do (but you'll be doing all the homeschooling). Emphasize that it will be very, very hard, but you are willing to make the sacrifice for the good of your children. (Say this dramatically and nobly. Practice until you can say it without giggling, because giggles ruin the effect of noble statements.)

Convincing a spouse to do the homeschooling

I have, for whatever reason, never had a woman tell me she wanted her husband to quit his job and homeschool her children. It might have happened, but none of them have ever emailed me. However, I have had a surprising number of men do this. There are men who want their children to be homeschooled, but who are married to women who would rather spend three years without chocolate than to teach their children at home. Now what? I'm going to address this section entirely to men, and if you're a woman with this goal, you'll have to mentally change the pronouns.

This is actually a much harder task than the one described previously, because you are trying to talk a woman into doing something she doesn't want to do. I'm sure, if you've been married for more than a year, you have figured out that women like to change others, but aren't fond of others changing them.

Before you ask your wife to take on this task, be certain

you know what you're asking her to do. Homeschooling is hard work. It's time-consuming. All the other mothers brag about those glorious five hours when the house is devoid of others, when they can paint masterpieces, clean house, and get all their work done in peace. They make very good use of these busy hours. If you ask your wife to homeschool, you are depriving her of those coveted five hours. If she were the sort of person who enjoyed homeschooling, she would rather be teaching during those five hours. However, if you are reading this chapter, she probably isn't.

With time, she may become that sort of person, but then again she might not. Homeschooling is not for everyone. There isn't anything wrong with not wanting to home-school. Your wife's insistence on sending the children off to school each day doesn't mean she's a bad parent. There are many jobs you consider valiant but don't want to do. Your wife may recognize the value of homeschooling but know it isn't the right life for her. She might also believe children belong in public schools. And of course, if she is employed, she may want to stay that way. If you are planning to do the teaching, you have a good reason to try to change her mind. However, if you want her to stay home and do the teaching, you will have to tread carefully and respect her decision. Homeschooling is most successful when the teaching parent adores her job.

You also must figure out why your wife isn't willing to homeschool and how important those reasons are. If she loves her job or believes in the school system, you may have to give up your dream. If she is only insecure about her skills, you have hope. There are many people in the world eager to give their opinions, but it's your opinions that matter most. What woman can resist hearing a sincere husband tell her how wonderful she is, how well she parents, and how talented and smart she is? Women long to be admired and valued by their husbands. This admiration, when offered openly and honestly, can sway a woman who is afraid. If she knows she has your support and help, she may be willing to try it out.

Work with her to make the plans described earlier in this chapter. Help her research the Internet and the bookstores for information. When I receive e-mail from a husband who is helping his wife seek materials, I know I am helping a family that will succeed because the parents are truly functioning as a team. Offer to help with some of the teaching and always step in to assist in the housework. Promise to take over the children for a few hours after work because she will be tired of them by the time you return. Homeschooling is intense and exhausting for both the teaching parent and the children, and all need a break from each other.

A trial period for both spouses

Regardless of who favors homeschooling, a trial period is an excellent way to test the lifestyle. You can find out how it affects your family and if you enjoy it. If possible, take your trial during the preschool or kindergarten years, when there are generally no laws affecting your teaching. If your children are already in school, run a summer school for two hours a day, three days a week. Although this is not an exact duplication of what you will encounter later, it's a good way to ease into teaching. The entire first year of homeschooling can be considered a trial. Even if you send your children back to school when it's over, the year at home will have given your children a break and you an extra year with them in which to share the joy of learning together.

When you are planning your trial, begin slowly. If you aren't homeschooling during the school year, you are not required to report your trial to anyone and you don't have to take standardized tests. This means you don't have to do everything you would do in a normal school. Make sure some of the activities are just for fun.

If you are teaching a preschooler, think about the educational things you already do. Perhaps you already read together, do crafts, sing songs, and go on educational trips. This is the beginning of an excellent preschool program. The only change is you will schedule a special time to do them.

A sample school day for a three-year-old might be two hours long. Initially, you may want to teach for a half hour and then work up to two or three hours, adding a half hour whenever your child seems ready. Following is a sample schedule:

9:00   Fifteen-minute lesson on the weekly or monthly theme (transportation, zoos, families, etc.). This is structured and involves listening, singing and learning.

9:15   Craft based on lesson.

9:30   Fifteen minutes of free play with educational toys set aside just for school hours, such as block building, puzzles, matching games, or flannel boards.

9:45   Science experiment.

10:00   Pre-reading activities: matching, alphabet lessons, putting pictures from a story in order.

10:15   Story time. This includes listening to books and stories, acting out stories with flannel boards, puppets, and toys, and telling or dictating original stories.

10:30   Large motor skills play: Running, jumping, skipping, etc.

11:00   Math activities: Counting, sorting, matching. These can be taught through games.

11: 15   Free play with toys meant just for school.

11:30   Music, including singing, instruments, listening and
dancing to music.

11:45   Cleanup and discussion of day.

This is a very structured preschool. You don't have to
structure to this extent, but if you are trying out homeschooling to see if you like it, or if you just enjoy playing school, you
can try various schedules until you find one that works. Kindergarten can follow a similar schedule. Don't, however, stick
to the schedule this closely. If you're having fun, go longer on
one activity and drop something else. If your child is bored,
shorten the lesson. Use the schedule as a guideline, not a
hard rule.

If you are doing a summer school program, you will have
to work a little harder to make it fun, since your children
may resent spending their summer in school. If your child
is learning disabled and behind his peers, tell him you are
going to help him catch up so school won't be so hard for
him. Promise to do something fun each day after the hard
parts are over. To ensure his cooperation, ask him to help
you choose and plan the fun lessons. What does he want to
learn about?

If he doesn't have ideas, help him brainstorm. Set out a
piece of paper and pen. Each of you can call out any ideas
that occur. Write the ideas down—even the silly ones. The
most important rule of brainstorming is anything counts,
and it counts without judgment, although you may both find
yourselves giggling. If the session gets too silly, put it off until later or stop and use the list you made before silliness set
in. Resist your parental temptation to scold for silliness. Just
tell him this is fun, but now it's time to choose. Have a list in
mind of fun topics to get the ideas flowing if necessary.

Once you've chosen your ideas, take your child with you on the first exploration trip to buy or identify materials. All learning doesn't take place through books and worksheets. Purchase crafts, games, foods, and other items that fit the theme and make it fun. Try to identify a field trip for the grand finale of your summer school. On your own, track down one spectacular learning tool and purchase it as a surprise. Drop hints to your child, but don't let him know what it is until the first day.

Summer school should be no more than two hours, officially, although you can usually sneak in extra learning during the day through normal activities. The first hour should be the academics, especially if your child is behind his peers. The second hour is the fun part, in which you study your theme for the session. Chapter 14 shows you how to build a thematic unit. Stick to one theme throughout the summer school session and choose a name for the school that relates to the theme.

As you conduct your trial session, keep a journal. Record what worked, what didn't, and what you are learning. Take special note of when you and your children are having fun and when you are not. Do you look forward to the next day?

How will I know if the trial was a success?

The first year of homeschooling is the very hardest since you are trying to learn your new job. Don't begin this trial insisting on perfection. There will be frustrating days as your children learn to think of you as a teacher, and as you learn to think of yourself that way. You aren't going to be measuring your success this first year by the usual standards. Don't decide it's time to give up because the lessons don't go the way you plan, the children don't always cooperate, or you feel overwhelmed by work. Don't decide you are failing because the children want to go back to school.

Remember, you'll get better with practice. Don't be upset when your children don't always cooperate because they are children, and few children always do as they are told. As they learn that school time is a time of increased discipline, they will improve their behavior. Your children may want to go back to school because for the first year, most children experience school sickness, which is similar to homesickness, no matter how much they hated school and how much they love homeschooling. There is a tendency to romanticize the past. Children will remember school as a series of parties and recesses and forget the tests and boredom. Change is always hard.

The benefits of continuing through the first year, even when you don't feel you are succeeding, are great. As you leave behind the unrealistic expectations you had the first year, you will gradually discover aspects of yourself you never knew existed. You will begin to get a sense of what will work and what won't. Your children will settle into a routine and usually do what is expected of them. You'll meet other homeschoolers and you will learn new techniques from them.

Watch to see if the children are learning and if you are interested in the process of becoming a teacher. Notice whether you enjoy spending so much structured time with your children. Think into the future and envision yourself doing this for a year or two. If you can, and you feel hopeful, continue. Be sure your spouse is aware of the progress you're making and of your feelings about what is happening in your home. This can be one successful way of convincing a spouse to allow homeschooling to happen.

Don't do a final evaluation until the first year is finished, and when that evaluation comes, don't ask if you are home-schooling perfectly. Ask only if you have made progress. If you have, you have done all that can be asked of you the first year. The following year, you'll begin with a better understanding of what you will face and you will do a better job. You won't ever be perfect, but you will always be improving. Don't give up too soon.

Convincing a noncustodial parent

This is a very complicated situation, and you should consult your lawyer if you suspect any level of disapproval from the other parent. Occasionally, a noncustodial parent will try to use homeschooling as a way to gain custody of a child or to "punish" the custodial parent.

If you want to homeschool and you are not married to your child's parent, it is essential that you meet with him or her to discuss this idea. Come prepared to be calm and to show how this will benefit your child. It may be wise to get an agreement in writing with the help of lawyers. This is not about your relationship with the other parent; it is entirely about the welfare of the child, so stay focused on this issue. Homeschooling is wonderful, but it is seldom worth a custody battle or damage to the child's relationship with either parent. If you can't gain approval, back away and try again later. You can give your child many of the benefits of homeschooling by afterschooling, discussed in Chapter 8. Afterschooling is enriching your child's education while he continues to attend school.

Convincing the grandparents

This is an issue homeschooling parents often gripe about. Of course, you don't need the permission of your child's grandparents to homeschool. They raised their children their own way and now it's your turn. In real life, however, grandparents often have to be convinced. Their support or disapproval can have a powerful effect on the success of your school because of the effect it has on your peace of mind, and because some grandparents sabotage your efforts through their comments to the children. Their support can help your children love their new school.

Grandparents want what is best for their grandchildren. Even more than parents, grandparents consider their grandchildren perfect. All you have to do is to show them homeschooling is the perfect school for perfect children.

How you approach the subject may depend on how the grandparents felt about their own schooling and how they felt about the educations their children received. Do they know how schools have changed over the years? The focus on high-stakes standardized testing has completely changed the ways teachers teach and children learn. Kindergarten now covers first grade materials. Express your concerns over any of these issues that bother you.

Of course, none of these issues may be of special concern for you. If your focus is elsewhere, express those feelings. Do you know what they consider important for children? Choose those factors to dwell on. Perhaps you want to emphasize the ability to spend more time with your children or to make sure they have more time to spend with extended family. Maybe you want to be able to include religion into your schooling. Perhaps you just like a different teaching style, one that is more hands-on or more self-paced. The self-paced argument is especially important if your child is ahead or behind.

When you are ready to start teaching, tell them you have found the perfect school. The class size is small, the curriculum is personally designed to meet the needs of each child, and you have complete control over what your child will learn. Doesn't that sound wonderful? Once they agree, you can tell them that the perfect school is a homeschool. Drag out all the facts you probably gathered for your spouse or yourself and share them with the grandparents.

A little flattery helps, especially if the grandparents feel they never get to spend enough time with the chil-

, dren. Homeschoolers have more time for grandparents. Even better, some grandparents get to help with the homeschooling. (As you'll learn later, some grandparents even do all the homeschooling.) If this interests you, you might say, "And you know, I've heard that grandparents are even getting involved by teaching a subject to the children. They say it really builds the grandparent/grandchild relationship. So, I was wondering if you would teach the children how to build model airplanes. And Jimmy is really interested in the war you were in, so I thought I'd send him over one day to talk to you about it. You can show him your medals again."

The nice thing about grandparents is that they want the very best for your children, and if you show them homeschooling will put their grandchildren ahead of their friends' grandchildren, and that your children will be given the best life has to offer, most aren't hard to convince.

Convincing your children
One of the deep secrets of homeschooling is that some children don't want to homeschool. Many children enjoy going to school every day. Many children who have never been to school think they want to go. Their friends are going, and they've heard about school on television and from relatives. Some children who hate school and dread it still don't want to leave their friends, or they may think homeschooling will be like homework.

People will tell you it's wrong to make your children homeschool against their will. Remember that many children are forced to go to public or private school against their will. Children have to do what their parents consider best for them. They may not like it, but there is a good possibility you didn't like all the things your parents made you do when you were young. They'll survive, just as you did.

However, you will need to decide if it's in the best interest of your child to homeschool him against his will. Begin by figuring out why he wants to go to school. The first home-schooling parent I ever met said her children wanted to go to school until they found out they weren't going to ride a bus since the school was a block away. Once their parents explained this to them, they lost interest in the whole experience. The reasons a preschooler wants to go to school may be simple and easy to resolve. If he wants a lunch box, buy him one. My children got lunch boxes and backpacks every year, and we used them on field trips or even packed lunches at home so they were ready at the end of school.

Children who are already in school worry they won't see their friends, they will miss out on parties, and they won't participate in an upcoming field trip or special day. These can easily be settled. Set up a schedule of friend visits, plan your own parties, and study the same fun subject they were going to study in school or go on the same field trip—perhaps even on the same day. Better yet, go on better field trips.

Join a homeschool group in advance and help your child make friends with other homeschoolers. He will get a chance to see that this is a perfectly normal choice many other children are making and he will start out with friends who share that lifestyle.

Homeschooling is best when it is a joint decision between parent and child, particularly if the child is being removed from school. A preschooler can just be told there are lots of places to go to school and his place will be at home. If you want your traditionally-schooled child to decide for himself to stay home, you will have to motivate him to make the choice.

Ask him to tell you about school. Take notes as he talks. When he's finished, ask him to help you place the items in lists of positive and negative things. Don't deny the existence of good in the school. Even the worst school experience probably has some redeeming moments. Be fair. Then discuss each list calmly and cheerfully. How does he think the bad things could be made better? Which list does he feel has the biggest impact on how he feels about himself and his learning? If he were in charge of the school, how would he run it?

This last question is the key. You want him to start thinking of the perfect school. Together, write his description of the ideal school. Then look the list over and tell him that some families do create their own schools right in their own homes, and that some of the things on his list could be done if you and he created a school of your very own. Explain how homeschooling works, emphasizing that he would get to help plan the school, although you would be in charge. Ask him if he would like to think about having a school just for himself. He is likely to ask if his friends can come too. Tell him they have to go to their own school, and that homeschooling is just for the family, but that he could invite his friends to join him for some of the learning he does, such as field trips or science experiments. Then suggest the two of you imagine what homeschooling could be like and make plans for what you would study and how you would learn. Together, build a plan for your school and give it a great name of his choice. You haven't asked him yet if he wants to homeschool, you've only worked together to plan an imaginary school.

When you sense excitement building, it's time to ask. However, don't ask unless he really has a choice. If he *has* to homeschool, just tell him this is what he will be doing. (There are situations where a parent is justified in taking a child out of school against his will, but these must be thought through very carefully and the child should understand the reason for your actions.)

If your child is immediately excited about homeschooling, you're settled. If he has reservations, discuss them with him honestly. If he is strongly *against* homeschooling, you may want to leave him where he is. If he has questions and you don't know the answers, say so—but promise to search for the answers. If it involves something only time will answer, be honest about that too. You don't want to start out with lies or false promises because they will damage the relationship you want to strengthen through homeschooling.

You will need to plan for this conversation. Think of subjects you can study the first semester that are especially exciting to your child and offer these throughout the conversation. (Toss them in when the conversation is slow, unless he thinks of them himself.) Also, come up with science experiments, projects, and field trips. Suggest a special lunch once a week. This is a fun way to wind up the school week and gives you a chance to discuss the week's learning with your children. Emphasize the good parts of homeschooling. Generally, elementary school children can manage with only 15 hours of school a week, spread over four or five days. Any additional hours your state might require can be filled during everyday life. This means children have more time for hobbies and family time.

If you are willing to let your child return to school someday, you might agree to a trial period. However, you may have already decided your child will not return to school under any circumstances. A child who is in middle school and not yet reading, a child who consistently skips school, or a child who is often the victim of bullies or who is a bully, may not belong in a traditional school. If you decide on a trial period, create a contract holding him to certain rules. Otherwise, you run the risk of intentional sabotage by a child determined to return to school. In these extreme situations, you may want to set conditions your child must meet before being allowed to return to school. For instance, he may have to read at a certain level, or demonstrate that he can obey family rules for six months.

Convincing friends and your own siblings

Once again, you aré dealing with people who don't really have a say, but who must be dealt with anyway. These people may also have a hidden agenda, and in fact, may not even be aware of their own motivations in challenging your choices. You will have to listen carefully to discover the true reasons for their concerns.

Naturally, some of them really do have your child's best interests at heart. They may have heard terrible things about homeschooling, or they might know the sister of the cousin of the aunt of someone who homeschools and is terrible at it. (Whenever someone tells you she knows a homeschooler who does one thing or another, ask who it is and how well she knows this person. It's often an interesting answer.) They might even adore the public schools and think every child deserves to go there. Many people have fond memories of their school days, whether the memories are accurate or glorified.

Those are the noble reasons. Unfortunately, some people have less noble reasons. I have met many people who have reluctantly or accidentally confessed they know homeschooling would be better for their child, but they just don't want to do it. There's certainly nothing wrong with that. Homeschooling is hard, and it isn't worth doing if it isn't fun. Of course, that's easy for me to say because I did choose homeschooling. Those who don't choose it, but believe they should, feel guilty.

One way some people choose to deal with guilt is by trying to convince themselves they don't really believe homeschooling is good for children. They certainly don't want their friends and relatives homeschooling because that poses a tremendous risk. If those children become smarter, better educated, or even better behaved than their own children, they will be forced to wonder if they should have homeschooled after all.

Why don't some people want to homeschool? If you understand the reasons, you can prepare sympathetic and supportive answers to their feelings. Although your detractors may not be supportive of you, you want to counter their challenges with love and support for them. It confuses them and it makes them feel guilty, but that isn't why you're going to do it. You're going to be nice in order to set a good example, to teach by love. You may have to battle with yourself to make sure that's why you are doing it, but that's why you ultimately will help your friends and family feel as good about their choice to use the public schools as you want to feel about choosing homeschooling.

How many times have you listened to parents complaining about their children being out of school? By the end of the first day of vacation, many parents are counting the days until school begins again and they get their schedules back. They complain the children are bored, they can't get anything done, and they have no free time. Many parents really value those hours and make very good use of them. It isn't necessarily selfishness, but a longing for order that makes them glad their children are gone all day. Many good parents, even those who are home all day, need that time alone and can't bear the thought of having their children with them every day.

Other parents work outside the home and can't or don't want to give up that income. The decision to homeschool is greatly complicated when income is involved and it's a decision each family must evaluate for itself.

Finally, some parents don't really enjoy parenting all that much or don't enjoy doing it all day. They have wisely recognized they are better parents when their children attend school part of most days. In addition, some children, particularly those with disabilities, are very demanding and the parent truly has to have time to rest, gather strength, and accomplish tasks that would be impossible if the child were home. There are also many children who simply enjoy school and like to be there. Generally, their parents don't suffer from feelings of guilt because of this, nor should they.

So, homeschooling isn't for everyone. For some of us, it's a great adventure and the extra time spent with our children is a blessing. For others it's not an option, and that's fine. I'm grateful there were public schools I could send my children to when I needed to do so, and I have needed to do so.

It's very important not to get into education battles with others, especially family members and friends we care about. It simply isn't worth the destruction of a relationship. If you think there is any chance you will be attacked by friends or relatives, plan your reaction in advance and rehearse it. Be prepared to listen with respect as they outline their concerns. Then say, "I appreciate your concern, and I know you offer it because you care, but I've given this a great deal of thought. I've researched it very carefully. I'm going to try it for awhile, but naturally, if it doesn't work out, I'm prepared to stop. In the meantime, I would feel so much better if you could support me in this. I will need to be able to bounce ideas off you and turn to you when I just need to talk. I want to feel you are there for me, and that you believe in me." The more loving you are, the harder it is for this person to attack you.

A loving response will not, of course, prevent all attacks. There are people who will not accept your decision, and nothing you say will change their minds. If possible, make an agreement with them to avoid this subject in order to preserve your relationship. If they will not back away, you may have to evaluate how important the relationship is and how much you're willing to accept from this person in order to be with them. You are the only person who can balance their behavior against the value of their friendship. If you choose to press onward, try not to let them affect how you see yourself or your choice.

A friend's criticism hurts, certainly, but some people really don't understand your decision and it isn't as personal as it might seem. It has less to do with you than it does with homeschooling, or even with them. Try not to let them decide who you will be or how you will behave. Treat them respectfully and kindly regardless of how they treat you. Then find a more accepting friend to turn to, someone who can make you feel good about yourself and your choices. Every homeschooling parent needs a loving circle of supporters. Choose yours soon and choose them well.

Your decision to homeschool will never please everyone

Few decisions you make in life will ever please everyone, but there are some opinions that matter. You have to respect the feelings of your spouse or of the child's other parent. Homeschooling without some level of support from this person is unfair to the child. However, you do not necessarily have to act on anyone else's opinion. Make your choice, be proud, and start teaching.

More Resources

➤ *Miserly Moms: Living on One Income in a Two-Income Economy, 4th Edition* by Jonni McCoy
ISBN: 978-0764206412
If you are leaving your job and will need to make dramatic changes to your lifestyle, try this book, highly recommended for those new to frugal lifestyles. Includes recipes, shopping tips, and even frugal cleaning.

➤ National Home Education Research Institute
NHERI.org
Founded by Brian D. Ray to provide quality research on homeschooling, this site offers statistics on the academic and social abilities of homeschooled children. A book with more information is available for purchase.

➤ *Mommy Life*
"Homeschooling—Memo to Parents"
MommyLife.net/archives/2009/01/homeschooling_-.html
An article directed at grandparents who aren't comfortable with the parents' decision to homeschool. It offers basic information about homeschooling and suggestions for being supportive. Print it out and share it with the grandparents.

➤ *Homeschoolers' Success Stories: 15 Adults and 12 Young People Share the Impact That Homeschooling Has Made on Their Lives* by Linda Dobson
Prima Lifestyles, June 2000
ISBN: 0761522557

Chapter 4

Laws and Support

BEFORE YOU DO ANYTHING else, you need to learn your state's homeschooling laws. Without this information, you won't know what you are required to teach or for how long. In some states, there are laws requiring parents to have a certain level of education—although they generally allow you to teach under supervision if you don't meet the requirements. Homeschooling laws are passed at the state level.

Find the website for a large, statewide homeschool organization in your state. These websites often tell you how the state really interprets the laws. They also usually have local contacts you can e-mail with questions about the laws. Remember that they are not generally lawyers, so you will still need to study the law yourself and decide how to obey it. (The resource list at the end of this chapter will help you find the laws for your state.)

Support groups
The resource list at the end of this chapter can also help you find a local support group. Support groups aren't essential, but they are helpful for a few months, at least, while you figure out how the law really works in your school district. When you attend your first meeting, you will generally find yourself surrounded by enthusiastic supporters who are

eager to introduce you to their passion. They can tell you how accepted homeschooling is locally and what options are open to you. They can, and many will, tell you exactly how to homeschool, but you can listen nicely and then do as you please. I respond to this type of advice by saying, "I'll keep that in mind. Thank you!"

Support groups vary dramatically. They are discussed in more detail later in this chapter. Avoid paying any fees to join a group until you have visited several and know which group meets your needs.

Official school resources

Whenever we moved, I contacted the school district to find out what they could tell me about homeschooling. The answers told me a great deal about the area. Then I called the county offices, and finally the state board of education. When you call each location, ask if they can provide you with a copy of the laws regarding homeschooling for your state. If they tell you homeschooling is illegal, you can thank them and hang up without identifying yourself. As of this writing, home-schooling is legal throughout the United States; but based on the responses you receive from your calls, you will know if your state or district is not very homeschool friendly.

It is probably easier to get this information today. When I was homeschooling, a state once had to track down the janitor to talk to me—he homeschooled his children and was the only person in the office who knew what the laws were!

Finding other homeschoolers

If you still have trouble finding homeschoolers in your area, visit your library. Homeschoolers spend a lot of time in the library, and because they are there during school hours, the librarians know who they are. Librarians have always been my best source for introductions to homeschoolers. They can tell me if there is a day the homeschoolers come to the library as a group or if a very nice homeschooler is sitting right there in the corner. They often know where the support groups are and when they meet, and some will even call a homeschooler and arrange a meeting. You and the librarian will be seeing a great deal of each other, so this is a good way to get acquainted.

Churches are another source of homeschoolers. Although homeschooling is no longer just a movement for the religious, many religious people still choose homeschooling. When we started homeschooling, we were the first in our congregation to do so; but later, whenever we moved to a new area, we found an instant support system in our church. Although you may want to seek out diversity in your children's social lives, it is sometimes nice to have a few friends who share both your personal values and your educational lifestyle.

Do I need a support group?

Some homeschoolers thrive on support groups and others hate them. It's perfectly possible to homeschool without one if you're the sort of person who doesn't really like groups. If there is more than one homeschool group in your area, visit as many as you can before choosing. If this is your first experience with support groups, you will not be sure what these groups are like and what makes you feel at home. Before attending a meeting, try to find someone to talk to or find out if the group has a website. Some groups are restrictive and you want to be sure you are welcome.

The most common support group is Christian-based. Many of these have strict rules about who is considered Christian and some ask you to sign a declaration of faith. If you are not sure your religion qualifies, ask—and be prepared to accept the answer. It's unlikely the group is open to debate. If you do qualify, you may find these groups to be a means for meeting other like-minded people and to get answers to questions about combining academics and religion.

Some religious groups are not restrictive. I periodically attended an informal group for members of my faith, but the activities were open to anyone. These groups, if they include a few members of other faiths, can provide a nice bit of diversity for your children.

Another type of restrictive support group centers on a specific method of teaching. Some groups are open only to unschoolers and others to structured learners. (See the glossary for definitions of these terms.) Some groups are closed to people who are only homeschooling temporarily or to those who use government homeschooling programs. If you try to infiltrate a group that promotes a method of homeschooling that differs from your own, you may find yourself fending off criticism instead of garnering the support you came for. Again, it's unlikely you will be able to change anyone's mind, so if you don't agree with its philosophy, find another group.

When you are beginning, you are not sure how you will homeschool over the coming years. You may start as a structured homeschooler and then move to unschooling. You may even change faiths. You and your children will form deep friendships within the group you select. If you no longer meet the criteria for the group, you may be asked to leave. This can be painful and stressful, so consider choosing a more open group for your first experience.

Inclusive support groups are generally open to everyone, regardless of faith, teaching method, or type of homeschool. Some of them even welcome afterschoolers—parents who use homeschooling techniques to supplement a traditional education. These groups have both advantages and disadvantages.

The advantage to an inclusive group is that you can be

whoever you want to be and teach however you want to teach. As you grow and change, you continue the friendships and mentorships you develop. You will have the opportunity to meet people who operate their homeschools in different ways, which allows you to learn more about your choices and to monitor how they work in real life. You and your children benefit from meeting people who live, worship, and homeschool differently than you do, and yet you all share a common foundation through your decision to homeschool.

One drawback to such groups is that despite the determination to be inclusive, many people become missionaries of a sort when they encounter those who make different choices. You may find yourself in the middle of a battle over methods. If you are not interested in debate, you can find these types of groups very tiring. Another drawback is that you may find you have less in common with those you meet, and when you are a pioneer, as homeschoolers still are, sometimes you just long to relax on common ground.

Support groups meet for different purposes, although nearly all strive to create a social meeting place for those who have chosen an unusual path. Some are almost exclusively social in nature, meeting for park days, field trips, and parties. They allow the children to meet other children who learn as they do while mothers help each other with their challenges in an informal setting. Others are more educational. These groups offer lessons for parents on the mechanics of homeschooling, and often exclude the children, or send them to a nursery run by the teenagers. Some provide classes for the children in subjects parents might find difficult to teach, and a few of these are nearly small private co-op schools. Give some thought to what you want from a group before beginning your visits. If you want a little of everything, look for a broad-based group.

Some support groups are national or statewide and others

are small and local. The larger ones tend to be more political and more expensive to join. They are usually the defenders of homeschooling freedom and are exciting for those who love politics and irritating for those who don't. Some small groups are formal, with leaders and schedules. Others are casual, and may even include weekly calls to find out "if we are doing anything this week." In these groups, leadership is unofficial. There is usually one mom who seems to plan the parties and another who likes to organize the field trips and so on. These groups are effective for parents who just want to relax with a group of friends and to provide their children with some extra social life or unusual experiences. They are less effective for parents who get frustrated when activities are cancelled, haphazardly run, or seemingly run without purpose. Informal groups are often free to join, although you may be asked to contribute supplies for activities.

If I had it to do over again, I would join a homeschool group. I am not a particularly social person and am quite content with my family and a few close friends. However, my children could have benefited from having more friends who were homeschooled. There were few homeschoolers in our day and they didn't know many people who shared their lifestyles. I probably flunked socialization. My children had plenty of church friends, and when they participated in outside lessons or volunteer work, they made friends there. However, they didn't have the range of friendships other children had. This was not a fault of homeschooling. It was entirely my own fault, for homeschooling the way I would have done it as a child rather than focusing on the way my children would want it. If you're not a joiner, decide whether your children need these associations—even if you don't.

A more recent development is the online support group. These are conducted by e-mail, chat rooms, or forums. In some respects, they are much like informal support groups in your own town because you make friends, get annoyed by certain members, and seek advice. It's surprising how well you get to know people in these groups, and some people I have met online have become very dear to me.

Online homeschooling forums seem to develop a personality over time. Some thrive on controversy and debates. Others are highly informative and focus on information sharing. Some are social get-togethers and may include chat rooms. Pay close attention to the moderator of the boards you visit. She often sets the tone by asking leading questions. She may choose to keep a close watch on her guests, insisting on a code of behavior, or she may allow discussions to flow naturally. A group that is not moderated often becomes rather heated, making visits uncomfortable for those who dislike arguments.

If you are shy or reserved, look for a group that is somewhat busy, but not extremely large. Those who are shy are easily lost in the crowds. Notice whether you are warmly greeted and if old-timers invite you to introduce yourself. Are your questions treated with respect and are members supportive and encouraging? Just as you must carefully develop your offline friendships, you must choose where you spend your time online. An invisible critic can be as damaging as one who lives next door. On the other hand, a friend who lives across the country can provide as much love and support as a nearby friend. Look for online groups that are warm, supportive, and accepting of your choices.

To find homeschooling forums, use a good search engine, such as Google. Type "homeschooling forum" into the search field. These are also referred to as message boards or even just boards. As you visit each forum, read the posts that have been made and notice the dates of the posts if dates are given. This will tell you how busy the board is. If you find one you are interested in, answer an existing question or ask a question, and then return several times to see how others react to you. Are you quickly answered? Are responders generally friendly? Do the people on the forum seem like people you would want to know if they lived in your neighborhood?

There is no organization that evaluates the legitimacy of any homeschooling forum. You must decide for yourself if the group meets your needs. Be careful about revealing personal information, since anyone can read what you post. Never give your address or telephone number on a forum. Identify your location by state, and use wisdom in deciding who to get to know on a personal basis. Don't discuss specific people or public schools by name or town, since these are public forums and you don't know who might read your words.

More Resources
➤ *A2Z Home's Cool*
A2Zhomeschooling.com
This is the ultimate in online homeschooling resources. Ann Zeise is constantly searching out the very best sites for homeschooling and those get priority on her site. There may be twenty sites that show what a letter of intent to homeschool looks like, but the one she lists is fast loading and, when available, has additional commentary to help you understand the document. She has listings for resources in every state in the United States, and for many countries as well. Check her page first when you need to find laws, support groups or advice. She also has many tools for simplifying your homeschool, and a wide variety of homeschool supplies for purchase. Start with these two pages:

- A2Zhomeschooling.com/laws

- A2Zhomeschooling.com/regional/support_groups_homeschool_worldwide

Chapter 5

Organizing Your New Life

WHEN I WAS TOLD my first homeschooling book needed organization, I had to laugh. Who would ever take organizational advice from me, the person who can't find a pencil or her other shoe? However, the powers that be insisted, and this chapter was the result. My first editor was a home organizational expert and I suspect my advice shocked her. (Organized people do not teach their children how to throw everything into a closet in the five minutes before guests are due.) She chipped in her own advice, some of which is included here. It turned out I was using my cabinet all wrong.

If you are already pretty organized, or only a little disorganized, this chapter is of no value to you. Purchase a good home organizational book and put together a normal sort of system.

If you have severe ADHD or are just severely organizationally challenged, this might help. If nothing else, when you see the methods I had to resort to, you'll feel competent by comparison. This is minimal organization for the totally hopeless. Read at your own risk and with a sense of humor. This advice has been deemed by desperate people to be helpful and by ordinary people to be bizarre.

The secret is to start out correctly at the beginning, before you have a lot of supplies. If you already have hundreds of items in need of organization, start slowly and gradually make changes as you have time.

You will be developing a very simple system that is not too difficult to maintain most days. The secret to successful homeschooling is not maintaining a perfectly organized "classroom," but to feel that your program is under control. You just have to be organized enough that you can find your supplies and feel calm in your surroundings. That level of organization will be different for each person. The method of organization is different for each person as well. What follows is merely a suggestion. Use these ideas to help you create strategies that appeal to you.

What do I need to buy?

You don't need to spend a lot of money getting organized. You probably already have some of the basics. Do not rush out and buy any of these items until you have read the entire chapter and decided what you actually need for your own circumstances:

- Four-drawer filing cabinet if you can afford it or cardboard or plastic boxes that can hold file folders if you can't. This was the most useful thing I ever bought for organizational purposes. I am a paper-collector.

- File folders (hanging and manila).

- Markers and pens.

- Notebook paper.

- Three-ring binders. You'll need a very large one for each child and a smaller one for each child if you prefer to have the current week's work in a separate notebook. You will need at least one for yourself, with the number depending on how you choose to use them.

- Plastic crates: one for each child and one for you.

- Index card boxes and index cards if you prefer not to work on a computer. (One or more boxes depending on how you use them.) These are for organizing term paper research, listing books you want to read with your children, and other brief information you might collect.

- Bookends.

- Shallow bins to hold construction paper, crayons, and other supplies.

Where do I put all this stuff?

If there is any way to manage it, consider obtaining a four-drawer filing cabinet. There will be things to keep track of, and they need to be kept in one place. If you can't afford one, find cardboard or plastic boxes and label them so you remember what they are for. Then, before you even begin to fill your filing cabinet (or cardboard or plastic boxes), decide where you will keep it. Don't say, "It can stay in the corner of the living room for now until I find a better place." If it starts in the corner of the living room, there's a good chance it will still be there when the youngest child is graduating from college. Don't leave it anywhere "for now" unless you are prepared to live with it in that spot forever.

Where do the filing cabinet or storage boxes go? In a place you can access any time of the day or night. (Some of your best ideas will occur in the middle of night.) The best place is wherever you will wind up when you are making lesson plans. You might have noble ideas about sitting at your desk, but if your desk has thirty-seven books, four days' worth of mail, fifteen cute knick-knacks, and a few candy bars on it—and you can't remember what color it is—you probably won't sit there to do the lesson plans. Where do you sit when you are reading, playing on your laptop, or doing your favorite hobby? That's where you will wind up doing your lesson planning, so put the file cabinet there. If you can't keep your file cabinet in that location, you will need a small, portable file box big enough to hold teaching supplies for the coming month. That can be taken wherever you land each day. Label it.

Don't run to the store yet! Read the rest of the chapter with a notebook in hand and write down what you decide you need. Some of the suggestions I make won't work for you, so you need to make your own list. If you can't find a pen to make these notes, find a crayon and add pens to your list. (Parents can almost always find a crayon.)

If you are impulsive, you don't want to set up file folders and make lesson plans, records, and schedules right now— you want to rush to the school supply store and buy everything you see and then teach it all the first week. Just this once try really, really hard to curb this impulse. If you give in, you will run out of money and not be able to set up your school correctly. You want this to work, so you have to be sort of organized just for a little while. You'll get to the fun parts soon enough, but first, you have to drag yourself through the boring parts and behave like an organized person. You can do it!

What goes into this big new file cabinet you own? You need to decide what goes into each drawer and label it. Use a removable label, because you will change your mind regularly for awhile.

The top drawer should have all your official paper-work. When you researched homeschooling, you found out what records you are required to keep. Copies of these go in this drawer. You will probably have folders for attendance records, lists of subjects studied, portfolios containing samples of your child's work, and anything else that shows what you studied. You will also keep a copy of any official document you were required to fill out when you registered as a homeschooler, if your state requires registration. These are the documents you'll need if you're asked to prove to someone you are legally homeschooling. You want to be able to access them quickly and easily. At first, this won't need a whole drawer. Use the back half of it to hold materials for subjects that don't need much room. This will depend on how you teach and what subjects you like best. The more you like a subject, the more *stuff* you will accumulate for it.

Science, history, and language arts usually need their own drawers. These subjects require crafts, worksheets, lesson plans, reading lists, and other extensive materials. They take a lot of research if you're building your own lesson plans, and research has to be stored so you can find it again. (You *think* you'll remember that you left an item in the china cupboard, but you won't.) All the other subjects can go into the top drawer. However, this is your file cabinet and you get to do it your way. If you are passionate about a subject, such as art or cooking, you may want a larger drawer for that subject.

Put one-fourth of the hanging file folders into each drawer. Inside each hanging folder, place a manila folder. The manila folder has the same label as the hanging folder so you will remember where to file it. When you remove a file, do not remove the hanging folder. Remove only the manila folder. Since they have the same label, you will know exactly where the file came from and can return it correctly. Before placing the file folders in the drawer, place a blank sheet of paper into each one. When you are filing, you will use this for cross-referencing. You may have materials that belong in both history and art, so you want to make a note that the actual materials are in the other drawer. (Don't say you'll put the blank paper in later, because you won't.)

If you're really disorganized, place a zippered pencil

pouch—the kind you place in three-ring binders—in the top drawer. Put a few pens in the pouch so you'll have something handy when you need to label a new folder. That way you won't have to waste time looking for something to write with and you won't skip the labeling step. If you're as disorganized as I am, tie a string to the notebook hole on the pouch and then tie the other end of the string to the drawer handle. Put the pouch in the front of the drawer and close the drawer. This is to make sure you don't pull the pouch out of the cabinet and then leave it on the floor; if you do, your children will wander off with it and you'll never see it again and it's back to writing with crayons. If you're the sort of person who won't remember there's a pen in the top drawer when you're working in the bottom drawer, put a pouch in every drawer. (If you have a "normal" memory, you can skip this entire paragraph.)

If you're working with portable file boxes, follow the same pattern. Keep the box of documents near the front door. The others can go anywhere that is convenient, but keep them in the same place every day unless you're working with them. You don't want to waste time hunting for them. Plastic boxes, purchased inexpensively at discount stores, are your best choice because they are sturdy and look a little nicer when they're sitting out. Cardboard boxes need to be very strong because those file folders soon become heavy.

Anything that doesn't go into file cabinets needs to go on shelves. If you have an empty closet (I know, but just in case . . .) put some shelves in there and fill them with your supplies. If not, come up with a bookcase or other shelving unit and stack art supplies and other teaching materials there. Small plastic storage containers or bins that fit on these shelves and are clearly labeled help you find what you need and help children figure out where to return the supplies they've been using. If your children can't read, place small pictures on the shelves and the same picture on the bins. They can easily match the pictures to return the bins to the correct spot.

Your first shelf might have a stack of construction paper, a stack of drawing paper, and shoeboxes of art supplies. Place the paper in shallow bins. You can set the entire bin on the table where your children are working, and then send one child to return it when you're done.

The second shelf might have science supplies carefully labeled, and the third might have research books for the unit you are currently researching, unless you're sure you can trust them to go on your desk. (They are on the bottom because you will probably find yourself sitting on the floor to go through them anyway. If you aren't a floor-sitter, they can go on a higher shelf.) On the top of the bookcase, line up the books you need to teach the current unit. Don't stack them. Buy bookends.

Each child can have a plastic crate for his or her own supplies. It will hold books, a pencil case, and his school notebook. Make sure everything goes back into the crate at the end of each day. In fact, at the end of each subject, have your child return any item he won't need for the next class.

Your crate will hold the supplies you need this week, including your own copies of textbooks and your teaching notebook. You can keep your own supplies on shelves, but it's often helpful to have them portable once you feel comfortable enough to homeschool all over the house instead of at a table.

Keep your system easy to use. You are very motivated now, but your motivation will vary. If your system is hard to use, you will stop using it. Take a little extra time now and think through your options. As soon as you notice something isn't working, stop and make changes. Every now and then, reorganize a shelf or bin. That way they won't get too far out of control all at once.

Organizing your day (more or less)

Many of us hate schedules. It is, admittedly, nearly impossible to have a firm schedule when you have children. A child who wants to learn to read right *now* doesn't care if the schedule calls for dishwashing, and a child who has hurt her knee can't wait for an open spot on the calendar to receive her bandage and kiss. Children have to be delivered and picked up, husbands come home early, and friends call. I have found, however, that a schedule helps me to get more done, even when I don't always stick to it. It creates a certain amount of structure and offers a plan for the day.

Remember those lists you made when you were trying to figure out if you had time to homeschool? Those lists can be the start of an organizational plan to help you manage your home. You listed all the things you do regularly and also noted which ones were not essential. To work out a loose schedule, which may be all you can manage at first, begin by charting out the hours you are awake for a week. You can make your own hourly chart, print one from the Internet, or buy one. It doesn't matter because, for now, it is only for you. You will want one sheet for each day of the week.

Fill in each task that must be done at a specific time—taking a child to gymnastics, for example. If you have something that needs to be done on a specific day, but not at a specific time, write it at the top of the sheet. Do you have three or four hours free each morning to teach school? While school can be done whenever you get to it, I've found most people need to choose a time and stick to it as much as possible. This helps the children move into school mode at a specific time, and keeps parents from getting so busy they forget to get started. No matter what else we don't get done, we want to hold school most days. Mornings seemed to work best for us. The children were awake and didn't have to stop a fun game to have school. I wasn't tired yet. If the world fell apart, it usually waited until school was over. We held elementary school from eight to twelve o'clock, four days a week, which still left plenty of time for play, chores, and planning.

Put the school hours on the schedule in bright red so you don't forget them. Nothing else can be scheduled for that time. You may discover you can do other things, but you should not plan to do them. School is the entire focus of your time and everything else is a bonus.

Now pencil in any other tasks you want to accomplish. Decide when you plan to grade papers and plan lessons. This will take quite a bit of time at first, but you will speed up when you are more experienced.

Mornings

If you can cope with an early morning, try to get up before your children. Do those things that help you feel under control and peaceful each day—showering, dressing, praying, exercising, or whatever you need for yourself. Then set up everything you need for school. Post a schedule on a dry erase board or a sheet of paper, look over your lesson plans, and review the supply checklist you will learn to make for each lesson. Now take fifteen minutes, at least, to catch your breath and relax before waking up your family. If you can't get up any earlier, you will need to do most of these things the night before.

Your morning with your family can begin with breakfast followed by a half hour of family housework. This way you start out feeling under control. Take a moment after each subject to put away whatever you won't need for the next class. The children may eventually learn to do this automatically, but you should remind them until that time. When school is over, do another half hour of chores, putting school things away and completing small tasks that didn't get done in the morning. Have the children help you prepare lunch, unless you had them pack lunch before school. After lunch, have them help you clean up the kitchen before they scatter for the afternoon.

Afternoons

If at all possible, use the first half hour after lunch cleanup as your own personal time. Put the youngest ones down for a nap and have older ones play or read quietly. However you let them spend this time, schedule it as your quiet time. Don't grade papers, make lesson plans, or clean house. Spend it doing something you love.

Parents often consider it selfish to take time for themselves. In reality, it's very unselfish and benefits your children as much as it does you. When you take time to indulge yourself a little, you are more peaceful and fulfilled, which makes you more fun to be with. You are also building toward a future.

When my first child was a demanding infant, her doctor warned me to take time for myself every day, keeping my hobbies in practice. He reminded me there would come a time when she would grow up and not want every moment of my time. As children get older, they want to become more independent and to have activities that don't involve their parents. It seemed impossible in those busy days, but sure enough, the children grew up and I had to find another life. Fortunately, I had one to put into place.

You are a much better parent when you give something to yourself each day. Even a half hour spent doing something that doesn't benefit anyone but yourself will help you remember you are more than a homeschool parent. It isn't that this isn't a rewarding and wonderful title, but it's not all there is to you. When your children graduate, you don't want to feel you've lost your identity. When your children see you giving some time to yourself, they will also learn to value them-

selves. They also need to learn how to be alone successfully. Declare a "My Special Time" hour for each member of the
family. During this hour everyone chooses something to do
alone, with the only rules being that it doesn't bother others
or break rules and can't involve watching television or using
the computer. They need to spend this time reading, doing
crafts, playing creatively, or just daydreaming. The activities need to be things that help them learn to enjoy their own
company. You may have to help them plan this time at first.

When Special Time is over, you should feel somewhat
recharged. Hurry and finish whatever tasks you have left
to do for the day. Don't forget to plan dinner, although it is
better to plan dinner at least one day ahead in case you get
busy. It's easy to forget all about dinner on a bad day. Try
to make a plan for your dinners a full week ahead. If you
don't want to plan the entire meal, at least decide what the
main dish is. You will find it harder, once you're teaching, to
rush to the store for a forgotten ingredient. These days, I'm
attempting to create a master menu plan—someday I might
even get it done. You, however, can assign it to your children
for Home Economics. It's delegation with a purpose.

Each day, take something from the freezer for the next
day. This way you are always a day ahead, and if your day is
awful and you feel out of control, you will at least know what
is for dinner. Suppose you have planned a meal that involves
doing something fancy with chicken breasts. However, your
day falls apart and there is no time for anything fancy. You
still have the chicken, sitting defrosted and ready to go in
your refrigerator. You can toss it in the oven without any
adornment, heat some vegetables, add some fruit, and you
have an instant emergency meal without rushing out for
fast food.

If you don't have time to really clean the house, do whatever makes it look like you did. Pick up the worst of the clut-

ter. Wipe off counters, sweep the floor, and vacuum the center of the room. Do enough to make yourself feel in control again, and don't do it alone. Make your children help.

Planning your school day

The house is as tidy as it's going to get. Dinner is planned and possibly cooking. (Let each child have a turn helping you cook. This is home economics, but its also bonding time.) Now you get to work on school. Begin each work session by getting the children out of your way. Try to avoid plopping them in front of the television more than necessary. If they are tired of playing, send them to read or let them play with a box of craft supplies. Traditional school may be out by now and your older children can play with their friends. If you can work with distractions going on around you, stay in the room with them so you can monitor problems and ask for their advice about upcoming lessons. If you have a baby or toddler, assign an older child to keep track of her, or place her in a safe place where you can see her.

If you are keeping a homeschooling journal, jot down your reactions to the day. What went right? (Always start with the good stuff; otherwise, you might find you're too discouraged to do it later.) Next, list what went wrong, but always follow this rule: You may not list more things that went wrong than went right. If you listed six good things, you may only list six bad things, and should list even less. Now, circle the one bad thing that worries you the most and the good thing you're most proud of. Write the good thing on a sticky note or file card and post it on your refrigerator to look at the rest of the day. Come up with a solution for the bad thing.

To come up with a solution, you have to word the problem correctly. Don't say, "I have a terrible temper." Instead, write, "I became upset when Jason dawdled during math." You can't do much today about having a temper. You can, however, come up with a solution to the dawdling and to your reaction to dawdling.

Now that you've handled that, plan the coming day. You will take one day each week to plan the coming week, but each day you should go over the upcoming day. If you didn't finish everything on your list, you'll need to adapt the schedule. You may make changes based on what you learned about yourself and your children that day.

Gather all the materials you will need and make sure you understand how to do everything. Practice anything you aren't sure of. Work a few math problems. Search for a new way to teach a subject. Make the craft. Listen to a recording of a song. Practice explaining the history lesson and read the stories in the reading book.

Evenings

When you feel sure of your upcoming day, stop and play with your children for awhile. By now, it's time to prepare for your spouse's return from work. Having him or her return to a reasonably under-control house and family is a nice gift to give. I was never very good at that, but I always thought it would be nice if I were. If you feel that way too, comb your hair, tidy the house, and get the kids settled down doing something quiet. Have some of them help you prepare dinner and set the table.

Whenever possible, keep your evenings free for family time. You have tired children and a spouse who is ready for attention. You may have lessons the children attend, but try to avoid the tendency to fill every afternoon and evening with outside activities. Until your children are grown, you may not realize how important this time will be to you and your family someday. Make the most of it and keep your evenings uncluttered and available for each other. Try to plan at least one activity the entire family can do together each night, and plan time for the children to share with their other parent what they did in school and in their free time. Most importantly, plan time when you and your spouse are alone together. The stronger the marriage is, the stronger the family is. The stronger the family is, the better the homeschooling is.

Homeschooling is more about family than it is about anything else.

Finding enough time

You may find that all the things you're supposed to do won't fit into this simplified plan. In fact, you will probably find that to be true. For instance, you probably signed your children up for lessons and joined support groups, and those take time. If your children are in elementary school, try to do all your work in four days. Use the fifth day to run errands, clean house, and take field trips. I tried to avoid leaving the house on our four school days when the children were young. Everything got done on Friday. You will save both gas and time if you only leave home once during the school week.

If you find yourself in situations where you have to wait, make use of this time. Each of my children had a backpack. We spent a great deal of time in doctor's offices. Each backpack contained drawing paper, crayons, pencils, a book, and other small, quiet items the children could entertain themselves with while we waited. I added school activities that were portable, which they worked on when we were forced to be out during school hours.

I had my own bag for these times. I used the time to read research materials or to write. You might use your waiting time to pay bills, work on crafts, or plan menus. Download a classic you've always wanted to read into your phone or e-book reader and read it when you find yourself waiting unexpectedly. By keeping a copy of *Huckleberry Finn* in my car,

I eventually managed to read a book I had always planned to "get around to someday."

Weekends

On Saturdays, set up your coming week. Use this day to plan your lessons for the coming week if you haven't already done so, and then forget about school. Prepare some emergency meals. Clean house. Do whatever makes you feel like you can enter the coming week in control, and make your family help you do it. Then do something fun as a family.

On Sundays, don't do housework or schoolwork. Use this day to recharge your personal spirit. Go to church, spend time writing in a journal, work on a quiet hobby, and do quiet activities as a family. Choose the activities that most help you feel peaceful and happy. Begin Mondays feeling refreshed and ready to learn.

When it doesn't work

This is not a complete guide to life management. You will need to experiment with various schedules and plans until you find the one that works for you. Don't get frustrated if you get to Friday and things didn't go the way you planned. Make a new plan and start over the next week. It was just an experiment. As you test various schedules and solutions, you will eventually encounter parts of the plan that work. When situations change, you will also change. You may never be perfect, but you will always be improving. Improvement is the goal.

More Resources

➤ *Managers of Their Homes: A Practical Guide to Daily Scheduling for Christian Home-School Families* by Steve and Teri Maxwell
ISBN: 0966910702

You can purchase this book and scheduling kit from the Maxwells' website: Titus2.com

This book comes highly recommended to me by some of my readers. The Maxwells have eight children and scheduling was naturally a concern. This is a time management kit for busy families that was tested on twenty-five families, whose experiences over the first year are recorded in the book. It shows parents how to organize their time so they can keep up with housework and other responsibilities, and takes into consideration the special challenges of homeschooling. The website offers continuing support and ordering information for the book.

➤ *OrganizedHome.com*

The most valuable section of this website is the printable home organizer. Print out pages that keep all your family's information and schedules in one easy-to-use notebook. The website also offers organizational tips for children's bedrooms, holiday planning schedules, and a special section for homeschoolers which has detailed instructions for organizing supplies. The printed pages require a fair amount of ink, however. You may want to use them as a guide to creating your own.

➤ *Confessions of an Organized Homemaker: The Secrets of Uncluttering Your Home and Taking Control of Your Life* by Deniece Schofield.
ISBN: 1558703616

"Organizing is the means whereby we can streamline those necessary chores, so we can get on with life's more pleasurable experiences." Deniece's book has helped me where others failed because I don't have to spend twenty hours setting up a complicated system before I can even start. Although I was in the middle of unpacking and settling into a new home when I first read this, I was able to pull out several suggestions and put them in place in just a few minutes. As I have time, I incorporate a few more. She is also the person who explained filing cabinets to me. The focus is more on using common sense to solve homemaking problems than on a minute-by-minute plan for organizing your life and the solutions are inexpensive and easy to create. She once required "a camel, a canoe, a priest and a tourniquet" to get through her home; now housework is just a tool to get her what she wants, which in our case is time to homeschool.

➤ *A2Z Home's Cool*
   "Must I Be Organized?"
   A2Zhomeschooling.com/beginning_home_school/help_
getting_started_homeschooling/organization_home_schooling
   "A homeschool mom with too clean a house either isn't interacting much with her children or has hired a maid, which isn't a bad idea, by the way." You'll love this article by Ann Zeise on homeschool organization that is realistic, laid back, and practical.

➤ *The Food Nanny Rescues Dinner: Easy Family Meals for Every Day of the Week* by Liz Edmunds
   ISBN: 093527877X
   This television cooking host specializes in helping parents who don't cook real meals to learn how. Her theme nights template makes meal planning easy and the recipes are for ordinary foods real families eat. I'm not much of a cook, but I haven't been able to mess up one of her recipes yet. That's impressive.

Chapter 6

Record Keeping

FROM A LEGAL STANDPOINT, record keeping is one of the most important aspects of homeschooling. It requires a certain amount of organization and effort to do correctly. Whether you live in a state that requires you to submit your records or one that does not, you must always have them and be ready to show them when asked. However, once you have your system in place, it's possible to keep the necessary records without too much effort.

Before you begin, find out what records you are required to keep by researching the laws for your state. You learned how to do that in Chapter 4. Keep all the records required by law, but keep others that will show you are a competent homeschooler. Your records should include:

- Copies of any paperwork you were required to submit to the government in order to homeschool.

- Attendance records.

- A summary of your educational plans for this year.

- A detailed outline of what you are studying this year, including the lesson plans already completed.

- Test scores if your child was tested by a professional tester or testing organization.

71

- A portfolio of sample work.

- Immunization records.

- A list of books you are using for school.

- A list of books your child has read so far this year (optional).

- A description of field trips, outside classes taken, and interesting projects or programs you have been involved in this year (optional).

- All of these records for the past two years or more, plus all records for every year of high school, because colleges often ask for them.

The most essential records, the ones you might be asked to produce immediately, need to be kept someplace you can access quickly. Today, you are much less likely to be asked to prove you are really homeschooling, but if it should happen, you want to know where those records are.

Attendance records

Keep attendance records showing the days you held school. Initially, this can be done on your calendar. Each day, write the number of hours you held school in the bottom corner. You may want to do this at the end of the day so you can summarize the additional educational time you spent outside of school hours. For example, you may have only held school for four hours, but you might have spent the afternoon at the zoo, which would count as a field trip.

At the bottom of each month's calendar page, record the total number of days school was held that month and the total days so far for the year. You can do this by recording it as a fraction: 23/180, with 23 being the number of days you held school and 180 being the number of school days your state requires.

It is essential that you follow the homeschooling laws of your state in order to avoid problems should someone official ask you to prove that you are complying with those laws. You will probably find, however, that your state does not regulate how you record the work that is completed. Should you be asked to present it, you could probably give them a summary or a list. Most likely, you will keep a daily log of your work, which will be enough to prove what you have accomplished.

Each month, transfer the information to a time sheet. Create one for each child. On this time sheet, write the month and year and record the number of hours each child attended school. You will probably have perfect attendance because you can draw on your hour bank to make up any hours you've missed. When you have more hours than you need, record them on a separate sheet of paper. This is your hour bank. When you want to take a day off, record the needed number of extra hours on your official time sheet, and delete them from your record of extra time. If your state requires a certain number of hours to be completed each year, or a certain number of days, divide these by the number of months you hold school. Then you can say on the form, "125 days completed out of 175 required. On schedule."

You might list on the top of the form what days you meet and which days you took off for official holidays: *School held Monday through Friday, weekly.* List the official school holidays. I simply copied the calendar of the nearest school and noted that I followed their calendar. Keep this record in your teacher's notebook, which we will discuss later in this chapter.

None of this takes much time. You only have to do this part once. The transfer from your calendar to the time sheet occurs only once a month. To help you remember, write a note to yourself on the last day of the calendar. If you have an organized older child, you can appoint her school secretary and let her do it. However, it's officially your responsibility, so check to be sure it gets done. You can't blame your child if the records aren't kept.

Older children can sign in and record their own hours. Train them to sign in just before starting school, and sign out when they're finished. They should re-sign in when they do anything educational later on, such as playing on a basketball team. Each morning when they sign in, they should total the number of hours they recorded the previous day. They don't do this until the next day in case they have anything to add later on, such as an hour spent reading before bedtime. Be sure to verify they did what they said they did. You should still make the transfer of their hours to the time sheet each month because that annual time sheet is your official record. They can keep their schedule of hours in their student notebook discussed later or in a central area of your school.

Description of this year's curriculum

At the beginning of the year, write a basic summary of what you plan to teach this year. This provides you with material to show officials right from the start. Following is a course of study submitted by my very good friend Brandy Ross, the mother of three of my favorite homeschoolers, including my goddaughter:

Math

The first grade math course is designed using the outline set by *Core Knowledge: What Your First Grader Needs to Know*. A variety of texts, workbooks, games, and worksheets will be used to master the skills. Place value, counting to 100, addition, greater than and less than, subtraction, and telling time are some of the lessons that will be covered.

Reading

Reading is an essential skill in life and this course is designed to encourage the student to embrace a lifelong love of reading. We will continue to master the necessary phonics skills to attain this goal. Reading materials include Abeka's K readers and beginning reader books.

Writing

Writing is another essential skill. Penmanship and letter recognition is practiced using lessons and writing tablets from Abeka's phonics system.

History and Geography

This first grade course is designed to take a deeper look at history and geography through the outline by *Core Knowledge: What Your First Grader Needs to Know*. This course covers ancient history beginning with the Ice Age and American history beginning with the Mayans. Materials will be various texts, articles, websites, and books.

Science

The first grade science course follows the outline set by *Core Knowledge: What Your First Grader Needs to Know*. This course is designed to give the student a deeper understanding of the animal kingdom, the ocean, the human body, the solar system, and the Earth. The lessons are backed up with workbooks, websites, and hands-on projects.

Fine Arts

This course is designed to aid the young student in gaining an early understanding and appreciation of culture, music, and art. The lessons expand on what was introduced in kindergarten.

Home and Life Management
The student of today may not be as well prepared for life and home management as youth of the past. This course helps to teach the skills necessary in life. Some of the lessons for the first grade course are manners, personal hygiene, room organizing, care of pets, yard maintenance, and tool identification.

Fitness
The fitness program has several methods to teach lifelong goals of overall good health. The program includes martial arts, golfing, yoga, meditation, aerobics, and various physical activities.[†]

Your teacher's notebook
Your teacher's notebook, a three-ring binder, will contain the details of your school. Choose the thickest notebook you can find—two to three inches—because it will fill up quickly, and buy tabbed section dividers for it. In the first section, include a copy of the documents your state requires. Although they are in your files, you want them with you when you're working so you can refer to them. Create two sections of your notebook for each child in your school. (If you have a large family, you may prefer a separate notebook for each child instead of one large notebook.)

On the first page of the first section, put the child's name and grade and a list of subjects she is studying this year. Following this page, in the same section, create one page for each subject your child will be studying. On each subject page, describe the curriculum in detail. You can do this easily by placing your lesson plans and unit studies in the notebook behind a description of the class. Print them from your

---

† Brandy Ross, personal correspondence with the author.

computer as you complete them and punch holes in them. At the end of the year, you will have a complete history of the year's studies. You don't need to make a different lesson plan for each child. If all your children will be working from the same unit study, simply print out one copy for each child and place it under his section of the notebook. If the unit study includes adapted assignments for each child, highlight the child's work on each page.

If you are placing your lesson plans in the notebook, the description for each class should have enough detail to explain what you are studying if you show the plans to someone early in the year. This will explain your plans until you have all your lesson plans written. "Kelly is nine years old and reading two years above grade level. Her writing skills are also above grade level. This year, her literature class will correspond to her history study of pioneers. She will begin by reading the entire *Little House on the Prairie* series. Field trips include a visit to a restored pioneer village and a workshop on making butter. Following this she will . . ."

Have your children keep a list of the books they read, including those they read on their own, and add copies of the lists to the notebook behind the page for English. They may be more motivated to record them if you let them place a sticker on a chart each time they record a new book. Another way to make sure you know what the child has read is to create a stack of bookmarks on your computer. Have your child write the name of the book and his own name when he begins the book, and have him use this bookmark to keep his place as he reads. When he is done with the book, he hands you the bookmark and you record it in your notebook.

The second section for each child will have grades, test scores, or any other method of evaluation you use to prove they are learning. This will be discussed more in later chapters. Even if you don't believe in grades, put something in there each month. Write a brief summary of how you think your children did:

"Kyle completed three chapters in math this month and showed complete mastery in his chapter exams. His reading is becoming smoother and he is able to sound out most words that follow the rules of phonics. He is beginning to read for pleasure. Kyle is becoming skilled at using maps. His writing is improving, and he is making fewer spelling errors. He has mastered the complete sentence. He still has some difficulty sitting quietly."

If your children have been in public school, or if you attended public school, you may recognize these as the "Kyle is a pleasure to have in class" paragraphs on the back page of each report card. Be sure to include the areas that need improvement, or your report may not be believable. You will probably want to give great thought to how you describe these challenges since the only people they really benefit are those who might be reviewing your work. School officials will want to know that you are paying attention, but they will be concerned if it looks like Kyle is having serious problems that you are not working to resolve. In the above paragraph, most people wouldn't worry that Kyle has trouble sitting quietly, because many children do. If he is doing well in his lessons, it will be obvious that his behavior problem isn't serious. But when you list problems, also describe what you are doing to resolve them in order to demonstrate that you are capable of handling these challenges.

If you were to create a table of contents for this notebook, it might look like this:

1. School documents, including immunization records, attendance records, homeschool registration forms, brief summary of curriculum.

2. Karen's curriculum. The first page includes her name, her age, her grade, and a list of subjects she is studying: reading, arithmetic, science, social studies, English, art, music, gym, drama. The second page is for reading. It includes the name of her textbook, a description of the reading club she belongs to at the library, and a list of activities not included in the text-book. Each week, the parent adds the lesson plans for the coming week. For example, *Monday: Pages 18–21 in text, read Chapter 3 of current early-reader novel, plan project based on this book.* When Karen takes a test, the corrected test is placed in the notebook. The end of the Reading section includes a list of books she has read for school and on her own. (There will be similar pages for each subject. They might be divided by tabbed or non-tabbed dividers, or printed on colored paper for easy identification.)

3. Karen's testing and evaluations. This includes her end-of-year standardized tests given by the public school district, because they show where she started the year. This also includes important tests Karen's mother has given to evaluate what her child has learned. A quiz would go under the specific sub-ject studied, but a midterm would go into this sec-tion. Each month, Karen's mother writes a summary of what she feels Karen has accomplished that month.

Following Karen's two sections are similar pages for each child.

Because this is your notebook, you should do it your way. Like everything else in this book, these are just sugges-tions. Your book should contain anything you feel you need to stay in control. My own notebook included lesson plans I was currently writing, and I stored these at the back. I also included articles on homeschooling or teaching that I wanted to study as well as a few motivational materials for the bad days.

I like to place a calendar in my notebook. I bought the kind meant for school notebooks, with holes already punched. Later, I made my own on the computer. I used these pages to note the themes for our unit studies and starting and ending dates for special projects. On each Monday square, I wrote the math chapters the children should be on if they were to finish the book by the end of the year. This is discussed in more detail in chapters covering lesson planning.

Be sure you know where this notebook ends up each day. You cannot afford to lose it because it contains the essentials for running your school. Start a new notebook for each school year and place the old one on a bookshelf, or transfer the materials to your file box.

Portfolios

Place folders in your file cabinet that contain samples of your children's work. This is called a portfolio. Many colleges request a portfolio of a high school student's recent work, and many states allow a portfolio to be evaluated as an alternative to standardized testing each year. This portfolio should contain stories, reports, book reports, math tests, science projects, and other materials that show what the child is doing and how well he does it.

The simplest way to compile the portfolio is to have the children keep all their work in a notebook. At the end of each month, place everything they have completed into their folders. You should keep at least two year's worth of records in your files and *all* high school records, but most parents prefer to keep the basic records and at least a sampling of work until their child is safely admitted to college. Find out if your state requires specific records to be kept longer than one year, and then keep those records at least a year longer than required. Having samples from previous years allows you to prove the child has made progress. It also allows you to go back and find out how much progress your child has made.

If your folders start to fill up, sort through them and choose an assortment to keep. Don't choose just your child's perfect papers or you'll have a credibility problem. Include tests or some other method of demonstrating how you measured learning and handwritten papers as well as typed ones. (If your child has a writing disorder, note this in your summary.) Include your monthly summaries and write an end-of-year summary as well. Use the portfolio to show that your child is working to grade level, or to the level expected of him by his disabilities, and also to show an interesting curriculum. If he is below grade level, show that he is making progress. Include photographs of art projects and outside activities. If you will be showing this to an official evaluator, talk to people who have been through the portfolio process in your area and ask them for suggestions.

Recording cross-curriculum lessons

If you are required to show your records to someone and must complete a certain number of hours in each subject, you may find the record keeping confusing. When I first began homeschooling, I used a school district program and I had to complete a chart every week. I often found myself staring at a report on Thomas Edison and wondering whether it was English or science. If the report was illustrated, was it also art?

Since you are the teacher, you can report it anyway you like. If you don't have to be specific, just list it as a thematic study or cross-curriculum study (lessons that teach several subjects at once) and list the subjects covered by the activity. Your listing might say, "Term paper on Thomas Edison: English, science, art." If you have to list it under one subject, assign it to the subject with the least hours that week. You may look over your week and see that you spent a great deal of time on science, but fall short of the required hours in English, so list your paper under English that week. The following week, if your child is still working on it, you can list it as science. These records are more for your supervisor's use than your own, so list it in a way that makes the supervisor happy.

Recording nontraditional learning

Sometimes we do things that are clearly educational, but not easy to explain. How do you record the half hour you and your son spent following a trail of ants? Place it under science and write something that sounds academic, such as, "Study of ant migration patterns," or even just "Entomology—ants." (Entomology is the study of bugs.) If you and your daughter spend fifteen minutes dropping things off the balcony just to see what will happen, talk to her about how fast they fell and whether their size or weight affected the fall. (Keep records.) Then list this as the study of gravity. Playing dressup? Theater. Playing with fire trucks? Career exploration.

Does this sound like cheating to you, as if you can goof off all day and pretend it's school? If you do nothing all day every day but play with fire trucks, it may well be cheating. Playing with fire trucks is educational, though, especially if you talk about firefighters and perhaps visit a fire station the next week. Go to the library and find some books on fire fighters and watch a video of them in action. You've taken a fun game and turned it into a thematic study. Children learn by playing.

You can't count everything, or at least you shouldn't. The standard complaint among those who disapprove of homeschooling is that homeschool parents take their kids to the mall and pretend it's a field trip. Don't count mindless cartoons or mall trips or anything that doesn't have a legitimate educational value. What counts also depends on the age of the child. A five-year-old can count playing with fire trucks as career exploration, but a ten-year-old probably can't. While an eight-year-old might really learn something from helping Mom make cookies, a twelve-year-old would have to make them for the first time to count them, and then they would be counted as home economics. Use your judgment and keep in mind that learning is the purpose, not hours on a time sheet.

Don't record everything
Children need down time, just as we do. There will be times when your child will want to build with blocks without listening to a lecture on architecture, or will want to waste time just because he's tired. Don't be a teacher every minute. Take time to enjoy being with your child. If you rush off to record every event on a time sheet, he will begin to wonder if you ever spend time with him just because you want to or if it's always just part of the job. You don't want that to happen. Let go and have fun.

More Resources
➤ *Young Minds Homeschool Forms and Scheduling*
DonnaYoung.org/forms.htm
Printable forms for everything a homeschooler could possibly need. Includes planners, record keeping forms, high school transcripts, portfolio pages, and calendars. Pages are available in several formats.

➤ *The Homeschool Mom*
TheHomeschoolMom.com/gettingorganized/planner.
php#unitstudyplanner

This website offers a number of free online forms for recording keeping, planning lessons, assignment sheets—even an unschooling record sheet.

Example Attendance Record

Year_____ Child's Name: _____

This school follows the same schedule as George Washington Elementary School, Generic Town, New Jersey.

Total Days Required: 180

September: School held 15 days. No absences. 75 hours.
October: School held 20 days. No absences. 100 hours.
November: School held 18 days. No absences. 90 hours
December: School held 12 days. No absences. 60 hours
January: School held 20 days. No absences. 100 hours
February: School held 18 days. No absences. 90 hours
March: (etc.)
April:
May:
June:
July and August: School not in session

Total number of days for this year:
Total number of hours school was held:
Total days this year: 170

Chapter 7

Homeschooling One, Many, and the Baby

WHETHER YOU'RE HOMESCHOOLING ONE child or seven, planning makes things easier. Even more important than planning, though, is the ability to be flexible. As homeschooling moms, we're running miniature education labs. A scientist starts with one theory but often moves to another based on what he learned as he tested his ideas. Getting it wrong the first time is not failure—it's education. If there was only one right way to teach children, all schools would use it and test scores would be incredible. That hasn't happened, and that tells us there are many ways. Our job is to find the method that works for our child and for us. Both factors matter because you teach more effectively when you're comfortable with the method you are using.

Homeschooling the only child

In some ways, homeschooling one child is more difficult than homeschooling many children, although it depends on the personality of the child. I began my homeschooling career by teaching only the oldest of my three children. I was new at it, so I was managing to make every mistake commonly made by homeschoolers; but I also faced the challenge of spending so much uninterrupted time with a child whose personality was as strong as my own. She and I clashed as I struggled to be the perfect teacher and tried to force her to be the perfect student.

When I was teaching one child, I put all my self-esteem, my goals, and my pride into this child's education. It was, I thought, her job to prove I could do what most people thought I couldn't do. Instead of starting out slowly and gradually getting used to what we were doing, I leaped in at full speed, partly because I was using a school district program that first semester and had to report to someone every week. I planned lessons that looked impressive to the supervising teacher instead of planning lessons that worked for my daughter. Since the two of us were alone all day, all my attention was focused on her. This was far too much pressure for one child, and it's a wonder we survived it.

Homeschooling isn't entirely about you or your reputation, even though it often feels as if it is. We can smother our child in the homeschooling process if we aren't alert. Sometimes this smothering comes from just wanting the very best for your child and trying too hard to achieve it.

When you are homeschooling a single child, it's often best to plan to do other things during the school day. When you are homeschooling several children, your full attention is needed most of the time; but when you have only one child, he needs time alone. That means you can occasionally sneak off to do a fast load of dishes or answer an e-mail.

Working alone allows a child to figure out a problem for himself. If you are there at his side, he will develop the habit of asking for help before trying to come up with his own solution. If you are busy you can say, "I'll be back in five minutes. See if you can figure it out before then." Your eventual goal, discussed in a later chapter, is to help him become an independent learner, so he must learn to struggle through difficult challenges on his own as much as possible.

You are also a distraction when you are nearby. You probably prefer to be completely alone when you need to accomplish a difficult task because another person will talk to you or be someone you can talk to. Your child will usually be more task-oriented if he is alone. If he has an attention disorder, he may need you there all the time at first, but you can gradually teach him to work alone by leaving for one minute, then for two, and then eventually for most of the assignment.

One of the challenges a homeschooling parent will face is trying to do group projects. Some subjects are more fun when done with others and some really require the presence of others. Most people need life experiences in carrying out group efforts. In some instances, you can be the group. If you are developing a project, work as his partner. Let him take the lead and make assignments. You can simulate reality by telling him you will pretend to be a child his age. Create a character and play the part. During one project you might be a whiny child, and in another a timid child. Let him figure out how to resolve the problems created by the partner. This can actually be more effective than working with real children, since you can openly discuss the issues involved without feeling as though you're gossiping.

Place your only child in a club, a church group, or on a team. There are many possibilities that allow him to work with others who are not just like him. You can also invite other children to participate in some of the activities you do in your school. When I home-preschooled, several neighborhood children came over on Tuesdays for science experiments and art projects. I also took field trips on days the traditional schools were not in session and invited a friend or two.

Offer your home for your child's friends to use when they want to put on a play, make a neighborhood newspaper, or develop a service project. Of course, you may have to suggest these things to your child first. Those unofficial, unsponsored events don't seem to be a part of the ordinary child's experience anymore. When I was a little girl, children were always getting together to put on a play in someone's backyard, or to have a club for whatever project interested them. Adults were neither welcome nor needed. There was no funding and there were no fees. Now a child who wants to do these things joins a club organized and run by adults, complete with uniforms and trophies. Teach your children and their friends to create some unofficial fun.

Veronica Ugulano, whose website, *Pontiac High School*,[†] features California homeschooling, is homeschooling an only child. She points out the importance of avoiding relationship burnout:

> My son and I spent all day every day alone togeth-
> er. Sometimes we needed a break from that. The
> most important thing to recognize is that parents and
> children **will** need time away from each other. Public
> school families look for ways to spend time togeth-
> er. Homeschooled families might need to look for
> ways to be apart, or to be with other people. We didn't
> have access to grandparents or other close relatives,
> so sometimes we each just took our project to opposite
> sides of the house to make space. He would read or
> play with building toys or listen to a book on tape, I
> would read or work on my forums or other computer
> work. The important thing is to give yourself *permis-
> sion* to need to be alone or separate.[‡]

When only one of your children stays home
Many families initially homeschool a child who is struggling

---

†   homeschool.priswell.com

‡   Veronica Ugulano, personal correspondence with the author.

in his traditional school. The siblings, who are doing well, continue to attend a public or private school. This creates a few unexpected issues for many parents.

Your children are probably accustomed to going on field trips at different times, or having a birthday party in one class but not the other. Because of this, many parents are surprised when the homeschooled child yells because his sister is going on a field trip, or his sister yells because he is going on one. Why is this suddenly an issue?

The child who left school is coping with "school sickness." This is the educational equivalent of homesickness. Even if he was miserable in school, it was familiar, and he wonders if he is missing something good now that he isn't there. When he sees his siblings having field trips, parties, and field days, and getting school credit for watching pointless commercial movies, he forgets the parts of school he hated and creates a fantasy of a school filled with day after day of play.

The greatest challenge is holidays. Homeschooled children can feel very picked on when their siblings come home with stacks of valentines. I occasionally had to ask my children if they wanted to go to school all year just to get thirty valentines in February. They didn't, but they *did* feel I should put them back into school the week before Valentine's Day, on Halloween, and on the day of the school Christmas party. They wanted to homeschool the rest of the year. I had to make it clear you couldn't go to school just a few fun days every year. They could homeschool or they could go to public school, but they had to make a choice.

You can help ease these days by planning a party of your own. If you belong to a homeschool group, you will probably be invited to a party anyway. If you don't, let your child invite his own friends over to exchange valentines. Suggest each child bring two valentines for each guest and then let them each make one more for each guest during the party. This will give your child a nice mixture of valentines. Plan something fun for the holidays the school children are celebrating.

The children who remain in school may resent the fun things you do with your homeschooled child. Even when they are having fun at school, they don't like the idea of their parent enjoying so much time with a sibling. They worry about favoritism and are sure you love that child best. They don't see a field trip or an educational game as a school experience. They see it as a family experience that excludes them.

I tried to plan field trips the same day my younger ones were going on trips. Furthermore, the entire family was allowed to use the educational equipment we purchased. I also told my oldest child, who was our first homeschooler, that it was not polite to brag about the fun things she did because it might upset her younger siblings.

You will need to spend some time talking to your children about homeschooling. Always discuss the events of the day as being schoolwork. Spend one-on-one time with the traditionally schooled children, and spend noneducational time with the homeschooled child. After awhile, everyone gets used to the changes. You may find after a year or so that the others ask to stay home as well. If not, they have made a choice to prefer school, and this will help the adjustment.

Homeschooling the large family

When I was a little girl, I loved reading books about one-room schools. When I found myself homeschooling three children, I realized I was teaching in just such a school—although the one room was an entire house. Still, I had to cope with teaching three children who were different ages and in different grades. I have known families homeschooling eight or more children at once.

If you are using a purchased curriculum, you may want

to have your children work in different rooms so they aren't distracted as you work with their siblings. You can also choose to train them to tune you out when you are working with someone else. Have each child start with something she can do alone. You can then move between the children, listening to them read, asking questions about their work, or explaining a math problem. Generally, you will need to start with the youngest children first. As soon as possible, teach the older ones to work independently so you only have to curl up and listen as they tell you about their day.

If you are building your own curriculum, which is discussed in Chapter 10, coordination will be your method of survival. As much as possible, everyone studies the same material, but at his or her own level. My two youngest are sixteen months apart in age, so they did their math separately. Since they both read above grade level anyway, we read real books instead of graded readers. This meant they could read the same book. All other subjects were studied together.

Suppose your family is studying endangered animals. There are materials available on this subject for every grade level, so it's a good choice for a coordinated curriculum. The basis of your unit study will be trade books (the books you buy at your bookstore for general audiences rather than textbooks meant for schools). Select books on this subject for every child in your school and have them read independently.

Many children can understand books they cannot actually read themselves. They just need someone to read the words to them and to discuss the concepts. This is particularly true of highly gifted children whose reading levels don't yet match their comprehension levels. Ask an older child to read the book to the younger child and to discuss it with him. This allows an older child to read a book he might be offended to be assigned, but which has valuable information in a simple format. In reverse, you can ask the older child to listen as a younger sibling reads to him. While this allows the younger child to practice reading aloud, it also allows the older child to experience a high quality children's book he might not have read when he was younger.

After your children have read their assigned books, let each one do a project or report on what he or she has studied. Discuss the books together at the dinner table, allowing every child to contribute what he has learned. If you discover the books contradict each other, make it a family project to find the truth (if there is a truth). If there isn't one answer the experts agree on, explain we are always discovering new things, even about the past. Encourage the children to make their own decisions about which theories are correct. Older children can write a paper defending their views.

Most thematic units offer wonderful possibilities for projects. A unit study on Shakespeare might include making a model of the Globe Theater, a puppet show version of a favorite play, and the creation of a Web page about the best children's books on Shakespeare and his plays. All of your children can work on these projects together. A teenager who is learning about black holes can teach what she learns to her younger brothers and sisters, who can understand some of the complicated ideas but who could not read the books that discuss them. She will discover, as you will, that the teacher always learns more than the student. You have to understand a subject very well to explain it to a younger child, and you have to have a clear vision of the major issues before you can create activities for the subject.

Coordinating the topics to be studied saves you time because you have fewer topics to research. You have to study Shakespeare yourself in order to teach your children about him, and you don't have time to study Shakespeare's era, the Revolutionary War, and the civil rights movement all at the same time. By teaching the same topic to all your children, you learn all about Shakespeare's world and you can make notes on what you can do for each child to make the lessons meaningful. You may still find yourself making three worksheets, but they will be similar worksheets that cover the same material and are adapted to the age of the child. If you have five children, you might find you can use one question for three children. If your children are close enough in age, they may be able to do most of their work together. My two youngest had very few assignments adapted to their grade levels.

Another advantage of coordinated learning is that it allows you to help an older child who is a poor reader. You can assign a book at a lower grade level, and explain that you want both children to read it, so you picked one meant for the younger child. The older child may be less embarrassed because he has an excuse he can give others. "My mom always makes me read baby books just so I can help my little sister. It's so embarrassing!"

My favorite reason for using coordinated learning is not really an educational one—it's a family reason. When the entire family is studying the same material, unity becomes a part of the school. We can all discuss the issues and curiosities we discover, we can take the same field trips, and we can remember together. My children enjoy recalling the experiences they shared in their early homeschooling days and they have a similar knowledge base for the debates they dearly love. The primary benefit of homeschooling is a closer family, and learning together is an essential part of building a great family.

Managing the baby and smaller children
One of the most challenging aspects of homeschooling is managing the children who are too young to formally homeschool. It's difficult to teach math while a toddler is taking

all the pans out of the cupboards or a baby is fussing. If you have little ones, make plans in advance so you don't find yourself struggling to cope. Although the plan may not always work, you'll have a starting place for handling the problem.

Since all my children were of school-age when I started, I turned to the experts for help with this one. Meg Grooms juggled little children, homeschooling, and a weekly column and still managed to remain sane and cheerful in the process. I asked her how she handled her youngest child during school hours.

> When I am working one-on-one with my older student my younger student often keeps herself busy with similar activities. If Cate is doing a math workbook, Emily likes to sit and write numbers or play with the scale. We also have a large set of felt characters and a portable felt board (aka, a [large] piece of felt that I was too lazy to attach to anything) that keeps her busy. Emily has her own "kiddie tabletop desk" that keeps her busy, a leap pad, and of course our last resort—the television & computer. Usually giving Emily a pair of scissors and a few magazines, as well as some stamps and markers, is enough to keep her happy. Emily also has a set of magazines that come in her name; they are her "school books."
>
> The hardest challenge is when I am talking with Cate and Emily interrupts. Emily has always been the "do it now" type of person and gets very angry when I ignore her or ask her to wait. I still don't have this 100% figured out, except to tell her to wait until it's her "school time" (when Cate is working on her own or playing on the computer). Cate and I also try to do most of her sit-down work when Emily is napping.

Next year I will have two official, reporting-to-the-state children. I expect to follow the same schedule we do now, just having two students taking turns with Mom's attention. Cate isn't a fluent reader and needs me to read her all directions, but she can pretty much do most of the work herself. I believe in having the child fix mistakes as soon as they are made, so I don't have her put her work aside for later checking, I check it when she's done. Thus, while Cate is doing her math workbook independently, I will work with Emily on hers. The children will complete science, social studies, art, literature, etc., together. The only individual subjects will be reading instruction and math. Hopefully. . . .[†]

It's important to note that although Meg hasn't entirely resolved the problem, she does have a plan, and she also has a good attitude about the days when things don't work out the way she planned. Although it isn't foolproof, her plan generally allows her to teach and to feel good about what she is accomplishing.

Little children like to be included in "playing school." At this age, they are very excited about learning—at least for awhile each day. Toddlers can sort, look at books, listen to music, and draw. Give them pictures of animals and ask them to put each type of animal into a pile. Teach them to do simple puzzles.

When my children were small, I found it helpful to have special toys that could only be played with when I needed to keep the children especially busy. Create a little school corner for your toddler and place in it learning toys she can only use during school. You may want several boxes you can

---

[†] Meg Grooms, personal correspondence with the author.

rotate when she starts to lose interest. If a box reemerges after several weeks, it will seem to be filled with all sorts of new toys, especially if you add something to it each time.

Meg added that her children love playing with craft boxes. She keeps a number of them for her children. "One is full of scrap material and foam; one is feathers and sequins; one is glue, a paper punch, and stencils; one has stamps; one has washable markers and crayons with scrap paper, etc. These keep the girls busy for hours."†

When I was teaching one preschooler to read and to do math, I began by setting up my younger child with an activity. I gave him ten minutes of teaching time and then settled him into his own activities. Just as no one could interrupt his ten minutes of teaching time, he could not interrupt his sister's fifteen minutes of reading or math instruction.

Some of your regular school activities interest preschoolers and they can be included in your lessons. If you are teaching a younger elementary school child, invite your toddler to join in the songs, the stories, the science experiments, and other fun events. By the time she is ready to go to school officially, she will be used to the school routine and you may discover she has been learning during this time. When my son was three, he was given some educational testing at our local school. The tester mentioned that he could add and subtract without counting. After I questioned him, I realized he had been watching his sister's math lessons as he played.

Toddlers also enjoy spending time with their older siblings. Ask a child to read to her little brother for awhile. The older child gets extra reading practice and learns an important lesson in service. The younger child gets some extra story time. If one child is reading to another, you are free to help a third child. This tactic is especially valuable when you

---

† Meg Grooms, personal correspondence with the author.

have a child who does not read well. A sixth grader with a reading disorder may be too embarrassed to read the second grade book he reads well, but if he is asked to read it to a little child, he can save face. Now he isn't reading a baby book; he is just reading to a baby.

The addition of a new baby can really confuse homeschooling life. Meg describes her plans for the first months after her baby will be born:

> I had Cate's annual evaluation done last month, so we have plenty of time to take a few weeks (or months!) off. Since the baby is a spring baby, it actually works out well because we use springs for more informal, child-led learning. It doesn't make sense for us to take summers off because everything is so crowded and it's so hot here. I would much rather have the cooler spring months off. I imagine the first few weeks after the baby [is born] will be an adjustment time and school won't be our top priority; however, I fully feel my children will benefit just as much from the trips to the pediatrician (they've already learned so much just going to the midwife with me), in the caring of the baby, etc. We will work harder through the summer to ensure that Cate's math curriculum for the year is complete, or almost complete.‡

Babies just want to be held and generally enjoy being in the middle of things. Assuming the baby is feeling peaceful, you can rock her while you listen to readers or tell stories from history. Babies will sometimes sit quietly and watch a good science lesson. In fact, as Meg points out, babies are a

---

‡   Ibid.

science lesson just by existing. They bring special interest to the discussion of growth and change. If you are teaching while the baby is crawling around, make sure you keep dangerous items out of her reach.

Of course, babies do get fussy, and they want to be changed or fed at impractical moments. Plan a curriculum that does not completely require your participation all the time. Be ready to change direction and send your children to do something alone while you tend to a fussy baby. Later in the book, you will learn to create an emergency thematic study that children can carry out with little or no direction. For less drastic days, simply have the schedule in mind and know which items can be done alone if you need to focus on the baby.

Babies sometimes delight in keeping their mothers awake all night. When the day comes that you are simply too exhausted to teach, either pull out the emergency kit or skip school. If you build a bank of hours, you can do this. Build a bank by recording every educational activity you do in your everyday life and how much time you spend on it. On each calendar page, write how many hours you should have completed by the end of the month, and later, how many you did complete that month as well as how many you've completed over the year so far. If you are ahead, you can take a day off. When your younger children nap that day, nap with them. The older ones can be instructed to read quietly. If the children accidentally do something educational, count it.

One additional solution for crisis days is to know a few responsible homeschooled teenagers. Homeschooled teens often build a successful business babysitting during school hours and doing their own work later in the day. If you are exhausted, hire a homeschooled teen to carry out your crisis unit study and to entertain the children while you sleep or care for a sick baby. Many homeschooled teenagers help teach their younger siblings and are quite good at it. They enjoy teaching new children and your children enjoy the change of teachers. Tuck some cash away for these days so you can afford them.

More Resources

➤ *Games Babies Play: From Birth to Twelve Months, 2nd edition* by Vickie Lansky
ISBN: 0916773582

This is a delightful book of learning games for the very newest homeschooler. Don't just keep your little one busy— teach her, too. Most of these games are so simple your older children can play them with the baby. The goal isn't to create a super-baby, just an alert and stimulated one.

➤ *The Toddler's Busy Book* by Trish Kuffner
ISBN: 0671317741

An activity every day for one year to keep your busy toddler occupied while you teach or clean. Many of the games require little preparation and little of your time. Teach your toddler through play. This author has a similar book for preschoolers.

➤ *PreschoolWithMommy.com*

My castle-themed website on homeschooling toddlers, preschoolers, and kindergartners. The website includes articles on parenting and teaching, lesson plans, and activity ideas.

Chapter 8

Less Traditional Ways to Homeschool

TRADITIONALLY, WE THINK OF homeschooling as involving a mother and her children at the kitchen table all day. In real life, of course, homeschooling is far more diverse than that picture, and the more popular homeschooling becomes, the more diverse it becomes.

Today, homeschooling is not just for upper-middle class moms. Nor is it all about religion. It's not even done at a kitchen table much of the time. Some people homeschool part-time and some just supplement their child's traditional education, a trend called afterschooling. Homeschooling is extraordinary in its diversity and its creativity. Every family is free to create its own school, even within the boundaries of the various state laws. In this chapter, we'll look at some of the possibilities for less traditional homeschooling—and in a few years, this chapter may well be outdated as these modes become more mainstream.

Homeschool dads

In all my years of homeschooling, I have met only one homeschooling father in person, and that was many years ago. However, they are out there and they are growing in number. Since I don't have any personal experience in this field, I'd like to introduce you to a great homeschooling father. Frank Domenico is an author, a columnist, and a homeschool dad, all at the same time. I had a chance to ask him a few questions and we'll let him speak for himself:

How many children do you homeschool? "I have successfully homeschooled four children. Two are now in college, one has enrolled in High School, and one is in the eighth grade."

How did you become the homeschool teacher for your children? "I am the follow-through parent, the 'bad cop,' and a good motivator and disciplinarian. My wife was climbing the walls staying home, so I worked her through law school and stayed home to raise the children."

What do you bring to homeschooling that is different from when Mom does it? "I think we have far more physical education, and we are more secluded as well. It is a little difficult to interact socially when everyone else homeschooling is a mom, and you're the only dad. People look at you askance."

Are there challenges you face that a mom might not? "I have had the police stop me because a "concerned citizen" reported that a man was running after a child. What was happening was that I was out at 11 a.m. jogging with my eight-year-old! People think you're home because you can't get a job, not because you chose to do these things. Even our Church-going friends are sometimes judgmental about the choices we've made."

Do you have advice for others in your position? "Do it. Despite the setbacks, this is the most wonderful experience of a man's life. You will not regret the time you stay home with your children. But you also need to find adult time and adult friends, or you may find you lose the ability to dialog with your friends."

Tell me something unique you've done recently in your homeschool. "I have motivated my son in the eighth grade to complete the entire math curriculum in three months. We also did a project where he had to determine 'If Columbus had sailed the Ocean blue in 1215 instead of 1492, which nations would have colonized The Americas?' His research and conclusions were fascinating, not just for a kid, but really for anyone. He astounded me."

Terrie's thoughts on homeschool dads

Even though homeschooling by fathers is becoming more common, it is likely it will be a long time before you find large groups of them in one area or have people stop acting surprised to find out you are one. Being a homeschool dad comes with challenges the moms don't have to cope with, such as the lack of a support system. Two homeschool moms can break up the isolation by team-teaching from time to time. A dad really can't do that unless he is fortunate enough to find another father at home.

Whenever I read about homeschooling dads, the general consensus is that they are more fun as teachers. Frank mentioned more physical education. Other fathers have mentioned more games and more hands-on learning.

If you're a homeschooling father, use the Internet to find online support. Finding local support may be more difficult, but if you join some of the larger homeschool groups, you may be able to find fathers who, if they aren't stay-at-home dads, at least actively participate in their children's homeschools. Then you can organize weekend and evening activities—father/child events and field trips. It's not quite the same as having daytime activities, but it can help you to meet other men who are actively involved in their children's lives and who understand homeschooling.

And if it's any comfort, most homeschooling moms are in awe of you!

"Being a stay-at-home dad can be overwhelming and

thankless, but trust me, your children will actually thank you for doing it," Frank reassures us.

Visit Frank's website (Wix.com/phranx/little-hawk)—he has a book on storytelling and every homeschool parent needs to know how to tell stories.

Homeschooling grandparents

Another growing trend in homeschooling is to have grandparents homeschool the children for their employed parents. Often these grandparents homeschooled their own children first. Some grandparents do all the teaching and some supplement what the parents do. This is a great way to strengthen the grandparent-child relationship and to bring something different into the education. I put out a call for grandparent homeschoolers and found Jeff Klick. Jeff is a pastor at Hope Family Fellowship and the author of books on the family and on morality (http://www.hopefamilyfellowship.org/first2.php). However, Jeff really just wanted to tell me about his wife Leslie who is the actual homeschooling grandparent. This good man thinks she deserves some recognition for her work. Here's what he told me about her:

How many children do you homeschool? "My wife actually does the teaching—we have two granddaughters, ages 7 and 5, that she teaches daily. My wife also assists our eldest daughter with her three school-aged children, sometimes in math and science."

How did your wife become their homeschool teacher? "Our son went through a divorce and even though the marriage did not work, both of the parents asked us to home school the children for a few years."

What does she bring to the homeschooling that is different from when Mom does it? "A vast amount of experience in multiple arenas. My wife has taught our three children all the way though high school and a nephew most of the way, in addition to the grandchildren now."

Are there challenges you face that a mom might not? "Discipline issues sometimes since we are not the parents. Since the parents are divorced, there are some emotional struggles that we are dealing with in the girls as well."

Do you have advice for others in your position? "Love the kids and invest whatever is necessary to assist for you may be the only one that can. We believe the sacrifice is worth it in order to hopefully help these young ladies walk with God."

Tell me something unique you've done recently in your homeschool. "Recently did some fun solar system modeling as well as tadpole feeding. From seed-growing to math, my wife tries to make this time special. The "Shoe-box" outreach to help poor children around the globe was also a big hit."

Anything else you'd like to add? "I have written two books, but my wife is the heart and soul of our family. Her sacrifice in the home education of my children, and now my grandchildren, is an excellent story worth sharing . . . she doesn't have the time to do so, like I do, thus I am the one sharing it."

Terrie's thoughts on grandparents who homeschool

Children today are increasingly isolated from their grandparents. They live far away and longer school days and longer school years limit the time they spend with their extended families. This is a sad fact of American life, because children need grandparents. They need to be comfortable with people of all ages. They need to gain the perspective on life an older relative can bring.

When homeschooling is done completely or in part by grandparents, it can bring something different to the experience. Grandparents are often more relaxed, more fun, and more willing to experiment. When the grandparent is homeschooling her second generation of homeschoolers, she has gained some perspective on what she did the first time around. She's seen the results and can make changes that benefit everyone involved.

If you're homeschooling grandchildren, work closely with the parents. Make sure they're comfortable with the curriculum and the homeschooling style you've chosen. For me, the hardest part of grandparenting is remembering that I had my turn as a parent—now the children's own parents get to make the choices. At the same time, since you're doing the work, you should be allowed to choose something you are comfortable doing. If your styles are very different, you may need to compromise, perhaps being highly structured for some subjects and unstructured for others.

Set out the ground rules on both sides before you begin. Who is paying the costs of the homeschool? How many hours will you be teaching? Will you be sending home work for the children to do? What are the parents' priorities? What about the teaching of religion and values? Is everyone comfortable with how it will be done? You don't want to find yourself uneasy with what you have to teach, but you also don't want the parents uneasy with what the children are learning. It's fine for children to learn that parents and grandparents don't always have the same opinions, but the differences should be handled respectfully.

The more planning you do, the better off you'll be. You're family—you don't want the same battles ordinary parents and teachers have.

Carschooling

Carschooling fascinates a lot of people. Families take their children out of school and head into the real world on an extended journey, homeschooling as they go. What better way to learn geography and history than to actually visit the places you're studying?

On a smaller scale, many families do homeschooling in the car on ordinary outings or smaller vacations. When my oldest took a creative writing class at the high school, my younger children and I often homeschooled in the car or the park next door while we waited for her. We also homeschooled in doctor's offices, church buildings, and anywhere else we happened to be.

If you're taking off on a long journey, you'll need to plan your school very carefully. First, you need an official address somewhere. If you're maintaining your home, that state's homeschool laws would apply to your school, no matter where you're traveling. If you plan to sell your home, you probably want to maintain some sort of legal address somewhere, and that place will determine the rules for your school. Make sure you're properly registered and if you're required to appear for testing, find out what to do if you won't be home at test time.

Have a plan in mind to make sure math doesn't get lost in the excitement of the journey. Your history, literature, writing, and other subjects will most likely tie in with your studies, but math usually doesn't fit and can be easily overlooked. When will your children do it? In the morning before you leave? During lunch break? At night? Having a plan prevents you from forgetting it altogether.

Some studies can be done in the car. Many traveling families use audio books and others take turns reading aloud. Children can play educational games as they drive. Everyone can study one aspect of a place you're visiting and then give oral reports as you travel. If you spend a lot of time on the road and sightseeing, some of the work will need to be done in the car. The suggested resources at the end of the chapter can help you find more information on successful car schooling.

Part-time homeschooling

Some children attend the local public school part of each day and homeschool the remainder of the day. We used this method with varying success, but it does have some advantages.

Well-meaning adults who insisted my child didn't know what he was missing worried my son. When he talked to me about it, I suggested he attend the local grade school part-time and find out for himself. He had not been in school since the start of second grade. We visited the school and arranged for him to attend for several hours a day, three days a week. A teacher volunteered to take on this unusual task and the school issued tests to be sure he could do the work, because he was a little young for his grade, having barely made the kindergarten cut-off date. A few months into the year, he decided not to return to school. He had found the experiment enlightening, but decided he wasn't missing anything he wanted.

This experiment worked for us because my son resented wasting learning time and he was too far ahead of his peers. He was startled to learn the teacher did not adapt the curriculum to the levels of each student. He resented the time the class spent on silly tasks and he hated the rudeness and misbehavior of the students. He began bringing his own books to class to work on when he was bored, and was soon doing his own work all day. He realized he was wasting his time.

Another child might have enjoyed this excursion into public school. My girls often attended school part-time and generally enjoyed themselves. They found two classes to be just right—a chance to take classes not offered at home, meet other students, and have lunch with friends. Then they came home and studied their academics at a more challenging pace.

If you decide to let your children continue their public school part-time, you should be aware of the risks. If your child has not been to school before, the novelty may appeal to him or he may enjoy the luxury of work that is too easy. If you do not intend to let him return full-time, make that clear from the start. Describe it as a supplement and nothing more. If you are trying to decide if your child should return to public school, tell the school officials. We found the schools gave us the best teachers hoping to win us back. They were always puzzled when my children told them they didn't want to attend full-time, but we got the best teachers anyway, because the officials were sure every child wanted to go to school.

We found that part-timing was not very effective in grade school. Although my son was supposed to be there for science and electives, the schedules changed constantly and he never knew what they would be doing when he arrived. The process was more successful in schools where students changed classes, because the schedules were more settled.

If your child has never been to a public school, or hasn't been in many years, you may need to prepare him for the experience. Make sure he can work in a noisy, distracting environment. Many children taking their first class are unnerved when they try to listen through sailing paper airplanes, passing notes, and whispering students. Spend a few hours studying at the library each week for practice. Your children need to learn to listen through noise and to tune out others when they are doing paper work.

Test-taking is sometimes a challenge for homeschoolers. We frequently don't give tests, since we know just how our children are doing. After all, we have only a few students and spend much of our time observing them, talking to them, and looking over their work. When we do give tests, we generally give the same type of test each time, based on what we consider important. My own tests tended to be weighted toward vocabulary and ideas. As you prepare your child to be tested by others, spend some time practicing other kinds of tests. Often, sample tests can be found online (using the methods described earlier in the book, search for "practice tests" and the subject you are teaching) or in test-taking books. Show your child the basics of public school testing: keeping his eyes on his own paper, filling in bubbles completely, following instructions, and meeting time limits.

If possible, bring your child to the school when you enroll him. Ask if someone can show your student around. Request that the guide show him how to work a lock if your school has lockers. This is one task many homeschoolers have not learned, and it's normally taught only to the youngest grade. Go over procedures to be followed if he is ill or injured, is the victim of bullying, or is asked to do something he knows he should not do. Unfortunately, schools sometimes cause children to violate family or religious rules by showing inappropriate movies, insisting a child taste a food he is not allowed to eat, or by expecting him to read foul language aloud from a book. You will need to ask the counselor how the child should handle the situation. We found the school counselor to be a valuable resource our children could turn to any time they felt uneasy about classroom issues.

Afterschooling

Afterschooling means you send your children to school every day, but when the school day ends, you supplement what they gained from school. Summers and weekends are also filled with learning activities. My parents raised me this way, and I raised my children this way for many years. Does afterschooling work? I can nearly always spot a homeschooler by his outstanding social skills with people of varying ages, his intelligence, and his excitement about learning. Afterschoolers often fool me into believing they are homeschoolers. While afterschooling doesn't offer all the benefits that come from learning at home all day, it does offer many of the most important ones.

Homeschooled children spend more time with their parents and build a closer relationship as a result. They learn to value education because the entire family learns together. These benefits can also be found in an afterschooling family.

A growing complaint about public schools is that they demand too much homework. Children attend school for an increasing number of days and hours in order to improve test scores, and then come home with even more hours of dull paperwork. As an afterschooler, you don't want to add to the paperwork load. Instead, your contribution will be to add hands-on learning to the bookwork your child is already doing. You can choose to supplement the subjects taught, or you can focus on material the schools don't offer.

If you want to focus on helping your child learn more about his school subjects, meet with his teacher early in the year to find out what the children will be learning. This allows you to formulate a loose plan for the coming months. Look for the fun aspects of the subjects your child is studying. If he is learning about plants, buy a microscope and plant a garden. If he is learning about endangered animals, take him to the zoo or a wildlife preserve.

In most public schools, particularly at the lower grades, subjects are introduced but never really studied in-depth. A child gets one chapter on the human body, one on astronomy, and another on plants. Each chapter might be studied for a week or two. Instead of trying to supplement every subject your child learns, select a few and dig in as a family. You might want to begin early so your child has a firm foundation when he begins the subject at school. Starting at the same time it's covered in school, however, allows the child to pick up the basics first and then build on that with you.

In-depth study is the key to developing a passion for learning. Children seldom become excited about a subject during a week of learning the basics in a fifteen-minute class. Enthusiasm develops as a child moves beyond the basics and into the exciting details, mysteries, and curiosities found in every subject. Look for books and videos that explore the basics and the fringes of a subject. What happened to the settlers who disappeared at Roanoke? Is time travel scientifically possible? What plant could become extinct in the next year? Theoretical topics have the power to excite a child's mind.

Look for a hands-on aspect to your subject. If your child is learning about plants, put in a garden as a family. If your child is studying nutrition, ask her to plan a healthy week of meals for your family. If she is learning about computers, do something new on your own computer. Learn together and have fun. You are telling your child that learning is important, and that you support the efforts her teacher is making.

When your child develops an interest in something not covered in school, offer to help her learn about it at home. Show her she doesn't have to wait for a class to learn something. Ask her to suggest ways she could learn the material, and then help her find appropriate resources and develop a plan. Encourage her to carry out the plan by participating with her and by discussing her progress.

Homeschoolers are often recognized for their ability to socialize well with adults. Children who spend their days almost entirely with peers and one adult often become very peer-dependent. They develop a desperate need to be with friends all the time, to please their peers, and to imitate them at any cost. A homeschooler learns to entertain himself while his friends are in school and also spends time learning from and getting to know adults. Try to add adults to your child's life. Let him approach experts on subjects he is interested in. Have him stay in the room occasionally when adults are visiting your home. Find a senior citizen who needs the companionship and help of a child and encourage your child to build a relationship. Let him seek out an older teenager (carefully chosen) for advice. Make sure he doesn't spend all his time with children who are his age and just like him. Friends can come in all ages and a surprising variety of personalities and backgrounds. Help your afterschooler expand his world and you will give him the social competence so much admired in homeschoolers.

More Resources

➤ *What the Rest of Us Can Learn From Homeschooling: How A+ Parents Give Their Traditionally Schooled Kids the Academic Edge* by Linda Dobson
ISBN: 0761519777
Linda Dobson is one of homeschooling's best writers. In this book, she shows parents who don't homeschool how to give their children many of the same advantages, including a joy of learning and a sense of belonging to the community.

➤ *Learn to Sign the Fun Way: Let Your Fingers Do the Talking with Games, Puzzles, and Activities in American Sign Language* by Penny Warner
ISBN: 0761532633
Languages make an excellent supplemental subject for afterschoolers because they are seldom taught in the younger grades. Sign language is fun for children because it's physical and is the fourth most commonly used language in the United States. This is the sort of book you want to choose, because it's filled with fun activities instead of a list of signs with no suggestions for learning them. You may want to find videos to show you how to move your hands like an expert.

➤ *The Science Explorer*
http://www.exploratorium.edu/science_explorer/
As an afterschooler, you want to spend your time having fun. This website has many experiments, interesting articles on science and books to supplement your child's school education. This is one of my favorites, because the science experiments are on topics that interest children, not adults. Take apart a computer disk, make a periscope, or look at an oozy substance that can't decide if it's liquid or solid.

➤ *Games for Learning: Ten Minutes a Day to Help Your Child Do Well in School / from Kindergarten to Third Grade* by Peggy Kaye
ISBN: 0374522863
These are simple games you can play with your child—no worksheets, no dull drills—just fun together-time that supplements your child's education. Peggy Kay also has books on games for specific subjects.

➤ *Carschooling: Over 350 Entertaining Games & Activities to Turn Travel Time into Learning Time - For Kids Ages 4 to 17, 2nd edition* by Diane Flynn Keith
ISBN: 978-0615309491
Don't waste the drive time. Learn chemistry, history, math, and even physical education through games while strapped into a seat belt.

➤ *The Home Schooling Father* by Michael P. Farris
ISBN: 978-0805425871
Michael Farris, the president of the Homeschool Legal Defense Association, writes a short book on homeschooling dads, one of the few books on this subject.

Chapter 9

Temporary Homeschooling

TEMPORARY HOMESCHOOLS ARE GROWING in popularity today. The most common temporary homeschool is the emergency homeschool, which begins because something is wrong at school or at home. A clash between teacher and student, a problem with bullies, or a family crisis—something just isn't working with the current school year. Some families can no longer afford a child's private school due to unemployment, and decide to homeschool until the parent returns to work. A family that is moving mid-year may decide to keep the children home one full year to avoid a transition challenge.

A newer form of homeschooling is the homeschool sabbatical. In this model, a parent decides to give the children a one-year break from traditional schools by homeschooling. They may travel for the year or they may simply want more time together. Some want a year to work on overcoming the challenges of a learning disability or to help a child catch up. Many just do it for fun. Some are testing the idea of permanently homeschooling.

Parents who begin homeschooling with the intention of returning their children to school have to approach homeschooling a little differently than permanent homeschoolers. In this chapter, we'll learn how to make the most of a year at home.

Because your children are going back to school in a year or so, you will have to pay more attention to what their schools are doing. You will need to be sure your children keep up with their class at school. It can also be more important to maintain their current friendships so they are still strong when the children return. If you want to do something special or have a particular goal in mind, you'll have to plan it more carefully to be certain it's finished or that you can complete it after the children go to school again.

Before removing your children from school, meet with the teachers and the principals if you can. Ask the teacher for details about your children's learning levels, their strengths, and their weaknesses. Find out how the teachers think your children learn best. Explain that you are going to work on making sure the return year is successful and this will help you set goals. You may not agree with everything the teacher says, but since you are leaving anyway, there is no point in arguing. Just listen.

From the principal, learn what your children need to have mastered when they return and what the return procedure will be. Are they automatically going into the next grade or will the school insist on a placement test? What subjects are the children in their grades going to study? Are there particular skills the children master in those grades?

Find out what you'll need to do to put them *back* in school. This allows you to keep the proper records right from the start. At the very least, you'll want to keep a basic record of attendance, immunizations, subjects covered, and tests taken. Maintain a portfolio of sample work—average work and a few of the best things. A scrapbook with pictures can help the next teacher understand what your child did during his year away.

If your relationship with the school hasn't been very good and you aren't comfortable meeting with them, gather this information by looking through your child's schoolwork and report cards and by talking to parents of children in the grades you need information on.

Starting without warning

If you are reading this book because you got mad during a meeting and pulled your children out on the spot, or if things aren't going well and you pulled them out with only a few days warning, you are probably overwhelmed right now. The contents of this book are more information than you really need. Read this chapter and the ones on laws and on removing your children. Skim through for the most critical information. You don't need everything in this book right at the start. For a step-by-step process of setting up a temporary homeschool, visit a website I created just for this situation—Emergency Homeschooling: http://www.emergencyhomeschooling.com.

This website walks you through the process of setting up an emergency or temporary homeschool without all the extra information I've included in this book. Once you're settled a little more, come back to the book to learn more about homeschooling. But for now, start slowly.

The important thing is to not try to rush into a full program of school immediately if you're not ready for it. Take a few days off and have fun. Then plan just a few activities you can do together that are educational. If you have a math book, start using it after your short break so you don't get behind. Don't worry about schedules yet—just spend half an hour a day on it until you have time to make a plan. Make sure every day has reading in it, including some fun library books on history or science. Do some art and music, include a little gym, and have a school planning meeting with your children to let them give you feedback on how they'd like school to operate and what they'd like to learn. Many of their suggestions won't work, but try to incorporate at least some of their ideas and one topic they are passionate about.

If you're feeling very insecure, consider a government homeschooling program. They're ideal for temporary home-schoolers unless they are really behind or really ahead. You'll be able to jump right in on most of them.

Choosing a curriculum

This is covered in more depth in other chapters, but as a temporary homeschooler, you need to give some additional thought to your curriculum. If you want your children to learn everything they would have learned in school, you may want to consider using a school district homeschooling pro-gram. Technically, this isn't homeschooling since the govern-ment retains control of the education, but I did this for awhile and I considered myself a homeschooler. You probably will as well. Leave the technicalities to those who like to argue such things and just proceed as a homeschooler. Even though the school is planning the work and overseeing it, you will be able to monitor exactly what your child is learning and be able to step in if he's learning something inappropriate or if he's having trouble with a subject. You'll find yourself very involved in your child's education, even when you're using a district program.

Using this program allows your children to keep up with their usual school. It also makes returning your child to school very easy since he officially never left the dis-trict. However, it gives you less control over what your child will be learning. If your child is behind or ahead, you'll face many of the same problems that may have led you to take a year off in the first place.

Another way to keep up with the school is to purchase the textbooks the school uses and put together your own lesson plans. I did this the first year I homeschooled on my own. However, it's very expensive and the books have so many mistakes in them that when I tried it, I wasted a lot of time researching and correcting the content.

A good compromise is to purchase the math book. Math generally requires you to know everything taught in the previous math book, so it will make your children's return easier if they've had the same book. You generally have more flexibility in the other subjects, so you can use any materials you like for those. You may also find a math program that is similar to the district's program. If your child is behind, choose one at his level. It is very possible you will be able to finish more than one book in the year, allowing him to get closer to grade level.

If your child stays at grade level for math and reading, he should have no trouble returning. The other subjects are flexible. You don't need the official reading book to stay at the correct reading level. You just need to read and to work on whatever word attack skills (phonics, sight-reading, comprehension) your child needs.

Although you might decide to cover the same history topic, you can put this subject together any way you like. For science, focus on getting your child excited about the world and don't worry too much about keeping up.

If you are working with a high school student, make sure he takes all the classes needed for graduation. Temporary homeschoolers who are in high school may want to use a district program for their year off to make sure there are no problems with graduation.

Making a plan to keep up

If your child is working at grade level in every subject, you only have to be sure you keep up with his class. Make a list of everything you need to cover this year in math. Then divide it by the number of months in the school year. This gives you a rough idea of your pace. You probably won't spend an equal amount of time on each subject, but you'll be able to monitor whether you're ahead or behind. If you're using a math book, divide up the page numbers instead of the topics. You can break the schedule down further to find out how many pages you should do each day.

Just because a page is in a math book doesn't mean you have to do it. You don't have to do every problem on a page, either. You can, if needed, do a page three times. Pre-test your child before starting a new topic to find out if he already knows how to do the problems. If he does, just have him do a few problems for review purposes and then move on. Periodically, send him back to that page to do a few more for additional review. However, don't spend a lot of time on anything your child can already do. This allows you to slow down when you encounter something difficult.

Follow the same pattern with your other subjects if you're concerned about keeping up with them. Purchase children's books that have reading levels printed on them and use these to monitor how well your child is reading. These may not be entirely accurate, but they are a good starting point. In general, don't worry too much about the official reading level of your child. Buy a variety of books and read them together. When you listen to your child read, write down any words he doesn't know. Notice what he does to try to figure out unfamiliar words. Does he attempt to sound it out? Does he try to figure out the word based on the content? Teach the words he misses and help him improve his word attack skills. By teaching him words he reads in real life, either for pleasure or in his school books, he will gain confidence as a reader.

Approach spelling the same way. Instead of worrying about what words he ought to know, just teach him the words he misses in his writing. Turn on spell check, but not auto-correct if he uses a computer, and then have him make a list of the words he misspells. If he isn't working on a computer, lightly mark misspelled words so he can make a list of words after finding out the correct spelling. It is far more sensible to teach him to spell words he actually uses. It probably won't matter much if he happens not to know how to spell a few words that were taught in the traditional school that year, so don't worry about following their lists.

For any subject where exact content is unimportant, decide what you want to teach and make a loose schedule. Adapt it based on how interested you and your children become in the subjects.

Making a plan to catch up in reading

If your child is behind in school, you want to get the most possible out of your one year at home. This means you need to focus on the subjects that are suffering. Your child may have trouble juggling six subjects, but if you focus on just two, you can make remarkable progress.

Reading impacts every other subject, so if your child is behind in reading, focus on that subject. You'll have to continue doing math, but all other subjects can be lightly taught through the reading instruction. Just intersperse literature with books on history or science.

If you're going to be teaching reading for three or four hours a day, you'll have to be creative to make it interesting. You can't just sit together reading books all day. Instead, mix up the teaching so there is a combination of reading silently and aloud, being read to, reading for practical purposes, and reading for subject matter. You can also spend time playing with books.

Oral Reading. While your child is fresh in the morning, have him read to you for a little while. Keep it relaxed and give him all the time he needs to figure out words he doesn't know. If he asks for help, guide him through the process of figuring out the words part of the time. The rest of the time, just tell him the word. Save the rescue for words that aren't all that important or that don't follow normal word attack rules. If you teach some words in advance, the story will be easier to manage. When he's struggling to learn the words, he won't remember what the story is about, so once he's mastered the vocabulary, have him read the story again.

Journaling. Tell your child the journal is not private and he can write an actual journal or he can write stories. If you prefer, have him dictate the entries to you. Type the entries once a week and turn them into reading books. I discovered children read better when they are reading words they wrote themselves. Use the journal as a reading book a few times a week.

Play a game that requires reading. This can be a board game or a learning game you purchased or created. This gives him reasons for learning to read, and it's fun.

Story time. Choose a book he can understand and enjoy, but that is too hard for him to read on his own. The goal is to show him how wonderful reading is and to motivate him to read for himself someday, so this time needs to be stress-free and fun. For a child who is far behind, story time lets you introduce him to the books his peers are reading.

Formal lesson on reading skills. This can involve any skill he needs to improve. You can find workbooks for this in most teacher supply stores.

Read from history and science books. He can read alone or with you. Devise a project based on the reading (making a model, playing a game, doing an experiment, etc.). Have your child write the project plan and then follow it as you carry it out. This combines reading and writing practice.

Cooking lesson that involves reading a cookbook. This is another way to teach reading through practical skills. Make lunch, dinner, or dessert together and be lavish in the praise.

Read comics. They aren't great literature, but they're fun.

Read instructions in textbooks. This is important for getting through the next school year.

Play with books. Whenever he reads a good book, have him play with it. He can act out the story with toys or puppets, make a craft, or do something the main character did. He can change the ending or rewrite a scene with himself in it. It doesn't really matter what you choose to do. Just do something extra that makes the book more memorable.

As you can see, reading is a fairly integral part of our lives. Reading instruction doesn't all have to be boring schoolwork. Some of it can just be fun.

Don't spend too much time worrying about the grade level. Just concentrate on teaching as many reading skills as you can, doing actual reading of all kinds in an emotionally safe environment. Show him how much fun reading really could be. Your child is likely to improve his reading this year if you give him lots of opportunities to read things he actually enjoys reading.

Teaching the advanced child

Homeschool sabbaticals are a wonderful gift to give the advanced child. Notice I am not using the term gifted here. It doesn't really matter what a child's IQ is. If he is very advanced in a subject, this year is your opportunity to let him learn at his own pace. Too often gifted programs give more work, but not more challenging work. They exclude children who are highly motivated but not gifted, and those who are not good at IQ tests, even though they may well be gifted. This section refers to a child who is well ahead of his peers or who is a motivated learner.

When you start evaluating your child's learning levels, you may discover he is far more advanced than you realized. A lot of advanced children hold back in order to better fit in. When my children first came home (a term homeschoolers use for children who stop attending traditional schools to homeschool) the principal told me my second and third graders were reading too well for any of the books available to the elementary school. I started them on high school books, but by the end of the year tests showed they should be reading college level books. At that point, we began using ordinary trade books. I didn't worry about grade levels. They just read whatever they wanted to read.

When you are working with advanced and highly motivated learners, you have to make some decisions, particularly if they are returning to traditional education in a year. If they are already advanced, making them more advanced increases the likelihood of boredom when they return. The further ahead a child is, the harder it is for a school to meet his needs.

On the other hand, I hate the idea of holding a child back just to make the schools happy. My children got a lot from the learning they did ahead, even though it also created some challenges. I feel children should be allowed to learn to the full extent of their abilities and interests. That said, it is a decision only a parent can make. If your child is old enough, you might want to discuss the problem with him. How does he feel about being ahead of the class? Does he get bored? Would he be willing to go to a higher grade for some subjects when he returned?

If your child really loves math, you might look at more creative types of math that wouldn't be covered in normal math classes anyway, such as brain teasers. This way, he is improving his math skills without getting too far ahead. Being advanced in reading is more of a problem for the youngest children because the first reading books are normally very dull. As the children get older, the stories may not be difficult enough, but they are interesting. You can provide your child with harder books for his pleasure reading.

If you're concerned about creating boredom, consider focusing your advanced work around history, science, art, or music. Dig deeper into those subjects and look into the mysteries and controversies. Let your child take the lead in figuring out what makes the subject fascinating to him.

The most important skills you can give an advanced child are the abilities to research and to analyze. Make plenty of room in your curriculum this year to get your child to think, imagine, and choose.

Planning one memorable thematic unit

Even if you're using a packaged curriculum, try to create one personalized program to carry out during your home year. Choose something your child is very eager to learn— and possibly something you're both eager to learn—something he is not likely to learn in school. You can choose an elective—any subject not part of the academic curriculum you'd like to learn together—or you can choose to focus in on one part of science or history. Do some serious learning, but make sure you keep it fun. This is your memory-making event, the one the children will still talk about when they grow up.

You don't have to spend money or make the lessons complicated to make them memorable. The memories come from creating a shared experience. A combination of books, videos, games, cooking, field trips, and that sort of thing will make it fun. The chapters on planning unit studies will help you with this. You can start it a few months into the year to give yourself time to settle in first.

Setting reasonable goals

When you know you only have a year, you may be tempted to pack too much into it. You get overly ambitious and plan too many exciting things or decide your children will completely catch up or get years ahead. This leads to stress for both you and the children and can spoil the year.

It's important to set goals for the year, but make them goals you can achieve. If you finish early, add an additional goal later. If your child is three years behind, you probably won't get him up to grade level this year. You might get him only two years behind. You might only manage to get him more confident and help him improve some skills, even though he's still just as far behind. Whatever you accomplish is more than he would have gotten if he'd been in school this year.

Put your goals into writing. Take a few minutes and list the most important thing you'd like to accomplish during the year and then shrink it into manageable size. Then choose a few more to work on. Try not to set too many goals—three might be plenty. For instance, you might list:

Have William progress one and a half years in math.
Help William learn to love history.
Have three memorable family learning experiences.

These are manageable goals and shouldn't put too much stress on the family. Alternately, you could set two goals for each subject, one on academic achievement and one on attitude toward the subject. Once a month, stop and evaluate how you're doing in progressing toward the goals. Sometimes you'll realize you set the wrong goal or made an unrealistic goal. When that happens, it's perfectly acceptable to change it and start over.

Ending your year at home

As your year at home comes to an end, take some time to evaluate how it went. The first year of homeschooling is hard and the first year is all you had, so you can't expect perfection. What can you reasonably expect from your year of homeschooling?

Perhaps the most important thing you'll take away from the year is that you will know your children better. You've had so much time during the year to find out who they have become. This should lead to an improved relationship overall. Even if the year was a bit rocky, you've learned enough to figure out how to make things better as time goes on.

Your ability to work with your children's teachers will have improved. Having taught them yourself, you now have a better understanding of the challenges the teachers faced; you also have a better understanding of how your children learn. This will improve your ability to work out any needed accommodations or help with homework.

Notice the areas where your children have improved in their schoolwork, their behavior, and their relationships with their family. These are some of the benefits that come out of homeschooling.

Plan a big celebration to end your year. Even if the year wasn't perfect, it was a major accomplishment for everyone. Do something special to finish it off.

Returning to school

Let the school know your children are returning in plenty of time so they can be assigned classrooms and take any evaluations the schools might require. You may want to ask if you can meet with their new teachers to go over your child's work. When my oldest returned from a year and several months at home, we met together with the new teacher. We showed him the books she had used and samples of her schoolwork and her creative writing. We went over special needs and he asked about her interests. She told him what worried her about returning to school and they were able to address those issues. This helped ease the transition back into school. The teacher started out knowing where the problems might be and what her strengths were. It also set a framework for home and school communications. I was able to demonstrate that I took her education seriously and had a realistic understanding of her abilities and needs. This led to a more peaceful school year.

Maybe you're not sure you want to end homeschooling

Although my daughter returned to school, the next year she decided to go back to homeschooling and her younger siblings asked to join her. When your homeschool year ends, you may discover you and the children enjoyed the year and want to continue. You can decide to become a permanent homeschooler or just continue for one more year. You don't have to make a final decision for the remainder of the children's educational careers. You can make the choice a year at a time.

If you decide to continue the experiment, take time to evaluate what you liked and what you didn't like about your homeschool year. This is a good time to make changes. Homeschooling offers a lot of freedom, even in restrictive states. You can change your method of operation every year until you find the one that is comfortable for you.

The second year will be far smoother than the first year because you'll have gotten past all the beginner's mistakes. You'll start your new year as an experienced teacher who speaks the language and has resources to draw from in developing an exciting homeschooling program.

More resources:

➤ *EmergencyHomeschooling.com*

My website on temporary homeschooling. An efficient guide to getting started at the last minute.

➤ *Suddenly Homeschooling: A Quick-Start Guide to Legally Homeschool in 2 Weeks* by Marie-Claire Moreau
ISBN: 9781936214402
This book has a variety of lists to help you move through the process of setting up a homeschool with two week's notice.

➤ *Love in a Time of Homeschooling: A Mother and Daughter's Uncommon Year* by Laura Brodie
ISBN: 0061706469
This book sparked a lot of publicity about the idea of a homeschool sabbatical. It's very honest and straightforward. I don't think she really caught the vision of homeschooling or realized the potential, but the book is enlightening in terms of some of the challenges and benefits of temporary homeschooling.

Chapter 10

Getting Supplies When You're Cheap . . . ummm . . . Frugal

THE FIRST QUESTION PROSPECTIVE homeschoolers usually ask is how much this is going to cost. This is a serious issue, especially if you are living on a single income in a world designed for two incomes. Fortunately, there isn't a set answer to this question. How much you spend depends on how you decide to homeschool, how much time you have, how much experience you have choosing educational materials, and how many supplies you already have around the house. It also depends on how much money you have to spend. The more money you spend, the less time you will have to spend. If you are willing to put the time into research and into making your own materials, you can homeschool nearly for free.

Purchased curricula can run hundreds of dollars, but building your own can cost much less. You can do as much from the Internet, your imagination, or the library as you can manage. Let's look at some of the expenses you will have and learn how to minimize them.

You have to have books. You don't, however, have to have textbooks for most subjects. Ordering standard textbooks is quite expensive and most are very inaccurate. There are many good trade books (ordinary children's books) available for nearly every subject, and these are much cheaper. There are also used curricula sellers online. Ask questions before sending money to these resellers. What do they mean by "like new?" If you are unfamiliar with the company, ask home-schoolers you know for recommendations since anyone can set up an Internet business. Be sure the company is trustworthy, and evaluate it just as you would any other company. Many areas also have curriculum fairs in the summer. Your local homeschooling group will know about these, or you can do an Internet search for the fairs in your area. These are like Christmas in August for most homeschoolers, so come with a budget and a list or you will spend far more than you can afford.

School supply stores have a smaller selection, but may offer less temptation. If you show up when the store is crowded, you can start a conversation with other shoppers and ask for their recommendations. People love to be consulted. Just look for someone who seems friendly and unhurried. If the person you choose turns out to be a professional teacher, don't tell her how awful your school experience was. Instead, act grateful to have the advice of a professional. Make a point of befriending the staff at this store so they will tell you the truth about which materials really work and will let you know when something exciting becomes available.

You can use thrift stores and other sources for used books if you're careful. Old science and history books are usually inaccurate, but old math and English books are often much better than their modern replacements. Old reading books are fine, too, as long as they match the way you want to teach reading.

Finally, become an expert on your library and get on a first name basis with a librarian. Librarians were my very best resources. They picked out wonderful books for my children, taught my little ones to use the library, and made suggestions for building my literature course. When I was teaching Shakespeare, they kept an eye out for interesting children's editions and ordered them from other branches without bothering to ask first. They just knew I'd want them. Be certain you know where those books go in your home, or the fines will cost more than the book. We kept a basket on the hearth and the books could only be read in the living room, which spared me the trauma of digging under dusty beds to find books buried among the dirty socks.

Supplies
Of course, you will need more than books. As I've mentioned, homeschooling takes a lot of *stuff*, and some of it costs money. You may already have plenty of art materials, office supplies, and educational toys. When you buy gifts for your children, make some of them educational. My definition of an educational toy is one that is messy, has lots of pieces, and encourages imagination. Toys with one neat piece are great for homemaking, but they seldom manage to teach anything. Tiny building toys are painful to step on in the dark, but they teach everything from creativity to geometry. Finger paint is hard on clothes, but is a fascinating method of exploring color and design. (Have you finger-painted recently? You may be surprised at how much fun it is.) Make sure you have storage containers for the parts and old clothes for the paint.

You don't have to buy all your supplies at once. Buy a few things each week and try to buy in bulk when you can. Anything public schools require is on sale in August and September, so set aside whatever you can afford for art supplies, paper, backpacks, lunch boxes, and calculators.

Following are some of the supplies you might want to gradually acquire for your school:

Art
Finger paints, watercolors, painting papers (although paper

bags and newspaper also work), crayons, markers, colored pencils, sidewalk chalk, construction paper, glue, glitter, a hole punch, scissors, yarn, lunch bags, and anything else that looks like fun. In addition to items you purchase, put together a box of interesting junk and give it to your children in art class. Include toilet paper rolls, scraps of material, colorful ads, leftover pieces of clean foil, sticks, cleaned fast-food boxes, bubble wrap, old magazines, and that sort of thing. The odder it is the more interesting the children will consider it. Let them make whatever they want with it and think of it as recycling. Use the backs of ads for casual drawing.

Science

Purchase a few good books about doing science with household items and then keep the items the books call for around your house. You might want to invest in a good (but not great) microscope and telescope, because children can spend hours peering at anything under the scope. A magnifying glass is inexpensive and easier for younger children to use than a microscope. Science is better done by hanging around places where science happens such as the ant trail in the back yard or the frog pond at the park than it is at a school desk.

History

Dress-up boxes with old-fashioned items can make history more fun. Buy these at yard sales and thrift stores and haunt your own closet as well. You knew there was a reason you kept your prom dress! Art supplies that can be used to make dioramas or posters are essential, especially for younger homeschoolers. We spent a fair amount of history time in the kitchen making food from the time periods we studied, but you have to cook anyway, so that doesn't count in your homeschooling budget. A newspaper is important for children old enough to monitor current events. (Even though they are online, consider a print newspaper for the experience.) Find both a globe and a map of the world as well as one for your country. When you teach, send children to point out every location you discuss on the globe and then on the map. If you are studying a specific country, get a map of that country as well. You probably need to buy those new, since countries change, but they don't have to be fancy.

Math

For young children, the most important tools are small items to count and to use in demonstrating a math problem. You don't need to buy the fancy manipulatives made for this purpose. (Manipulatives are items children use to make a visual demonstration of a math problem or concept; they cost a fortune in school supply stores.) Use toys, buttons, or candies for basic counters. Have some yarn handy for circling sets (groups). Have various measuring tools such as rulers and tape measures as well as measuring cups and spoons (which you probably already own). Calculators are important for technology-related math. Begin with very simple ones, but your older students should have a good calculator and those cost a lot of money, so plan ahead. (Keep in mind that you would have had to buy some of these items, including the calculator, even if your child was in public school.)

Music

For small children, you can build an inexpensive supply of children's music, which is often available on clearance racks. They are happy listening to music, dancing, and perhaps drawing what the music makes them feel. Make homemade rhythm instruments using household junk (for instance, filling a toilet paper roll with rice and covering it with whatever is sturdy and handy). Older children should listen to classical music and have videos of orchestras. Expose them to a variety of musical styles. Some of them will want to study a real instrument.

Beyond these basic supplies, you can use your imagination. A computer is important, since children are expected to know how to use one. If you can't afford one, make sure you take them to the library to practice using computers there. If you can afford one, buy it and subscribe to an Internet service. You will save a great deal of money and build a support network by pulling lesson plans from the Internet, learning new homeschooling methods, and meeting other homeschoolers in online discussion forums. Throughout this book, you will learn a variety of ways to use the Internet in your homeschool.

If you an afford it, consider buying a printer that is also a copier. If I could change one thing about my early homeschooling, I would have skipped the shiny textbooks and clever workbooks and bought a photocopier. I spent so much time and money preparing additional worksheets that the copier would have paid for itself. You can reuse workbooks and you can make copies of diagrams in library books. You can create coloring books and other teaching supplies.

As you get to know other homeschoolers, you will be able to reduce your budget. You can trade materials and books and purchase supplies your friends no longer need. You can also find out what worked for others before you spend the money. As often as possible though, look for materials that have more than one use. When I became more experienced, I chose educational games the children would continue to enjoy long after the unit study ended. Art supplies were fun as well as educational, and books had to have enough value to read just for fun. I searched my home for items I already owned and tried to imagine new uses for them. Building toys taught geometry and then became ordinary toys. Even if you are spending the same amount of money, you won't spend it on items you only use once.

More Resources

➤ *Homeschooling on a Shoestring: A Jam-packed Guide* by Melissa L. Morgan, Judith Waite Allee
ISBN: 087788546X
This book shows you how to cut your homeschooling costs, but it also shows you how to cut the cost of living in general, and how to earn money from home.

➤ *A2Z Home's Cool*
"Homeschooling on a Budget"
A2Zhomeschooling.com/materials/homeschooling_curriculum/budget_curriculum_shop/livelihood_issues_while_homeschooling
Links to various articles on frugal homeschooling and on homeschooling costs. Many homeschooling supplies are also available on this site.

Chapter 11

How Am I Going to Teach?
How Are They Going to Learn?

BEFORE YOU START TEACHING, you need to decide how you are going to approach your homeschool. Do you want to buy a curriculum? If so, how do you choose which one? Which of the three most common homeschooling methods (unschooling, structured learning, and eclectic learning, which are discussed later in this chapter) will you choose if you decide to put together your own curriculum? You have made many choices as you've prepared to homeschool. The best part of this decision is that there is not a "right" answer. It's a matter of preference and budget, and you can change your mind at any time.

Do I need a curriculum?
A curriculum is a collection of the subjects you teach your children and the materials used in that teaching. You can purchase one ready-made, buy books that give you guidelines for building your own, create everything from scratch, or use a mixture of materials. As mentioned earlier, your choice will be based on cost, time, ability, and pleasure.

A purchased curriculum can be expensive and may not work for a specific child, even if it worked for all your other children. Some curriculum providers don't allow you to reuse materials or to mix and match. This is a challenge if your child is six years old, reads at a fourth grade level, won't read about children who are so much older than he is, and can't write. On the other hand, a curriculum that is parent-proof and complete is a great way to get started if you aren't sure what you are doing and are too nervous to build your own lessons for awhile. You can begin with these materials and gradually introduce your own lesson plans as you build confidence.

Using a curriculum the first year lets you find out how a subject can be taught and allows you to watch how your children learn. As you use the materials, you will begin to see what your child enjoys and what frustrates him or bores him. If you later choose to create your own materials, you can use what you learned to create lesson plans your child will really enjoy. This option allows you to reduce the amount of time devoted to homeschooling as you adapt your schedule to your new lifestyle.

Don't feel uncomfortable about purchasing a curriculum. Many parents use them quite successfully, either as a permanent method or as a temporary option. Many children enjoy them and like to help select the program they will use. If you are employed or have many small children and very little time for preparation, these materials are ideal. They are also a very good option for parents who are insecure about their ability to teach certain subjects or to plan lessons. They provide access to current trends in teaching methods. Many of these programs also provide good support for anxious parents and accountability for parents in homeschool-unfriendly states.

If you want a purchased curriculum, search for reviews that tell you about the materials and about the kinds of children who enjoyed or hated them. Go to your Internet search engine and type: *"homeschool curriculum" reviews.* There aren't any guarantees when you read the opinions of others, but this is a starting point.

Now try to visit a curriculum fair and look at the materials. You might also look up publisher pages on the Internet to learn more about the packages. Remember that anyone can create and sell a curriculum, so study the author's credentials, his experience with homeschooling, and the opinions of those who have used his program.

Think about your child's needs. Many packaged programs are just workbooks. Some children work very well with textbooks and workbooks and others get bored. Some programs have a great deal of drill, which many children need. Others focus more on understanding the concepts being taught.

Can your child work quietly at a desk for long periods of time? Does he like to do that? If so, a reading and writing package may be just right. Does he need to do something hands-on in order to learn? In this case, a quiet package will be frustrating for both of you.

Be sure to look carefully at costs. Some packages are very expensive. Some allow you to hand down materials to younger children, only replacing consumables. (Consumables are materials you use up, such as worksheets.) Others insist you re-buy the entire package for each child. Some packages come with record keeping, grading, and the assistance of a teacher if you need it. Be sure you understand what is included in your program. Find out if you are required to submit the completed work to the school. Don't be afraid to ask questions by telephone or e-mail before you purchase a program.

Evaluate the amount of time needed to complete the program. If each subject is taught separately, you will need more time than if subjects are combined, and your day will feel choppier. A thematic unit, which allows children to study all their subjects around a theme, makes a day flow more smoothly, but may be a challenge if your child is not at the same grade level in all subjects.

Notice how the program teaches each subject. This is particularly important in math and reading. Some math books teach chapter by chapter. You learn one subject in the first chapter and then move to a new subject in the next. Other books teach a little of each thing and then review old subjects. A newer trend is to simply introduce everything with minimal drill, repeating every subject every year. This is designed to create high scores on standardized tests rather than having the child actually learn the material.

Reading programs vary and styles come and go. As a homeschooling parent, you are free to ignore trends and fads in reading instruction. Be sure the program appeals to you as the teacher and seems appealing to the child. Decide whether your child has the background to start the program. Some programs presume a child arrives with certain skills you may have assumed would be taught in school.

If you have been able to find other homeschoolers, ask them about the programs they have tried and ask to see the materials. A face-to-face discussion with someone you know may tell you more than reviews from complete strangers.

You are not locked into any method for life. Many parents begin with a purchased program the first year, particularly if they have to begin unexpectedly. They have the entire year to decide what to do the coming year, and this can be a tremendous relief to nervous new teachers. If you feel extremely insecure, start with a popular homeschooling program. (A few hours of research on the Internet will tell you which programs are currently popular, because they will be mentioned again and again on homeschooling websites.) A few months into the year, introduce a subject you want to teach yourself. Find out if you enjoy preparing lesson plans and teaching. If you do, consider creating some of the subjects yourself.

Gathering prepared materials from many sources

An in-between way to teach is to use a variety of materials and lesson plans created by others. The Internet is a wonderful source of lesson plans. Many were created for public school classrooms and take a little adaptation; but as you practice, you will become more skilled at doing this. As homeschooling grows in popularity, the number of lesson plans made just for homeschoolers also increases. To find lesson plans, go to your favorite search engine. Type the words "lesson plans" in quotation marks. Outside the marks, type the topic of the lesson plan you are looking for. Your request will look like this:

```
"lesson plan" George Washington
"lesson plan" turtles
"lesson plan" endangered turtles
```

You use the quotation marks to make the program search for the entire phrase. You will still get pages you don't want, but it will narrow down the choices. Experiment with different terms until you get exactly what you want. Becoming an expert search engine user is worth the time involved in practicing. Don't send your young children to search, because even seemingly innocent searches can turn up some scary or immoral pages.

You might create a lesson plan on turtles by finding a book about endangered turtles at the library, finding a thematic unit book with ready-made worksheets in your school supply store, and purchasing some videos. When you have enough lesson plans in a certain area, you have a curriculum for that subject.

Will these materials work?

How do you know what to use for your children? At first,

there is a lot of guesswork involved. I made many mistakes when I started out because I didn't understand how my children liked to learn and I didn't understand how I liked to teach. If you're not buying a complete package, try to buy small amounts of materials at a time while you experiment. If you make a mistake, sell or give away what you can't use. The only serious mistake you can make is to blame yourself instead of the materials. Nothing is right for every child and even after years of teaching, I sometimes guessed wrong. Just move on and don't take it personally.

Still don't know what you want? Keep reading. We'll discuss ways to teach each of the subjects soon, and you may notice yourself becoming interested in certain teaching methods. When you see what captures your imagination, you'll know what to choose.

What kind of homeschooler do I want to be?

If you've already attended a homeschool support group, you may have realized homeschoolers speak a foreign language. There are so many new words, or old words used in odd ways. Knowing those words gives you a sense of belonging and superiority as one "in the know." Having a shorthand language also simplifies conversation. (That's the official reason for the odd language we speak.) The words aren't hard to learn, though, and in this section we'll cover three of the most common and toss in a few more as we go along. There is also a glossary at the end of the book. In no time at all, you will be talking like a professional.

There are three types of homeschooling commonly in use—with about a thousand variations. You don't need to know all of the variations, but you should be familiar with the three main categories. Not knowing these words will quickly brand you as the very newest beginner. Of course, these types have various names, but you'll pick those up as you go along. These names change periodically, so listen carefully when you hear homeschoolers talking to see if an exciting new method is really an old method with a new name.

Structured learning

This is also known as "school-at-home." Structured learning imitates the methods used in a small public or private school. Often, the day begins at a specific time and starts with a ceremony or routine (a prayer or a flag salute, for instance). Then the children head for desks or the kitchen table to complete a traditional curriculum planned by the parent or purchased from a curriculum company. One subject carefully follows another using standard teaching methods.

Most homeschoolers start this way. After all, you've never done this before and you know nothing about it. You may not even know any other homeschooling parents. To ease what is already a high level of nervousness, you imitate what you are comfortable with.

Structured learning is effective, controlled, and peaceful for many families. It soothes fears and looks understandable to outsiders. If you are new to homeschooling and scared, this is an excellent way to begin. If you are in a state that is not homeschool-friendly, this is the easiest type of home-schooling to explain. It is my preferred way to teach because I like lesson planning and teaching. It's not the most popular method, at least not publicly, but it's perfectly respectable. If you want to be structured, don't let others talk you into something you're not comfortable with.

If your children have already been in school, talk to them about what they did all day, what they liked, and what they didn't like. You can use that to create something that works for you. Remember, you're in charge. You are the teacher, the principal, the school board, and the parent. You get to do this your way. If something traditional is uncomfortable for you, don't do it. If you are doing it one way and get tired of it or it doesn't work, stop doing it that way.

You should be aware that the most militant homeschoolers deeply oppose structured learning. Of course, someone opposes every method of homeschooling, but for some reason, structured learning tends to get made fun of, even though it's quite effective. So if someone asks if you are structured and you say yes, be prepared to defend your choice.

One possible answer is to smile and say, "We're new at this. We're starting out with what I know and then gradually branching out. Who knows what we'll be by next year?" You may still get a sales talk about the virtues of unschooling, but you probably won't get laughed at. Your companion may grin and say you're a typical beginner, but you'll learn. And you will. What kind of homeschool parent would you be if you weren't learning new things?

Always remember: this is your school and these are your children. You decide how to teach. Don't allow others to take advantage of your insecurities and talk you into doing something you aren't comfortable with. I let myself get talked into unschooling, and although it worked out okay, I'm sorry I did it. There's nothing wrong with it—it just wasn't right for me.

Unschooling is a method to be worked up to if you're unsure of your abilities and worried about your children's educations. If your children went to school first, structured learning is often the best way to begin. They may not be excited about knowledge yet, and you'll need some time to help them reach a point where they're once again curious about the world. After awhile, you'll know how much structure and freedom you're comfortable with.

Unschooling

This is the other end of the extreme. Unschooling is also

known as natural learning, child-led learning, and various other names people think up to describe this very popular homeschooling method. Unschooling means the children learn what they want, when they want, and the way they want. They might spend all day playing in the mud or they might spend hours on a workbook. It's their choice. Radical unschooling is even more extreme—in some cases, it means no rules. Although the media loves to cover it, few people are radical homeschoolers.

Despite what an unschooler might tell you, many of them really aren't quite that casual about it. Many homeschoolers structure math for awhile, and some also structure reading instruction until the child reads well. The other subjects are unstructured. But even in these areas, some parents sneak in more structure than might be apparent.

Suppose you wanted your children to study astronomy but you knew they would rebel if you just said you were going to study it. You want them to think it's their idea. How would you go about it?

I would begin by taking them to a planetarium. Then I'd follow up with a movie about space or astronauts. A few days later, I would read some books to them about the stars and perhaps buy a telescope. Soon, the children have the night sky on their minds and are beginning to learn about it on their own. The better they've been trained to be curious about the world, the more likely this is to work. Technically, you're following their lead when you help them track down materials, crafts, and field trips related to the new topic of study, because they've now shown an interest in the subject. Unofficially you, well, we don't want to say you tricked them into it or manipulated them into it—perhaps you sparked their interest? That's it! Through good parenting techniques, you sparked an interest in astronomy.

Although the unschooling method seems to be easier because you don't have lesson plans, papers to grade, or hours of structured teaching, it's actually a complicated method. As the parent, you must work to be sure your children are involved in meaningful activities. If they haven't learned to have an enthusiastic love for learning and exploration, they may plop down in front of the television all day and do nothing. Unschooling parents pay close attention to what their children are doing and guide them to quality activities. You may need to make a few rules, such as banning television and video games during certain hours, or even asking children to describe and carry out their learning plan for the day. An occasional day of doing nothing won't hurt them—I like those myself—but five or six of those days every week will. However, watch closely to decide if what passes for doing nothing is really learning time.

Eclectic learning

Eclectic learning is a combination of structured and unstructured learning. This method allows you to mix various methods together to create a complete curriculum personalized to the way your child learns, the way you teach, and the materials you have access to. You might choose to structure the reading and math, and then let the children study whatever they like for science.

You might use a math textbook, hands-on learning for science, and a mixture of materials for history. Children can cook a Chinese lunch, read a book on China, play Chinese games, and visit a museum display, thus learning about China without ever touching a textbook. This method is fun for parents who like to prepare lessons. You can give the children as much freedom as you're comfortable with and gradually add more.

As an eclectic learner, you can find your materials anywhere. I gathered textbooks from thrift stores, bought new materials from school supply stores, traded with other homeschoolers, and bought computer programs. Sometimes I used materials made by others and other times I made my own. Sometimes I gave specific assignments. Other times I said, "I need you to show what you have learned about Beverly Cleary and her books. How do you plan to do that?"

Telling others you are an eclectic learner usually doesn't cause any reaction. It's the method most homeschoolers use, because it allows them to structure any subjects they are particularly concerned about and keep other subjects relaxed. It also allows them to switch between methods without having to explain the changes to other homeschoolers. Even if you plan to be structured, you can safely say you are eclectic if you do anything in the normal course of a day that counts for school.

For example, you may not bother teaching gym, since your family is active anyway. Your gym class is unstructured. Cooking will most likely be done as a daily task, not a subject. Home economics is unstructured. Do you let your children choose their own bedtime story? Literature is unstructured. You can see that it's very easy to truthfully call yourself eclectic if you choose.

When you want to sound very knowledgeable, especially to nonhomeschoolers who won't know what you're talking about, say, "We are eclectic learners with structured leanings." Translation: We do whatever we want, but we're more structured than not." Later, if you adopt a specific homeschooling style, you can add more homeschoolese: "We use a Charlotte Mason approach, although we have a preference for Saxon math. However, we are gradually moving toward a Classical Approach." Don't worry about translating that one. By the time you get ready to say something like that, you'll be a seasoned pro.

If all of this feels overwhelming, don't worry about it. Tell people who ask that you are eclectic and then do whatever you want to do. In time, these words will become comfortable to you. One day, you will attend a homeschool meeting and realize you speak the language as well as any native.

Does it matter which method you use? Not really. There have never been any studies proving one method works better than any other. You will teach better if you use a method you are comfortable with. I have used all three methods and it doesn't seem to make any real difference in how much anyone learned, even though it mattered to my own comfort level. Choose whatever you want and have fun!

Learning styles

Children don't all learn the same way. This is probably one of the most important reasons homeschooling works. In a classroom with thirty or more children, even the best teacher would find it difficult to give each child a personalized education. Who has time to prepare thirty different lesson plans each day? The best the teacher can do is to use a variety of methods and hope for the best. With the incredible pressure placed on teachers to achieve high test scores, integrate special needs children, cope with behavior challenges, and teach many subjects which ought to be taught at home, teachers are limited in their abilities to do even this.

We have only a few students, and it's much easier for us to accommodate our children's learning styles. We can use as many methods as we like to teach a subject and, if something doesn't work, we have the time and freedom to start over with a new method.

As you wander the library and bookstore shelves in the reference areas, you will find many books that explain the learning styles of children. The styles have fancy names and can seem a little intimidating. You don't need to know those fancy names. You don't need to be able to describe how your child learns as long as you can teach him. Later, when you've mastered the basics of homeschooling, look for an easy-to-understand book on the subject if you are interested. It's fun to study, but it isn't essential.

You could, of course, pay to have your child tested. An "expert" would give you a printout telling you how your child learns and what to do about it. A much less expensive way to figure this out is to teach your child. Choose a method for teaching and then watch your child at work. If he learns the material, and seems comfortable, you have found one method that works. There may be more than one, and there may even be different methods for different subjects. In fact, you will find that what works one day will not work the next because your child is in a different mood. When you prepare your lessons, have alternative methods in mind in case one is not working.

In this section, we will explore some of the ways children learn and how you can teach using these methods. I'm not using the fancy terms, because they change often anyway. We'll use everyday words you can remember.

Hands-on learners

Chances are you already know if you have this sort of child. He's the one who is getting into everything, taking the clock apart to see if it works, and taking the measuring cup out of your hand to try it for himself. He never listens; he jumps in and tries things. A less outgoing child who is a hands-on learner may seem clueless when you are explaining things to him. If he seems to glaze over as you speak, it may be that he finds it difficult to learn from what he hears.

Most little children are hands-on learners, also known as kinesthetic learners. They nearly always learn better by doing something. As your child becomes older and more experienced, he may need less opportunity to touch and do, but he may never outgrow it.

Teaching a hands-on learner is fun, but it also requires more planning and more of your time. You need to think about how to allow the child to touch, smell, and try the topics you teach.

For example, many children can learn to add by doing a few worksheets that have pictures of objects the child is asked to add. A hands-on learner will learn best if you initially use real objects instead of pictures and if he handles those objects himself. Set up three toy cars and circle them with yarn to make a set. Then set out two toy cars and circle them with yarn. Have him count how many toys are in the first set. Put a card with the number of items under the set. Do the same thing with the second set. Add a card with a plus sign and another with an equals sign. Now have him count the total number of cars and put a number card down to show the answer. Finally, you will do the problem again and show him what the written problem looks like. Make sure he understands what he did by having him do it himself with different numbers. Only after he has done dozens or even hundreds of calculations with real objects will he be ready to tackle the workbook. By this time, he is essentially reviewing, not learning.

You can see that any young child can benefit from learning this way. For some children, this is good teaching, but for others, it's essential teaching. If your child needs hands-on materials in order to learn, use them. Periodically, let him try learning another way. He will not always be allowed to learn with his hands and he needs practice with other methods. Let him try less physical methods of learning when the material is less important to know. You might also try other methods in his best subjects, because he will already have a good sense of the material.

Spend lots of time doing science experiments with this child. When you study history, try on costumes, eat the food, and play the games. Bring out toy soldiers to help visualize the details of a battle, and toy historical figures to act out other events. Don't learn about computers—use one. Look for the action in everything you teach. Chapter 12 discusses adding movement to your lessons, and these tips can help the kinesthetic learner as well as the hyperactive child.

Visual learners

Some of the techniques that help kinesthetic learners also help visual learners. These children have to see something in order to learn it. They are often described as poor listeners, spacey and inattentive. This may be the result of a learning disability, but it may just also be the result of a learning preference. For young children, this means books, pictures, writing, and doing. You won't be able to say, "First add the right hand column and then add the left hand column." You will need to sit beside the child and do the problem as she watches you. Then she will have to try it herself.

An older child may find lectures challenging. While it's unlikely you will be lecturing your child (well, not about history or science, anyway), she may want to go to college or accept a job involving meetings. This child needs to become an expert note-taker. Have her take notes at meetings she attends, or have her watch a lecture on television or the Internet and record the important information. When she writes, she will find it easier to pay attention. When she sees her notes, she will be better able to remember the material.

It often helps older students to diagram material. If a student reads an article on the rotation of the planets, she may need to sketch it so she can visualize it. While it's possible to find a pre-made diagram, she will improve her skills by making her own. Ask her to read the material, and then, working sentence by sentence, lay out the arrangement of the planets as they are described in the article. At first, you may have to do this with her, but she should eventually be able to do it herself. Being able to make simple sketches will allow her to follow spoken lectures more easily. Don't worry about drawing skills or extensive detail—she should just put it into a format she can understand.

Homeschooling is very conducive to visual learning. Since you aren't trying to teach thirty children, you don't spend a lot of time lecturing. Most of the time you're reading, writing, or doing. The visual learner will find homeschooling much more successful than she did public school education. Your only challenge will be to make sure you strengthen her auditory (listening) skills as much as possible. Have her listen to books on tape. Attend lectures. Put on music as you work. Hold long conversations with her about school and life and teach her to listen to you.

If your child finds listening nearly impossible, you may need to train her. Read aloud a paragraph and ask her to tell you, in her own words, what you said. Gradually make these readings longer until she has fairly good concentration. You may find she never reaches what you would consider a satisfactory performance level. Help your child figure out her limitations and what she has to do to overcome them. When a child has a disability, she should participate in the solution.

Auditory learners
These children are good listeners. They will have a wonderful time in college where most teaching is done in a lecture hall. In a homeschool, however, they may struggle a little if they're using traditional homeschooling methods. They have to hear something to really learn it, and yet most homeschooling is done by reading, writing, and doing.

This is simple to fix. Have your child read his textbooks into a tape recorder. This gives him oral reading practice. When it's time to study, he can listen to the tapes. If he doesn't read well, you may want to read them yourself. Many books are on commercial tapes as well. Naturally, you can't let him listen to everything on tape. He does need to learn to read. However, if he does the initial reading himself, either silently or aloud, he can master the material by listening later on. Often, just hearing himself read aloud as he records will be enough to add an auditory component.

Spend a great deal of time talking to this child. Ask him about his studies. Discuss author Bruce Coville over dinner or in the car. Go for a long walk to talk about the origins of the universe. This child will enjoy videotaped lectures, which can be found online, and may "watch" them with his eyes closed, to block out visual distractions. As long as he isn't snoring, you may want to allow him to do so—at least occasionally.

Gradually improve his ability to learn in other ways. Give him plenty of reading material. Show him diagrams and have him explain them. Teach him to read a map. Play a scene in a movie and have him describe what he saw. (You may have to turn off the sound so he doesn't gain all his clues from his ears.) As he becomes more comfortable with visual symbols, he will become a stronger student. As long as his reading skills are good, however, he will struggle less than other people in school and in employment. Teaching a child to listen is much harder than teaching him to observe.

Now that I know all this, what do I choose?
Take advantage of the flexibility of homeschooling. Take into consideration the ways your child likes to learn, the ways you like to teach, your budget, and your time, and then just choose. Despite what you might read as you research, what you choose really isn't going to be the deciding factor in whether or not homeschooling is successful for you. What will matter is the time and attention you give your children

as they learn and the personalization you add to the lesson. It will be your excitement about learning and your longing to share knowledge with your child. Don't stress over the testimonials that insist there is only one right way. The right way is the one that works for you and your child. Choose and have fun!

More Resources

➤ *The Well-Trained Mind: A Guide to Classical Education at Home* by Jessie Wise and Susan Wise Bauer
ISBN: 0393047520

Classical education has developed a large following among Christian homeschoolers. It focuses on the relationship of our society to ancient western societies, and teaches students to analyze. The focus is not on what you learn, but the actual process of learning and evaluating. This book's author is a homeschooler who was once a professional teacher.

➤ *Core Knowledge Series* by E. D. Hirsch, Jr. (Editor)
Series published by Delta Publishing.

This series of books is extremely popular with homeschooling parents of elementary students. It does not have lesson plans, but it outlines the material children need to know at each grade level and includes literature samples, documents, discussion questions and other resources. This should be used with other materials, since there is not enough to comprise a full curriculum. However, it can serve as a guideline for what should be taught. Critics say it does little more than introduce. Fans say it helps a child become familiar with all the essentials of society.

➤ *What Your Kindergartner Needs to Know: Preparing Your Child for a Lifetime of Learning*
ISBN: 0385318413

➤ *What Your First Grader Needs to Know: Fundamentals of a Good First-Grade Education*
ISBN: 0385319878

➤ *What Your Second Grader Needs to Know: Fundamentals of a Good Second-Grade Education*
ISBN: 038531843X

➤ *What Your Third Grader Needs to Know: Fundamentals of a Good Third-Grade Education*
ISBN: 0385336268

➤ *What Your Fourth Grader Needs to Know: Fundamentals of a Good Fourth-Grade Education*
ISBN: 0385312601

➤ *What Your Fifth Grader Needs to Know: Fundamentals of a Good Fifth-Grade Education*
ISBN: 0385314647

➤ *What Your Sixth Grader Needs to Know: Fundamentals of a Good Sixth-Grade Education*
ISBN: 0385314671

➤ *Home Learning Year by Year: How to Design a Homeschool Curriculum from Preschool Through High School* by Rebecca Rupp
ISBN: 0609805851
A year-by-year guide to what children should be taught using standard guidelines. While Rebecca presents a comprehensive curriculum guide, she understands the variations in how children learn, and this book won't give you daily lists you can't possibly follow. This guideline can be followed exactly or used as suggestions for creating your own curriculum. Very popular and well done.

Chapter 12

When Your Child Is Behind or Ahead of His Peers

MANY CHILDREN WHO BEGIN in the public schools are behind their peers when they start homeschooling. Other children are not quite ready for academics when they reach kindergarten or first grade. Some children are far ahead of their peers. In this chapter, we will discuss ways to help a child catch up or get ready. We will also learn how to help the advanced learner.

Catching up
If your child is nine years old and still can't read, or is threatened with the possibility of being held back once again, you may have questioned the school's ability to help him. Special education has been tried unsuccessfully, and you have decided you couldn't do any worse than the schools did. But now you're starting out with years of learning to make up. Where do you begin?

Begin by studying the tests and reports you received from your child's school. Try to understand what went wrong and when. Did he fall behind right from the start or did something go wrong later in his schooling? What did the teachers blame for the problem? (The teachers may not have always been correct, but this is a starting point.) Ask your child to read and try to find clues as you listen and watch. Does he act afraid when he makes a mistake? Is he the victim of a teacher who belittles him when he makes a mistake or is he perhaps a perfectionist who can't bear to be wrong? You may have to begin by building up his confidence.

Does he know how to sound out a word? Can he read some words from memory? Does he read with expression? Can he tell you about the material he just read? If he is missing skills, you may need to back up and start over. However, there's a more important step that must come first.

LuAnn Lawhon, who has taught many children to read, suggests parents who realize their child can't read focus first on the love of reading. "One of the best ways most kids pick up on reading is to be read to and read with; working together with lots of discussion, keeping it informal without pressure.

"Sometimes kids get behind because the pace is too quick or too soon for some learners. They panic and build a block against it because they haven't had any early success. I'd develop the love of reading first. I suspect there are often emotional factors involved with the inability to read. Kids are so full of feelings, and if something is forced on them too soon, it can take a long time to get around the negative feelings."

LuAnn's words are wise advice for loving parents. You might feel tempted to sit your child down and shove words into him as fast as possible, to prove you can teach him, and to help him catch up. Instead of preparing for a test or a judgment, focus on the child. Why do you want your child to read? You want him to be able to learn, to succeed in employment, and to love books. If you are a passionate reader, you may be embarrassed to have a child who doesn't share your love. Remember: this isn't about you. It's about your child and his future. If you can bring yourself to back up to the days when you read to him as he curled up in your arms, you can restore what was taken from him in school.

What went wrong when he went to school? Although some children are victims of a bad teacher, I suspect most children are simply victims of a bad system. Schools have pushed academics to start too soon, and kindergarteners are now learning what was once taught in first grade. Many children are not ready for formal academics yet. It has absolutely nothing to do with intelligence. The brightest child may not be ready for academics in kindergarten because that may not be where his heart is at that moment. Too many people equate academics with IQ and forget there are many kinds of brainpower. Every child has her own built-in pace, and pushing her to match the pace of another is dangerous. Just as a tiny child cannot keep up with her long-legged daddy, a kindergartner may struggle to keep up with an overly ambitious school board. High test scores benefit schools, not children. Your children are home now, and you may not have to answer to a test. If you don't, ignore the pace set by the school and focus on the pace set by your child. If you do, try to balance your approach, and keep careful records that show what you are doing to help your child.

Think about how to make reading special for your child. Make your story time as cozy and important as possible. Turn off the telephones, don't answer the door, and don't let anything get in the way of reading together. Making reading time a priority tells your child that reading matters and he matters. If it's cold, wrap up in a blanket together. If it's warm, read outside under a tree—or in a tree. Keep books in your car, in your child's backpack, in the bathroom. Keep them all over so your child can't manage to avoid them.

Reading is the most important academic skill because it makes all other learning possible. Make it a primary focus of your day and incorporate it into all you do. Show your child what reading can give him, and let him read what interests him, within reason. When you're ready to teach formally, smile, relax, and praise. Give him a sense of ability.

Writing is the second most important subject. Your child needs to be able to communicate through the written word. Even if he has a writing disorder, teach him to form the letters. He may have to do most of his written work on the computer, but he should be able to print when he needs to, and to sign his name. If he has a difficult time communicating through writing, let him dictate his thoughts as you write or type. Then read his words to him so he can see what he has created. Let him read his own words as his reading lesson.

Finally, tackle math. You may find, as with reading, you must back all the way up to the beginning. However, you will be able to move more rapidly if you review only the parts he doesn't understand. Many children just have gaps. Begin with the basics and have your child do one problem of each type. Have him do them as you watch and keep the numbers small so he doesn't get tired. When you find something he doesn't know how to do, stop and teach it. Have him work at it daily until he can do it for three days in a row without first reviewing. Then begin testing again. After three days, have him do a few problems of the first type he missed. If he has forgotten how to do them, back up again. If he remembers, test him again in a few days. Once he is consistently passing his tests, review periodically. It is less important to zip through the book than it is to be able to have the math in long-term memory. If you are reviewed by someone each year, you may need to explain this philosophy to the tester. Tell her that your child studied many types of math problems but remembered few of them when he was in school. Your goal is to study fewer pages, but to remember everything. Assure the tester your child will seem to progress more slowly, but will actually finish sooner because he won't need to relearn everything every year.

If your child is behind in all or most subjects, it may be more effective to begin slowly, introducing one subject at a time for a few weeks. History and science can be incorporated into the reading program instead of being an extra subject.

Helping your child believe in herself

Your biggest challenge won't actually be catching up. This is often easy enough to do if you are patient and follow your child's pace. The challenge is to build your child's confidence. If your child sees herself as stupid, this will block her ability to learn and slow her progress.

It's essential that your child see herself as capable of learning. It is nearly impossible to learn if you really believe you can't learn, and too many children leave their schools believing they can't learn, or that they are lazy or inferior. It's often the very brightest children who struggle with this the most. If they are told they have a high IQ and are capable of doing the work, but they know they can't do it, they may suspect the IQ test was inaccurate. In their minds, the only possibility is that they're not as bright as everyone thinks. They may struggle to hide this fact by intentionally not trying, not studying, not completing assignments. Many children who take pride in their giftedness would rather be thought of as lazy or uncooperative than to have people find out they might not be smart. Other children are told they aren't very bright or are treated as if they weren't, and they act the way they're treated. Whatever inconsistencies they see are pushed aside. They may be aware that few children their age read Shakespeare, for example, or that none of their peers can discuss the origins of the universe, and yet they continue to believe this is some sort of odd quirk, not proof that they are bright.

It takes time to restore a child's belief that she can cope with her schoolwork. It really doesn't matter what her actual IQ is. If she is at all capable of learning, she needs to know that. False praise only makes the situation worse since the child may believe you're lying to hide her lack of ability. Instead, set up situations in which the child can be successful. Initially, start behind where the child is and let her do some easy tasks. As she succeeds at these, continue to move forward. Each success will build confidence.

My children read early and we used an ancient set of readers to help us. The first five stories of the primer and above were review stories—there were no new words at all. These were followed by the teaching stories, which were harder. As we neared the end, the children would get discouraged and decide they couldn't learn to read. But the last five stories were review stories and, as they read those, they suddenly felt like the best readers in the world because they knew all the words. I learned to regularly insert review stories instead of just waiting until the end of the book. They need easy lessons once in awhile so they can realize just how much they really know.

Don't be afraid to give the struggling child a difficult task. Think of experiences you've had that made you feel great about yourself. Often these were the times you accomplished something you believed you couldn't do. If your child struggles with a difficult assignment and succeeds, she will realize she is capable of far more than she imagined. In the initial days of recovery, you may want to keep the tasks manageable, but they can gradually become more difficult.

Think carefully about the praise you offer a hurting child. Children need praise, but it must be valid and moderated. If you make a giant fuss over the tiniest accomplishments, or over things the child didn't really do, you may cause the child to believe she really isn't very capable if such a little task can bring such great praise. A simple, "Good job" is enough for little things. Save the giant celebrations for the big events, when your child has struggled and succeeded. Praise in accordance with the level of accomplishment, but do give praise. Notice the good. It can be difficult to focus on the good parts when you are struggling with a child who is struggling with herself. Building a history of noticeable successes, though, can help a child to gain a more positive, more accurate view of herself.

Learning disabilities

A child who has learning disabilities faces a few additional challenges in catching up. Your first task, after figuring out what his disability is and how it really affects him, is to decide how to explain it to your child. The explanations he received in school may have been helpful, or they may have been damaging. Research the disability together and learn all you can. Be sure to point out the positives you encounter, such as stories about people with this disability who have succeeded or studies showing it is possible to have a high IQ and a learning disability at the same time.

If you must submit to a standardized test, be sure to bring in proof of the disability and to request, in advance, accommodations during the testing. Accommodations are changes in the way a test or assignment is completed in order to compensate for the child's challenges. For example, a child who cannot write may be allowed to take the test on a computer, and a child who cannot see may be given the test in Braille. Insist that verification of the disability be attached to the results. This may protect you from any unwanted queries if the scores are low.

Find out what accommodations are typically used for this disability. Many parents are told an accommodation is a crutch. Since you would not deny a child with a broken leg a crutch or a child who cannot see a guide dog, why would you deny a child with a learning disability an accommodation of his own? While a learning disability is not necessarily an excuse, it is an explanation. It's nothing more than recognition that some part of a brain is damaged and the person with the challenge must find a new way to do the task.

We easily accept the reality of a physical disability, and yet some so-called experts try to claim learning disabilities are make-believe. While it's true some people abuse the term, there are many children with learning challenges, and it's unfair to deny them the help they need. Over the years, experts, parents, and children have devised simple and creative ways to help people battle the effects of a learning challenge. Find out what they are and try them out. Use only those adaptations your child really needs, and try, when possible, to diminish the need for some of them. Accept that a child with a disability can do what other children do, but may have to do it differently.

When a child learns to see his challenge as nothing more than a nuisance requiring some extra creativity and effort, he understands he is just as capable and wonderful as any other child. The additional challenges and heartaches that might accompany a learning disability can become a way to grow. Some successful adults even credit their disabilities as a deciding factor in their success. What they learned in the battle made them strong, flexible, and creative.

Starting out behind

Some children are not ready for academics when they begin kindergarten or first grade. In many states, kindergarten is optional, so parents are not required to submit to supervision. This makes it easier for you to wait until your child is ready, although you may have some catching up to do when test time comes.

In most cases, intelligence isn't the cause of being unready for academics when a child turns five, just as it isn't always the reason a child learns early. Preparation plays a part, but a parent can take all the right steps with a very bright child and still realize he isn't going to learn to read or calculate this year. At one time, this wasn't an issue. Kindergartners weren't supposed to read and calculate. Those lessons belonged to first grade.

Today, however, since more children are in daycare and more parents send their children to preschool and choose to make their child compete with others, these first-grade skills are taught in kindergarten and even in preschool. It's difficult, if the state tries to make your child conform, to avoid the damage caused by forcing academics on a child who is not ready.

One option is to begin reporting as late as possible. Find out what the deadline is for your child to be in a grade that must be reported or registered. Use that as your official starting date. If a child is not required to report to the state until age seven, you can start homeschooling whenever you like, but don't tell the state until he is seven. Then assign him to the lowest grade possible. This gives you some room for challenges. You can always have him skip a grade later.

If you must teach your child some academic skills, teach them using as many fun, hands-on methods as possible. Avoid placing him at a desk to do hours of worksheets. For example, you can teach the alphabet by making a child spend hours looking at worksheets that have the letter *B* at the top and rows of letters below, teaching him to circle all the other *B*'s. Or you can just play a game. Try this: Purchase some index cards or make cardboard squares from old cereal boxes. Make sure all the cards are the same size, shape, and color. Select two letters that look and sound very different from each other, such as *B* and *M,* or *H* and *C*. Notice that I've chosen one letter than has only straight lines, and one with curves in each set. These are the first two letters you will teach your child. (You

B

don't need to start with *A* and *B*. In fact, some educators believe it's better to teach the letters out of order.) You can also start with the letters in the child's name. Make at least ten cards for each letter. There should be nothing on these cards except for the letter you are teaching.

Give your child the cards with those two letters and ask him to sort them by letter. He probably does not know how to do this unless you have sorted in the past. Help him by putting the first card down and telling him what the letter is. Then bring out the other letter. Point out the ways the letters are the same and different. Tell him the name of the new letter. Put it down a short distance from the first letter. Now select a third card and ask which pile it goes into. He probably won't know at first, but talk about it and help until he can do this alone. Don't make it a test and don't worry about how fast he learns. It may take a very long time and many days of playing, but be sure it's always fun. Call it the letter sorting game and keep your attitude cheerful. In addition to this game, find other ways to play with letters. Try making letters from a variety of materials and letting him touch and play. Make your bodies into the shape of letters. How can you turn yourself into a *T?* Look for letters in your environment, and enjoy alphabet books together. Give your child two letter cards and have him put them behind his back. To the tune of "Where is Thumpkin?" sing, "Where is *B?*" Let him bring out the correct letter when you sing, "Here he is!"

Count real objects and read real books. Teach him to read

a single word and then, when you encounter it in books, let him be the one to read it. (He may be reciting, not reading, but it doesn't matter.) Label items in your house. Put words on cards and show him how to make sentences. You will be teaching academics, but because you're playing, you're not pressuring him to do what he is not ready to do. Spend extra time on the science, history, stories, and games that build readiness. Teach him to stand in line at the grocery store and bank, to sit quietly in a restaurant, to wait his turn in the home, and to focus on a task until it's complete. When you see he is ready for more formal learning, move into it slowly.

In the meantime, don't panic when he is behind his peers. Many children resist reading for years, and suddenly, at age nine, something clicks and they read as well as any other child. Continue making reading, math, and other types of learning a pleasure so he will want to learn to do them some day. There will come a time when you must be stricter in order to please whatever powers you report to, but stall if you can. The world wants our children to grow up fast, but *we* are better able to judge the timetable that is appropriate to our child. Stay in charge as long as you can.

When your child is ahead of his peers

Initially, this hardly seems like a problem, especially to parents whose children are behind their peers. In truth, it's less of a problem in a homeschool than it is in traditional school, but being advanced is still an issue that must be taken into consideration. Children who are bored in their traditional school often end up homeschooling because they aren't challenged, and bored children either lose interest in education or stretch their minds by thinking up creative ways to drive their teachers crazy. Thomas Edison and Albert Einstein were both considered troublemakers who asked too many questions, and both were eventually homeschooled by their mothers. Given the era, it's doubtful that their mothers were scientific wizards, but they still managed to educate their precocious and inquisitive children.

They know more than I do!

Intimidation is a serious problem for many parents of children who love to learn. What will you do when your child passes you up? If you already struggle to explain to a first grader why the moon doesn't fall from the sky, you dread the harder questions ahead. Physics, Shakespeare, calculus—the world is filled with intimidating knowledge you're sure you can't teach.

This topic is covered more in a later chapter (Chapter 24) on teaching children to be independent learners and has been discussed a little in an earlier chapter (Chapter 2) on teacher intelligence. As we've seen, you don't have to know everything to teach everything. True education is discovery and exploration. When your child wants to know something hard, he will learn to research it himself. Until he learns to do that, you will help him. I didn't know a thing about dinosaurs my first year of homeschooling, but the children were determined to make that our first science unit. We learned about dinosaurs together. Later, they learned about physics and trigonometry alone, because I chose not to accompany them. I faithfully read all my oldest daughter's physics books and said, "I don't get it." She just rolled her eyes and said, "I do." The two youngest didn't even ask me to read their physics books. They just asked for a ride to the bookstore to choose books and then asked a scientist at church to explain what they didn't understand.

Get to know a lot of people. We moved often, but as soon as I was settled, I started finding out what everyone at church did for a living, what their hobbies were, and how they felt about teenagers. My children were quite happy to take their questions to others. Many colleges run "Ask a Scientist" programs, which allow you to e-mail questions to science students. My children used those as well.

Master the art of asking questions. When my daughter wanted to have an in-depth discussion on Charlemagne, I nodded my head and asked good questions. My specialty is American history, not world history. You don't really have to know much about the subject to ask questions.

"Why did he do that?"
"How did that discovery change the world?"
"Do you think that was a good idea?"
"How would you have done it?"
"What does that word mean?"

In other words, you need to ask questions that allow your child to put the subject into terms even you can understand. This helps her clarify what she has learned. You also need to ask questions that help her analyze and think. In many ways, you can help her more this way than by knowing the answers. I took an independent study course on women's history one year from a wonderful teacher who didn't know much about women's history. He let me tell him what I'd read that week, but interrupted with a barrage of *why* questions. Since he didn't know the answers, he wasn't tempted to tell me what they were. Instead, I had to find the answers myself and he just told me if my answers made sense.

Early readers
When my oldest daughter read a novel at the age of three, I was, as are most first-time mothers, pleased. We cheerfully read through books about Ramona, Paddington, Winnie the Pooh, and the few other novels that appeal to little children. Soon, though, I was struggling to find material

for her. She was a typical little girl in every way, except she liked to read. As she explained to her sympathetic kindergarten teacher, "The books at my level are about big kids. I don't want to read about big kids. I want to read about kids like me."

Children who read well have a somewhat easier time now, because beginning chapter books allow children to read chapters sooner. However, it's still a challenge to find good books for them. Many of the plots in books for fifth graders are completely inappropriate for kindergartners or preschoolers. We discovered there were a number of older books that were appropriate for young children. It hasn't always been considered nerdy to write a moral book, and older books are often less sophisticated. Look for an experienced librarian to make suggestions. It's a good idea to read the books yourself to make sure they don't have material that makes you uncomfortable.

Another challenge faced by preschoolers who read early is that many of them can't read smaller print, even though they understand the story and the words. We found that the first editions of books by Carolyn Haywood were ideal for this problem. They were typeset in extra large print with large spaces between the lines. The first Betsy books take place when Betsy is three years old and all of Haywood's books are appropriate for little children. These can often still be found in older libraries, thrift stores, used bookstores, or at online sites that sell or loan collector children's books. A librarian once told me, although I haven't verified this, that they were written with early readers in mind, and that's why they were published as they were.

Children who enjoy math are often stopped by their inability to write. Most preschoolers or kindergartners aren't ready or willing to sit at a desk doing worksheets. Most children shouldn't be doing this, either. (However, there are always exceptions; some little ones adore worksheets.)

The math of interest to little children can easily be done without writing. Make small cardboard squares with the numbers and mathematical symbols on them and let your children "write" the problems using these. Spend a lot of time doing real-life math, and then, if they are interested, write the equations or symbols on a chalkboard so they know what they look like. Use appropriate math terms so your children learn the language of math. As your children learn to read numbers, begin building a number line around the top border of their bedrooms. Add each number they learn until you have circled the room. They may enjoy finding the numbers you call out to them.

Even the most gifted young child will probably not be ready for the amount of writing she may long to do. Allow her to dictate her stories, her writing, and her journal to you. Consider teaching her to type. I made word cards out of index cards for my preschoolers as they learned to read and even included punctuation cards. They enjoyed "writing" sentences with their cards, and making up simple stories. Naturally, they found it more fun to write "I have green hair" than to write that they had blond or red hair, but we weren't fussy about accuracy. They were little, and we were just playing.

Emotional challenges of giftedness

Many children who realize they are better at schoolwork than their peers become somewhat egotistical. While we want them to be proud of their accomplishments, we don't want them to believe they are better than other children. I often reminded my children that all children were learning. We talked about the subjects their friends were learning that they were not—gymnastics, art, music—and then discussed how each person had specific interests and talents. No one has every talent, and one talent is not necessarily better than another. "It doesn't matter *what* you learn as long as you learn," I told my preschoolers. My school-aged children realized that it didn't matter when you learned something as long as you learned the things that were important to know. Help your children notice and appreciate the talents of others while continuing to value their own.

Children who find learning easy face one other educational challenge. For many of them, everything comes so easily they soon expect *everything* to be easy. When they finally encounter something hard, they panic or become angry. Many gifted children try to abandon a difficult task. A piano teacher told me these children were the very hardest to teach because they expected to be able to sit at a piano and instantly play.

Capable children must learn to struggle through challenging tasks. There is no possible way they can get through their entire lives without encountering something they can't do well, and it's better for them to learn how to work hard at something while they're still young enough to receive your guidance and encouragement. Seek opportunities for your children to try new things and when you encounter something that doesn't come naturally, insist they stay with the project or class. When they plead to quit or lose their tempers because the subject isn't going well, be gentle and encouraging—but firm. Show them how to tackle the project and demonstrate the correct attitude as you teach. Set the example by tackling something outside your own comfort zone. Naturally, you will have to choose their challenges carefully because you don't want to destroy their confidence, but they should learn to stretch.

Teaching a capable child can be very exciting for a parent because these children are often enthusiastic about learning. It requires a great deal of work for the parent (who is always struggling to keep up with the rapid pace), but it's also highly rewarding.

A word about pacing

Whether your child is ahead, behind, or right on schedule, one benefit of homeschooling is your ability to work just at your child's level and to teach the way your child learns. Don't pay too much attention to assigned grade levels and don't worry much about intelligence, which is an extremely inexact science. Intelligence does not determine success. It's your child's own determination to succeed that will matter in the long run. Teach him what he needs to know when he needs to know it. An enriching home environment and an enthusiastic teacher will do more than any test preparation book to get your child properly educated. Just have fun and make the world a curious and fascinating place to live in and to study.

More Resources

➤ *Creative Homeschooling for Gifted Children: A Resource Guide* by Lisa Rivero
ISBN: 0910707480
Gifted children have unique educational needs and this is considered one of the best guides to teaching a bright child. The book includes a resource guide by ability level which is especially helpful when children read well above grade level.

➤ *LDOnline.org*
This is the most important online resource for teaching children with learning disabilities. The site has academic articles as well as articles for the general public. Read first-person stories, find definitions and accommodation ideas, and discuss your child's needs on the discussion forums, including one monitored by disability professionals.

Chapter 13

Using Ready-Made Lesson Plans

TODAY'S HOMESCHOOLER HAS A tremendous advantage over the homeschooling pioneers because the Internet offers thousands of lesson plans on every subject imaginable. In addition, there are a tremendous number of ready-made curricula for purchase. These are wonderful time-savers for busy parents with demanding family lives and careers. However, these lessons were written for generic children and we are not raising generic children. Our children may have disabilities that make it difficult to do certain aspects of a curriculum or we may want to teach the lesson to a child much younger or older than the plan is designed to teach. If the lesson plan is written for a public school class, we must adapt it to the single child or multi-age homeschool family. Sometimes a purchased curriculum is boring and we want to supplement to make it more exciting or more hands-on.

Learning to adapt a lesson takes a little practice, but it's very good training for the parent who wants to eventually design her own curriculum. It's less scary to change one than to create it from scratch. I usually combined pieces of various plans to create an entire unit, just to save time and prevent over-taxation of my brain.

Adapting ready-made lesson plans

Let's look at some typical aspects of lesson plans and think about ways to change them. Suppose you want to do a unit on the Middle Ages. You find a lesson plan that is fairly appropriate for your children and you like it, but you can see some things in it that won't work. How do you fix the problems? Following are some sample elements of a lesson plan and suggestions for altering them.

Read the Magna Carta. Your children may be too young to do this. You could skip it, but if you're creating a challenging, in-depth curriculum, you may want your children to know what this is. Perhaps you will create a simple list of the highlights of this document's laws and discuss them with your children, comparing the laws in the Magna Carta to your own.

Write a story about a typical woman in this time period. A child with a writing or language disorder may find this too challenging. If the child is too young to write or has a writing disorder, he can dictate it; but if he has a language disorder, this may not be an option. Instead, you might have him draw pictures of a woman's life or act out a typical day. Since I had a boy and a girl working together, I usually adapted these assignments so each wrote about his or her own gender. They then shared their stories with each other. Younger children prefer to write about their own gender or age.

Give a speech on how young men became knights. Have your children prepare reports and present them to the family using visual aids.

Study paintings and other artwork done during the Middle Ages. If your child is visually challenged, paintings may not be particularly meaningful. You might let him try creating more tactile forms of artwork or tell him about the most important, just so he knows about them. He might also prefer to do a report on an artist which will still introduce him to the paintings.

Visit a reenactment. These are wonderful learning tools, but you can't visit one if there isn't one happening. If your lesson falls during the winter when there are few such events, watch a good video instead. Your children can also hold their own reenactment by eating the food, playing the games, and acting out the lives of those they are studying. Perhaps a puppet show would let them experience life in the Middle Ages.

Effectively adapting a lesson plan is merely a matter of figuring out the purpose of the activity. You probably want to accomplish the purpose, but you may have a better way to do it. For example, the requirement to give a speech is designed to teach children to prepare and present material to an audience, but this can easily be done within the family. The child may have other opportunities to speak publicly without needing to do it in this unit.

A requirement to attend a reenactment is offered for the purpose of bringing the past to life. There are many other ways to do this, and many are more participatory than the typical suggestion. When you encounter a suggestion (and that is all these items are), look for the purpose. Make a list of all the ways you can accomplish that purpose and then make changes that fit your needs and the abilities of your child.

Putting action into your lessons
Many people envision homeschooled children sitting at a kitchen table all day long. This amuses most homeschoolers because public school children are normally the ones spending long days at a desk. Most homeschooled children are too busy to spend much time sitting at the table. Whether your child is hyperactive, just a wiggly child, or even a typical child, she will benefit from activities involving action. Chil-

dren learn from doing, and they learn best when they aren't sitting too long. It simply isn't natural for a healthy six-year-old to sit all day long in one spot. If you buy a curriculum that is all reading and writing, add some action. Get out of your chairs and play!

Math is generally thought of as a quiet activity that is taught primarily through worksheets. As we discussed earlier, many math lessons can be taught through real life experiences, and these will have action in them. Even dull drill and practice can be livened up with simple movement. If you have a long hallway, you can place a chalkboard or dry erase board at the end of it. Write a problem on the board and let the children race down the hallway to record the answer. For variation, take the board outside and have them roll or tumble to the board. If your yard is full of dandelions, or even grass, have them gather the correct number of plants and present them to you when you call out a problem.

If you are homeschooling several children or can borrow some extras, try a game of math tag. Call out a math problem and charge after your children. If you approach them, they have to call out the correct answer to avoid being tagged. Play freeze tag and require them to solve a simple math problem to be unfrozen. These games can be used to review material for almost any subject.

Draw a large hopscotch on the sidewalk or patio. Have children spell their spelling words as they hop; one letter per square. You can use this same hopscotch to drill math problems. Write the problems on the square or just outside it. You can record these games as gym class if you choose.

Write letters on large cards and have your children organize them into words, or put words on cards and place them into sentences. If you spread the words or letters around the room, they will be moving to gather them. If you have the time, hide the letters and tell your children to find them. Children can learn to read the letters of the alphabet the same way.

Try a treasure hunt. Place a question, perhaps from history or geography, on your child's desk. Place word cards all over the walls of the house. Have the children try to find the correct answer. If you are doing a geography hunt, the first card might ask for the capital city of California. All over the house, post the names of cities. When your child finds one he thinks might be the right answer, he can take it down and look on the back. The back of the card has the question this card answers, and the next question. You might have a small reward at the end of the game, such as a sticker or the promise of a story.

Question 1: Who wrote *Ramona the Pest?*	*Answer: Beverly Cleary* Question 2: Who was Ramona's big sister?

Children love secret codes. When you have to introduce dull facts, write them in code. To simplify this, type them normally into your word processing program and then change them to one of the fonts with pictures.

Normal type: This is a secret code.
Wingding Font: ✳︎〰︎✻✦ ✻✦ ♋︎ ✦♏︎♍︎♌︎♏︎✦ ♍︎♌︎♋︎♏︎✎

You can type an entire lesson on something, such as mountains, in Wingding and let your children try to decipher it from the key. To make the key, type the alphabet, and change it to Wingding. When they have had more experience in codes, let them try making up their own.

Studying map skills? Cut maps into puzzles and let your children assemble them. Get a giant floor map and let your children "drive" a toy car along a route to become more familiar with the layout of the country. Hide the pieces of a map puzzle so your children will have to find them before they can assemble them. Lay out a map puzzle of the country, and leave one or more states out, hiding the missing pieces. Have the children guess which states are missing and then locate the missing pieces. Encourage them to work as a team rather than to compete.

As you gain more experience preparing lessons, you will begin to think of movement automatically. If you can't think of a way to put movement into your lesson, your children are likely to have good ideas. The real challenge will be to grasp the pacing. If you put movement into every activity, your children will become over-stimulated. Spread out the action and put it where you feel it's most important. Between times, assign the children quiet activities and even boring ones. Children need to learn that sometimes you just have to do something even when it isn't fun.

More Resources

➤ *Teacher Created Resources*

TeacherCreated.com and BuyTeacherCreated.com

The Teacher Created Resources company sells a variety of curriculum materials. I used these materials with my own children many years ago and their books can still be found in most teacher supply stores. Each thematic topic, such as ancient Egypt, sea animals, or fairy tales, is taught through each of the major academic subjects. There are even thematic units on unusual topics, such as chocolate and quilts. The books include worksheets, games, experiments and other elements that you can choose from to create a unit study. Most unit studies have separate books for the upper and lower elementary grades, and some are available for older students as well. Even today, when I have no homeschoolers, I have to restrain myself from buying them because they are so much fun!

➤ *Education-World.com*

Although this is a site for professional teachers, I have used it extensively in homeschooling. The site has many lesson plans created by teachers and homeschoolers, as well as articles about teaching, 50,000 Internet resource lists by topic and age, and templates for awards, planners, and learning tools.

➤ *e-LearningLinks.com*

A fast-loading and easy to use website listing free online resources for homeschooling. The website includes links to online flash cards.

Chapter 14

Building Your First Lesson Plan

YOU PROBABLY THOUGHT WE'D never get around to the fun part, didn't you? If you look at all you have learned in previous chapters, however, you will realize you already know a great deal about creating lesson plans. We've covered aspects of it in many of the earlier chapters as we discussed adapting lessons, adding action, and putting in variety and pacing. Now we're going to pull all of that together.

Initially, you may find it too overwhelming to create an entire thematic unit. If you are using thematic unit studies prepared by others, select one from the program you are personally interested in. Choose one aspect of the topic you would like your children to study in more detail. Prepare a single lesson plan for this unit and insert it into the plan given to you in the purchased plan. After you have done this several times, try to create your own thematic unit study. A thematic unit study is nothing more than a collection of single lesson plans on a subject, and building individual lessons will give you the confidence to create an entire unit. When you are planning a thematic unit study, you will first outline the unit and then plan individual lessons; but for now, you just need to practice creating simple lessons. Then you will feel ready to build a complete unit study.

If you don't have much teaching experience, your first lesson plans will take much longer than you expect. Use as many prepared materials as possible until you become more comfortable. Gradually increase the number you are doing by yourself until you are preparing as many parts of the lesson as you are comfortable with.

First, a word of caution: homeschooling parents tend to be impulsive. We get easily carried away once we stop being scared, or we cover our fear with elaborate lesson plans that are fun to create but nearly impossible to carry out. Start out slowly. Make your first plans simple and then, if you are having fun, make them a little fancier. You may discover you have a flare for fancy plans, but don't make every lesson fancy. As we've discussed before, too much excitement overstimulates children. It's okay to be dull and ordinary on a regular basis. One fancy lesson plan tucked into an ordinary day stands out much better than ten fancy plans taught in one day. *This sentence stands out because it's the only sentence in the entire book written in 14-point Brush Script font.* If all the sentences were in this font, you wouldn't notice it.

Let's start with some generic instructions on lesson planning. Afterwards, we'll apply what we've learned to a specific lesson plan. Finally, you will create your own lesson plan and test it out on your children.

Choose the topic
The first thing you have to do is to choose a subject. When you prepare your first lesson, select something you are comfortable with and enthusiastic about. It's a little less scary to teach something you already know pretty well or are interested in learning. Besides, it takes some research on your part, and research is more fun when you enjoy the subject matter. As the teacher, it's your duty to have some fun, too. A

happy teacher is a much better teacher! Since my favorite subject is history, I will use history as the focus of my lesson plan. Most homeschooling parents use literature or history as the centerpiece of their curriculum, although you can use anything at all.

Narrow the topic

You are only creating one lesson right now. Later, you will learn to make this lesson part of a larger thematic unit study that contains many lessons on the same theme. However, when you are only teaching one lesson, you have to narrow the focus. Choose one small part of your topic to write your lesson on. For instance, let's return to the earlier-mentioned unit study on the Middle Ages. This section will cover only one portion of the unit, but you may wonder how it fits into the whole. (Would you like to see how I created a Middle Ages unit study? I've offered ideas for this theme throughout the book and you can see the completed lesson plan on my website.)[†]

I certainly can't teach everything about the entire Middle Ages in one lesson, so I'm going to focus on teaching the steps to becoming a knight. Even this may turn out to be too much for one lesson. As I research, I will find out if I can teach this all at once or if I should break each step into a separate lesson. For now, though, I will research becoming a knight.

Write a statement of purpose

Write a statement of purpose. What do you want your child to learn during this lesson? "Students will learn the steps a boy took to become a knight in the Middle Ages." Let's look at other sample statements of purpose:

---

† TerrieBittner.com/history/Middle_ages_thematic_unit_study.html

- *My children will be able to design a science experiment using the scientific method.*

- *My children will learn about courage by studying Laura Ingalls Wilder's experiences during the hard winter.*

- *My children will understand the real-life uses of fractions.*

These statements show what the child will learn during the lesson. The purpose can be academic, moral, or motivational, or even a combination of all these. The courage lesson teaches a moral value through an academic approach—the reading of a quality children's book. Write this statement at the top of the paper or document screen. You might also want to put it on a separate piece of paper and post it over your desk. Everything you plan for this lesson must help you achieve your purpose. For example, don't decide it would be fun to have the children make covered wagon dioramas of Laura crossing the plains, because she isn't crossing the plains in *The Hard Winter*. Stick to the purpose.

Research your topic

For me, this is the exciting part of the lesson. I love to do research. If you don't love it and aren't secure in your ability to research, go to that librarian you've made friends with and ask for help. Most reference librarians adore research.

Begin your research at the library's computer catalogue. Search for the topic of your lesson. Write or print out all the books that show up and start looking at them. In your teaching notebook or in a notebook you prepare just for lesson planning, label one page: "Children's books for research only" and another, "Children's books to share with my children." If you prefer to keep everything on one page, list all the children's books on the same page and put a star by the ones you might want your children to read. If you have several children, put their initials by the books you think they would like. Be sure to record the location of the book, including the reference number, so you can find it again.

You may want to read a few adult books on the subject as well, to get a more complete background. Take one or two of them home. You don't have to read the entire book unless you want to. Use the index at the back to find just the pages you need. Take several of the children's books home also. Be sure to include some fiction as well as nonfiction. The librarian will be able help you find the most interesting books.

As you read the children's books, evaluate their accuracy, how much you think your children would like them, and whether they accomplish what you want them to accomplish. Make sure you are comfortable with the values being taught. Are the pictures interesting and accurate, based on your research? Is there racism, stereotyping, or any other factor that makes you uneasy? (You can still use the book, but you will have to decide how to handle that problem.) If the book is fiction, are the characters interesting and like-able? If the book is nonfiction, are all the topic-specific words defined? Are the facts explained clearly? Is it appropriate for the ages of your children? Will you need to read it to them or can they read it alone?

Remember, you are only planning a lesson, not a unit, so you won't need all these books. One picture book is plenty, and one chapter book is enough if your children are older, although this lesson may only be about the first chapter. Save the rest for the thematic unit study you will create later on. Choose the children's book that best suits your statement of purpose.

In my lesson, I realize the topic I chose was much too large, so I decide to focus on the work of a *page*. Little boys could become *pages* around the age of seven, when they were sent away to live in another castle, usually the castle of a relative. It was believed parents would be too soft to properly train and discipline a child. The life of a *page*, one of the early steps to possibly becoming a knight, might seem glamorous, but they were really just glorified servants. They waited on tables, studied etiquette, helped with the care of the horses and stables, and served the women of the castle. I want to make sure my students understand that all children didn't become *pages*. These were children from "good" families. Later, when I have their attention, they will learn about the lives of the peasants since there is far more to the Middle Ages than the romance we see in fairy tales. I started with knights because children like knights and I want them to be interested in this theme.

Organize your research
You need to get your research in order, so choose a method for doing so. If you don't use a computer, use the method described in Chapter 19 on writing reports. If you do use a computer, put the facts into a word processing program. As you read, notice categories for your lesson. If the categories aren't apparent as you research, you can use the copy and paste functions of your word processing program to move material into the correct section. For my lesson, I might have sections on who becomes a *page*, how a boy becomes a *page*, what he did when he worked, his schedule, his food, his play, and so on. I would write these headings in bold and leave a little space between each one. As I find information, I would place it into one of these sections. If I take a little extra time during this research phase and decide where it best fits with what I already have, I will finish with an organized batch of information. (If you are really ambitious, you could turn this into a personalized textbook.)

Once you have put your information in the order you want to teach it, you are ready to decide how to teach the lesson.

The Life of a Page

1. **Who becomes a page?**

    a. Boys from good families became pages.

    b. Purpose: to prepare him to be a knight.

    c. Why he left home: Parents believed to be too soft to discipline correctly.

2. **How does a boy become a page?**

3. **What does a page do?**

    a. Waits tables.

    b. Serves the women of the castle.

    c. Horses? (Find out if pages took care of horses.)

4. **What is the page's daily schedule?**

5. **What does a page eat?**

6. **What games might a page play?** (Note: Choose some games we can actually play.)

Choose teaching methods

You might have far more research now than you can really use. Don't panic. You don't have to teach your children everything you know, but the extra research will allow you to answer questions you are bound to be asked and will help you understand the topic better. One of the best things about homeschooling is that you get a chance to learn, too.

Don't tackle the entire lesson at once or you will feel overwhelmed. Move each category you have outlined onto a separate page and print the first one. Read it over and, if it helps, make an outline of the most important information. Think of all the ways you could present that information.

The first thing you have to do is to get their attention. Whatever you do first will set the mood and tell the children what sort of lesson they are about to receive, so this is the section that should be the most interesting. Your children may still have their minds on their last lesson, their breakfast, or the soccer game they will have later on. You don't want them thinking about anything but your current lesson, so you need to draw their attention to this subject. For our lesson on *pages*, I might show a picture of a noble knight and ask my children how a man became a knight and whether girls could be knights.

This serves two purposes because it focuses the children on knights and lets me find out how much they already know. After I've listened to their answers, I will tell them the process of becoming a knight starts when a child is just seven years old. If one of my children is seven, I will point that out. If they are older, I'll ask them to tell me about their lives when they were seven; and if they are younger, I will ask them to tell me how they think children that age spend their time. Then I will tell them the seven-year-olds who wanted to become knights led lives that were in some ways very different from the lives of children today, although some aspects were the same. The big difference is that these children lived away from home and had full-time jobs. This will capture their attention, because children this age think they would enjoy being all grown up. History is more understandable and interesting when there is a connection to the child's life. Each portion of the lesson will be compared to my children's lives.

Introduce the basics
Once you have their attention, you're ready to introduce the

facts. You know what material you want them to learn, but there are many ways to teach every piece of information. I often began by reading a good picture book to them or with them. I like them to understand that knowledge comes from books. We'll read it together slowly, talking about both the text and the pictures. I'll ask them how they would like to live this type of life.

You could also show a video, talk to them, or play a game. I like to use games, however, to reinforce the facts rather than to introduce them. Review is much less interesting than learning new material.

If you have older children, you can assign a reading to be done before you begin your lesson. A controversial reading, if it fits your topic, can spark a good debate. Once your teenager has seen that the issue is unsettled, you can provide him with tools for evaluating the arguments. He can then read articles on both sides of the issue.

If you are teaching a mixture of ages, you can still use the youngest child's picture book as a tool to introduce the very basics. Ask the older child to read the book to the younger one. I begin my own research in the children's section when I'm reading completely unfamiliar material. Not only is the material presented in a more interesting way, but it's written at a level I can understand without any background. Children's books generally introduce the sort of facts that bring a topic to life but that aren't usually included in an adult book. Once I'm interested, I'm ready to tackle the more complicated material found in adult books. Your older children may not be willing to admit they enjoy a child's book, but may be unexpectedly willing to read it to a sibling.

Work with the material
Once the material has been presented, you want your children to spend as much time with it as possible. The more

time they spend playing with the facts, the better they will remember them. Following are some ways to work with our lesson on *pages*:

Worksheets
These aren't creative but they are a traditional way to learn, and there is nothing wrong with assigning a few of them. Everything doesn't have to be fun. Your child needs to become familiar with the types of questions found on tests, and worksheets are a good way to practice without the pressure of testing. The upcoming chapter on evaluation (Chapter 22) will show you typical question styles.

Worksheets don't have to be boring; toss in an unexpected element every now and then. When I taught grammar to my youngest children, I would include instructions to act out the list of verbs found on the sheet, or to list their favorite red nouns. Just for the fun of it, toss in an off-beat question: "If you were a rebellious *page* and decided you wanted your job description changed, what is the first thing you would insist your boss change? What would probably happen to you if you did this?" "If our country decided to start a *page* system for children your age, who would you want to work for?"

These can be mixed in with the traditional questions about which of the following chores were not done by *pages* or what a *page* might have for dinner. Your children are less likely to get bored if you offer a chance to do a little imagining in the middle of all those uncreative facts.

Create new materials
Assign your children to make a simple book, design a Web page, or make a chart of the facts. Have them make quiz questions for their siblings, placing each question on an index card. Let them turn those questions into a game they invent together. Have them write a story or puppet show that

teaches the information. For instance, they might do a show on a day in the life of a *page*.

Do a craft
You have to do art anyway—why not tie it to the lesson? The children can make a diorama, paint a picture, or make a clay sculpture related to the lesson. Let them try making paper dolls or puppets. A science lesson can include a biography of the scientist, and the children can recreate a scene from the moment of discovery. Children reading *Wrinkle in Time* can build a tesseract model.

Live the lesson
Have your children participate in some aspect of the topic. They can cook food from the time period, make a pioneer rag doll, do a science experiment, create a costume, or do a service project. If you are learning about the environment, pick up trash. If you study birds, build a feeder. Is nutrition the theme? Plan a week of healthy meals. Did you read a book about lions? Visit some at the zoo. Bringing the lesson to life makes it unforgettable.

Organize and make final plans
If you are feeling indecisive, make a list of all the possibilities. Don't worry about whether your ideas are good or not. Just write down everything that comes to mind, no matter how silly it seems. This is called brainstorming, and it's most effective when you really let yourself go and have fun. In fact, putting down really goofy ideas on purpose will make it easier to list ideas you aren't sure of.

So, if inviting King Arthur to come to dinner pops into your head (because it's been that kind of day), write it down. Put a happy face by it if you're worried someone will see it and think you're losing your mind. Sometimes a silly idea will inspire a better one. For example, you can't really invite King Arthur to dinner. However, you could have the children dress in medieval costumes and have a medieval dinner. (They ate with their hands, so consider having it on a picnic table.) Or, Dad could study up on the king and pretend to be him at dinner. Your children could write stories about King Arthur being transported to their time and landing on their doorstep at dinnertime. None of these idea occurred to me until I wrote about inviting Arthur to dinner. Train yourself to take large leaps of imagination.

Once you have your list, choose one or two of the ideas that most appeal to you and seem to best carry out your statement of purpose. (Did you forget that statement of purpose? Go back and read it before you choose.) Keep in mind that a lesson should be carried out in one day. Some projects, such as a puppet show or large craft, may be carried over into the second or third days to complete, but the project will be introduced on the first day. Don't choose three big projects that take weeks to carry out. You should be able to finish all but one project on the day you start this lesson. Don't put in any more long-term projects until you finish the first one. The exception might be to read a novel related to the topic that you will read throughout the unit study. When you have more experience, you can consider putting in additional long-term projects, but for now, keep it simple. It's hard to know how to time long projects and you'll have difficulty making a lot of projects end all at the same time.

Next, put all the elements in order. For this lesson, I will first show a picture of a knight and ask the children what they know about knights and the process of becoming one. After we discuss it, I will use the introduction I described earlier, beginning a comparison of the lives of little boys from good families in medieval times to the lives of boys in our time.

I will start a chart with two sections on my large dry erase board. The first section will be labeled "Pages." The second will be labeled: "Seven-year-old Boys Today." (If I have a boy that age, I will use his name instead.) As we study, we will list what we learn about the life of a page and, in the other column, list what the boy today would do in the same category. For instance, a *page* was taught religion by a priest, but he was seldom taught reading and writing because it was considered unmanly. A boy today might be taught religion, but he would also learn to read and write because all children should be taught those skills. He would not, however, learn about his religion at school unless he went to a private religious school or was homeschooled.

We will read a book about the life of a *page* as our basic information source. We will read it straight through once, and then return to it to fill out our chart. Then we will compare and contrast. This is an important school skill which means we will figure out what is the same and what is different about the lives of the two boys. We will put a symbol to represent what is the same and what is different for fast reference.

Our next step will be to start a project. Since the lesson has been a quiet, sitting-still sort of thing so far, I want a little action. Let's imagine I have three children: an eight-year-old and an eleven-year-old, both boys, plus a four-year-old girl. I will suggest that the two oldest children choose a way to teach their little sister what they learned today and offer a few ideas, such as the puppet show (can you tell I love puppets?) or a book. I will make it clear they have to work together on this. This teaches them how to do group projects. While they work on their project, I will help the preschooler (who was sitting in on the story) make a little project of her own about the lives of girls in that time period. She will get to teach her big brothers what the girls were doing while the boys were waiting on tables.

And that's all there is to the lesson! That wasn't so bad, was it? You only need a few elements to the lesson, because your class probably won't last more than twenty minutes unless you need more time for the activity. You can see lesson plans don't have to be fancy or complicated. This is a very simple lesson plan, but it will teach all the material and the children will enjoy it.

You don't have to be overly creative to teach children. If you have more ideas than you can teach in one day, prepare some additional lesson plans and make the section on *pages* last a week or two. If the *pages* are the ages of your children, they will be very interested anyway, so you will want to spend more time.

Chapter 15

Turning Lesson Plans into Unit Studies

THE IDEA OF WRITING your own thematic unit study may seem intimidating, especially if you want it to last a month or more. Such a large project can seem overwhelming, but we are going to break the process into very small steps to make it feel manageable. Let's look at how I first wrote this book. This will help you understand how to approach your thematic unit study.

When I first began writing this book, I was extremely frightened by the number of pages I would have to write. To keep myself from panicking, I reminded myself that for several years, I had written a homeschooling column and each article was one thousand words. Because I've been writing one thousand word articles for many years, that length doesn't make me nervous. A chapter might be ten pages, but I often wrote a series of articles that came out to ten pages. I convinced myself to think of the book as a collection of articles. I can only write one chapter at a time.

I wrote my outline first and then pushed all but the current chapter title to a later page I couldn't see. All I had in front of me was my current chapter. I can only write one page at a time, so I started writing on the subject of the chapter. Although I had a plan for the total book in the form of my outline, I forced myself to focus only on what I was doing that very moment. Broken into smaller chunks, the book was less intimidating and the page count grew steadily. I didn't think I could write three hundred manuscript pages, but I did—one page at a time.

You have written a single lesson plan already. Your thematic unit study is nothing more than a collection of single lesson plans. Some days, in the course of a long unit, you will not even need a full lesson plan because you will watch a video or take a field trip. If the children are working on a long project, they may not need any other plans for an entire week. Don't be afraid of your unit study. After you have done the initial planning, just think a day at a time.

Statement of purpose

Start by writing a statement of purpose for the entire unit study. It will be similar to the one you wrote for your lesson plan, but it will be broader since you'll be doing this unit for awhile. Following are examples of statements of purpose:

- *The children will understand the lifestyles and major events of the Middle Ages.*

- *The children will learn to apply the Scientific Method to create their own science experiments.*

- *The children will understand how the childhoods of six important scientists affected their adult lives.*

How much time do you have?

Now decide how long you want this unit study to last. If you outlined what you wanted to cover t-his year, you probably broke it down into months so you could make a vague schedule. You are allowed to change your mind. The year we studied the Middle Ages, I allotted half a year to that and the

194

other half to the Renaissance. We were having so much fun when Christmas came that I decided to continue our study of the Middle Ages and save the Renaissance for the following year. This is a luxury homeschoolers have that traditional schools do not. Make a plan, but don't panic if it doesn't work out. You can shorten the time if you and the children are bored, or lengthen it if you are having fun. The schedule you are going to outline is just to help you plan. Your experiences will be the deciding factor.

Outline your unit

Make an outline of the unit. For instance, if you are doing the Middle Ages unit, you might list the major events you want to discuss, the people you want to learn about, and the aspects of daily life you want to explore. You will have to do some research to figure this out, but many Internet sites have outlines and so do most history books. Put the events in order first. Now fit the people into the events they were involved in. Finally, mix in the information about everyday life. This is the fun part, so spread it out. Remember, not everyone lived in a castle. You will want to discuss the lives of the peasants too.

Locate materials

Now head out to do some research. You want to find out what is available to help you. First, go to the library. There is no point in paying for something if you can get it free unless you want to start building a personal library. Talk to both the children's librarian and the adult librarian and then stroll the shelves. Don't forget to check the magazines. Next, look around the Internet and see what you can find there. If you have friends you trade materials with, talk to them.

Next, you're going to head into the danger zone because you are going into stores. *Don't buy anything yet.* I always wanted to buy every cute thing I saw on the theme I was researching and often did at first. Later, as I began to plan my unit, I often realized that about half of what I bought was pointless. I often found something better at the next store. Right now, you're just going to look. Take along your teacher's notebook and write down what you find, what is in it, how much it costs, and where you found it. You want to be sure you can find it again if you decide to buy it.

Decide what to buy

Now go over your list and mark those things you want to use in your unit study. Add up the costs and figure out if you can afford all the things you marked. Make sure you have material for each part of your unit. If not, you'll have to eliminate some of your choices. This may require you to return to the store to look at the materials again. Once you have chosen which items to buy, go shopping. Take your list and don't allow yourself to get sidetracked. If you need to, take someone with you to make you stay on track. If it's breaking your heart to leave something behind, remember that you can always get it later. I often picked up one new item each week out of the grocery money. If you're planning ahead, you'll be able to buy a few things at a time and not have to come up with a large amount of money all at once. I often bought the absolute minimum essentials for the entire unit at the start just to be sure they were there. Then I bought one or two additional items each week.

Organize your materials

Try to have all your materials at home at the same time for awhile. This may be a problem if you're using the library, but you can take the books you purchased to the library and work there. If you use a library book, it may be checked out when you need it. Plan ahead and be sure you know how many times you can renew the book. You should also be prepared to skip that book and come back to it later if necessary or to switch to a less desirable book. I usually borrowed the library book while I made my lesson plan. Then I returned it, but I checked on it a few weeks before I needed it to make sure it was available. If it was checked out, I put my name on the wait list and found out when it was due back. I checked it out one week before I needed it just to be sure I had it.

Next, look at each item you have purchased or borrowed for the unit. You can only look at one thing at a time. The logical choice might be to look at the first item on your outline and to find everything you have that fits there. However, you will spend a great deal of time wandering through each book again and again. Instead, go resource by resource. To do this, work on your computer (if you have one) so you can insert information easily, or list each item of your outline on separate pieces of paper set out in the order and numbered the way they are on your outline. Keep your papers in a three-ring binder so they don't get lost or mixed up.

Pick up the first book, pamphlet, magazine, or other information source you put your hands on. Don't waste time obsessing over which one you should look at first. You're going to stay in control of your impulsiveness and indecisiveness for an hour or so. (Take a deep breath—you can do this). Open the publication up and look it over. If it all fits into one category, write it on that part of the outline. A picture book will be used in one place whereas a book of thematic unit study activities will be used in many parts of your outline, so you will have to go page by page and write down the name of the book, the page, and what is on that page that applies to the appropriate sections. For example:

Middle Ages Activities, page 12, medieval clothing for nobles. (Handout describing clothing.)

When you list library books, be sure to write down the call numbers and which branch they were at if you visit more than one. If you list an Internet page, write the URL even if it's saved on your computer—you may lose your favorites file and not be able to find it again.

You now have your list of activities and resources divided into topics. The next step is to put the entire unit in order. Remember, you can only work on one section at a time. Take the first topic on your outline and look at everything you have for that section. If something is missing, you will need to find material for that section. Otherwise, put the items you found into an order that makes sense.

Pacing and scheduling

It's important to think about pacing as you work on the order of the activities. If you do something dull, follow it up with something fun. Don't put too many exciting things together or you will over-stimulate your children. If you have already made lesson plans for other subjects, check to be sure you don't have too many exciting or dull things on the same day.

If you're doing most of your subjects through this unit, make sure you cover all the subjects. You don't have to cover each one every day, but you should do them each several days a week. For instance, one day you might read about scientific advances, do a science experiment based on one of those advances, and then read a story about a child in the Middle Ages who worked for a scientist. That covers history, science, and literature. The next day you might have a creative writing assignment in which children write a short puppet show about how someone used the invention, and that covers your writing subject. Making the puppets is art. The following day, they may start rehearsing the play, and that is drama. You might not do any science at all the last two days, but the first day, even though it was listed as three subjects, was really all about science. In fact, this entire section is mostly science, although you are teaching it through the other subjects. For the records, however, put something under science at least two to three times a week.

The final step

You need your unit study in a format you can use. If you created it on the computer, you may want two copies. Put one in a small notebook you can refer to as you teach. Put the other in the section of your teacher's notebook that holds your curriculum.

The first page of the unit study should be a basic outline of themes for each part of the unit. For a unit study on knights, you probably divided the unit based on each stage of becoming a knight, and then had one or two sections on the lives of knights. Having this as a list helps you keep the larger picture clearly in mind as you work. Behind that will be each lesson plan, divided into one-day segments. At the start of each segment, list the supplies you need to teach that lesson. Check this list on your shopping day to see if you need to purchase anything.

Leave a space at the end of each day's lesson plan to make notes on how the lesson worked out in practice. What was especially successful? What didn't go the way you planned? This will help you improve your teaching over time.

Simplifying the process

This process may seem too overwhelming to you at first. If this is the case, find a good book on the subject your children can read. A chapter book that is fairly thick can be used as a textbook. Having this as your basic resource will cut down on the number of other materials you need to have. Today, there are good children's books on nearly every subject. Now, your outline will be the chapters of the book. Each chapter is one section of your unit study. The materials you gather will only have to supplement. Your children will read a chapter, either alone or with you, and then do a few activities based on the material in the chapter. If they read a chapter about King Arthur, they can follow up with a research project to decide if he was real and write a paper on their decision, or they can make a shadow box showing a scene from King Arthur's life. You might also have them read a fictional book about King Arthur for literature. You don't have to be fancy—just have fun.

Chapter 16

Teaching Math When You Can't Even Do Percentages

MANY HOMESCHOOLING PARENTS ARE afraid of math, especially if they were terrible at it in school. From the day they decide to homeschool, they are asked what they will do about higher math. They are asked so often that sometimes they begin to think they can't teach preschool until they've mastered calculus. Teaching math can be a little challenging, but we can master it if we overcome our own fears and take a little time to learn math ourselves.

Conquering your own math phobia

When I began homeschooling, I worried about algebra. My fifth grader was good at math and was nearly ready to start this subject. I had failed it three times in my early years as a high school and college student, and I didn't know what to do. Finally, I gathered my courage and signed up for a basic algebra class at the community college.

The first day I walked into class with my shiny new notebook and sharpened pencils, the teacher eyed me with knowing concern. I was literally shaking, my eyes on the ground, my heart pounding. Anyone watching would have been certain I was attending at gunpoint. At the end of class, the instructor asked me to see her in her office the next day. Great. My first day in school and I was already being sent to the office!

She told me she taught classes each summer on conquering math phobia, and I had the worst case she'd ever seen. At her request, I shared my terrifying mathematical history, from being laughed at by a teacher to staring in horror at a test I couldn't begin to take. She had me work a few problems and then diagnosed my challenges. Over time, with many hours spent in her office, I gradually gained confidence and learned how to overcome the problems caused by my disability and my insecurity. I received an A in the class, my first ever in math.

What I learned in that class was that I could do math if I really tried—and if I believed I could. I had a few challenges to overcome and I had to work harder than everyone else, but I did it. Following are some of the discoveries I made that year about math that helped me overcome my fears.

Math is not a foreign language: When I faced my first algebraic equation, I stared at the numbers and symbols in confusion. My teacher pointed out that every symbol had a word attached to it. I am comfortable with words. Since I knew how to diagram sentences, she had me diagram the mathematical equation. First, she taught me the word for each symbol. Then she had me label each symbol. Oh! Those were verbs! Every symbol said, "Do something." When I learned what to do when I saw the symbol, the sentence began to make sense. I memorized very basic statements. Memorizing those basic little tidbits and learning the definition of each symbol (not long definitions, but one-word instructions, such as *multiply*) turned the strange-looking equations into English. So, to make math less baffling, learn the language.

Don't do everything at once: When faced with a long problem, I tried to do all the steps at once. I have organizational challenges, and doing a long problem is really just a matter of organizing. I learned to look at the problem and choose one step to do. Most people can combine steps, but I have to do one at a time. In algebra, I memorized the order of operations. I followed them faithfully, one step at a time. Each time I did a step, the problem became a little shorter, and I felt a sense of accomplishment.

Playing with Story Problems: When I encountered story problems, even the simpler types younger children are given, I tended to make the same mistake. I'm a good reader, but the presence of numbers caused my brain to shut down and I didn't even try to solve the problem. I taught myself to write each fact as a separate sentence and to make a note telling me as to what I had to do. I tried to write a numerical statement or at least to simplify what I was learning. Then I organized the steps into the correct order and dealt with one statement at a time until I had created the numerical problem.

For example: *Jason is four years older than his sister, Susan. Susan is two years younger than her brother Joseph. If you add their ages together, they total 12. How old is each child?*

There are a number of ways to resolve this issue. I probably take the longest route. Your child might be able to think of a faster way. The first thing I do is to put the children in order by age so I don't get confused. The oldest child is Jason. We know this because he is older than Susan. Susan is younger than Joseph, which means Joseph also has to be younger than Jason, since he is only two years older than Susan and Jason is four years older than Susan. Did you follow that? From oldest to youngest, the children are Jason, Joseph, and Susan. Write that down.

Now what? We don't know how old any of the children are, but we know their ages total twelve. Jason plus Joseph plus Susan equals twelve. Let's see if we can create some statements. After studying the problem, I decide I'd rather work youngest to oldest because I like addition better than subtraction. Let's line them up.

Susan + 2=Joseph. (We are talking ages here.)
Susan + 4=Jason.

What other statements can you think of? How many years apart are Jason and Joseph? The problem doesn't say, but we can tell by looking at how far apart Susan is from each of them. You don't absolutely have to know that, but it might make you feel more secure. When you have lined up the statements, and feel comfortable, solve the problem. You can plug in numbers and guess. That is perfectly acceptable and if you do it often enough, you will figure out faster ways to solve the problem. Write the problem with the names of the children in order, showing the total as twelve. Choose an age for the youngest child. Add two for Joseph. Then add two more for Jason.

Example: Susan + Joseph + Jason=12

1+3+5=9. Nope, that's not right. Try another combination. Because the answer was too low, you need to start with a higher age for Susan.

Do you have it? Susan is two. Joseph is two years older, so he's four. Jason is six. That wasn't so bad, was it?

Learn how to do the math problems before you have to teach them to your children. If you have a preschooler, start learning right now. Spend as much time as you need on each step. There aren't tests or grades, so relax. Convince yourself it's a puzzle. For problems like the one above, buy little books of logic puzzles. They are just algebra problems, but they have easy charts to help you solve them. Learning to solve them will build confidence.

Sometimes it doesn't matter if you don't understand: Every once in awhile, I encountered a problem that made no sense. No matter how hard I tried, I couldn't understand why something worked. As my anxiety levels rose, my teacher told me to just learn to do the problem. It's helpful to understand, but not essential. Memorize the steps and hope the explanation will become clearer as you gain experience.

How to teach your younger children

Little children can learn math by using hands-on games, real-life activities, and fun puzzles. Visit your local school supply store and look at all the ways children can learn math. The typical grocery store workbook will not work because they're meant to supplement a school textbook and they skip steps. When you're ready for books, look for materials that break the steps down so children aren't overwhelmed with too many things all at once, especially if they aren't good at math. You also need lots of review because you don't want the children to forget what they learn. At the same time, you want them to learn why they need to know the material, and you want them to practice using the math in real-life situations. You also want to have a little fun. Finally, you want them to learn to think.

That means sometimes they need problems that don't have obvious answers. Look for books of brainteasers or math challenges. Give them one of these each week to solve, and let them spend the week playing around with it. Allow them to use any method except getting help, unless your children are close in age and you sometimes want them to work together. If you choose this method, be sure each child is contributing. You will still want them to spend some time solving problems without help.

Math is best taught at a child-led pace. At the start of the year, you will want to figure out how fast you need to move, but this is only so you know how you're doing. If you are sub-jected to testing, you may need to adapt to this schedule. If you are not, move exactly as fast as the child is ready to move.

The first day, give your child a problem similar to the ones in the first lesson. Does he already know how to do it? If so, let him do a small number, perhaps five, as a review, and then test on the second lesson. When you find something your child can't do, start teaching. We preferred to study on a wipe-off board, one child at a time while the others did independent work in another room. The advantage of a wipe-off board is that mistakes are simply wiped away, and there aren't any frustrating red marks or pencil erasure marks. I hoped it would make math less intimidating than it had been for me.

Teach your children a proper attitude toward encoun-tering something they don't know. When your child comes to something he can't do, say, "Wonderful! Now we know what you need to work on. We'll get to it first thing tomor-row." Waiting until the next day gives you time to plan the lesson and to look for something fun to include.

There is almost always a fun and practical way to teach math in the younger grades. If you're teaching fractions, for instance, bake cookies and talk about the fractions. Look for other fractions in your life and find excuses to practice them. By the time you get to the actual lesson, your child will have some sense of what to do with the knowledge he gets and a fair understanding of how the concept works. All he needs now is practice.

Memorization

Some educators feel memorization is a waste of time since calculators are so easily available. I disagree. Your child may need to do a calculation when he isn't near a machine, or the batteries may be dead. I feel it's always important to be able to do at least practical math in your head or on paper, even if you seldom do it. Memorization does not have to be dreary. Almost anything can be a game. Adding a hands-on component often makes a drill feel like a game.

Let's talk about multiplication tables as an example. The first step is to teach children the *commutative property*. This term means the mathematical rule that tells us three times six has the same answer as six times three. The reason your child wants to know this is because he will have to memorize far fewer multiplication facts if he knows them. You can teach the basic facts through the times twelve tables, and after awhile, you have only a few new problems. Your child will learn all the times zero tables, all but one of the times one tables, all but two of the times two tables and so on. Before long, he is rushing through them because there are so few new problems to learn.

Make several sets of flash cards with all the times table problems on them. You can purchase them, but most of the manufactured sets have a problem on each side of the card and those are less effective for games. Make sure all the cards are the same color, shape, and size. Now let your child help you think up games. We played these:

Game #1
Give each person playing the game a stack of flash cards that are the same size. They should have the math problem on one side and nothing on the other side. Have each person lay out the top card in his own stack. Every player solves the equation on his card and announces the answer. Other players can challenge if they think the answer another player gave is incorrect. The person whose answer is the highest number in the round wins. If someone successfully challenges another player's answers and then correctly solves the problem, the challenger wins. The winner of the round gets all the cards. If you don't want the challenger to win the round,

choose another reward for successful challengers, such as extra points added to his score for the round. (For example, if the sum of his addition problem was twelve, you might add three more points, so his total is now fifteen. Fifteen is the number he would use to determine whether or not he won the round.) The goal is to get the most cards.

As an example, Madison and Jackson are playing. Madison reviews her cards and sees that she has addition problems that, when added, have sums of 8, 13, and 15. She chooses fifteen as the card to play. Her brother's highest card only has a sum of 12, so she wins. In the next round, Madison announces her winning card to have a sum of 19, but Jackson points out that 9x2 is eighteen, not nineteen. Because he successfully challenged her answer, he wins the round and gets Madison's card.

Game #2

If you want to play noncompetitively, begin each round the same way, but place the card with the lowest answer in the center. The goal is to get every card in the center. The lowest card is placed there because it's usually the higher totals children need extra practice on and the children will have to recalculate the answers on remaining cards in order to decide which card to put in the center next. In this way, they will solve each of the higher cards multiple times before placing them in the center. You might time the game and keep tabs on how quickly the children finish. The family is still competing as a team, but trying to improve its score. If Madison and Jackson decided to play this version, they would look at the cards they each have. Madison would notice her lowest sum is two, and Jackson would notice his was four. Together, they would decide to put Madison's card into the center. They are trying to add quickly, because they have just five minutes to get as many cards into the center as possible.

Game #3

If your children like to move, hide the cards around the room. Tell them they have two minutes to find as many cards as possible, and without removing them from the location, solve the math problem on each card they find. At the end of the two minutes (use a kitchen timer to avoid arguments), have each child retrieve the card he solved that had the largest number as an answer. Whoever comes up with the highest scoring card wins that round. (Make up a rule to resolve situations where more than one child finds the same card.) To make it noncompetitive, give them one minute after the timer goes off to decide together which card to present to you. (Don't tell them how to decide.) After five rounds, total the points they've earned. A card that has an answer of eight (2 x 4 = 8) is worth eight points. To make the game more challenging, have them try to beat their highest score each time. Suppose Madison and Jackson have six problems on the wall. Between them, they solve all six of the multiplication problems and then get together to decide which card to bring. If the answers to the problems are 6, 12, 15, 18, 21, and 24, they bring their mother the card with the product of twelve. If they bring 24, they will have to end the game after the first round, and the total score for the game would be 24 since there are no higher answers. If they bring their mother the card with the answer of twelve, they can bring cards all five rounds and have the highest possible score. They would choose not to bring the card with the answer of six. Do not tell your children the strategy—one goal of the game is to have them figure this out on their own through trial and error.

Game #4

Music is a fun way to help children memorize, but they will have to sing the entire song to get to the correct answer. You can purchase recorded music that teaches math problems or make up your own. Your children can also make up the songs. It should only be one tool of many and is best used at the beginning of the memorization process.

Your children do not need to completely memorize the math facts in a given chapter before moving to the next chapter. Make memorization one portion of your math day. It may take years, but you will always be moving closer to your goal.

Because of my disabilities, I got through school by memorizing a number of times table problems a distance apart and then mastering the art of counting to the problem I actually needed. If your child is really struggling, you may want to teach him some counting skills. He must learn to count in his head in patterns. For example, I knew five times five was twenty-five, but I didn't know the answer to five times six. When I came to five times six, I thought, *Five times five is twenty-five*—then I added five more—*26, 27, 28, 29, 30* to get to the correct answer. I had memorized the information that five was two groups of two with one left over. I taught myself to count silently in that pattern. I had a similar pattern for each number in the multiplication tables that I couldn't memorize and I practiced them that way.

If you do not have a learning disability, you might feel I could have just as easily memorized the remaining times tables, but for whatever reason, I couldn't. I didn't learn the rest of them until I was older and stumbled on to a method that was physical enough to work for me. I learned my multiplication tables while on five months of bed rest during my first pregnancy. However, I had needed those problems thousands of times before my brain was ready to learn them, so I was grateful for the compensating techniques I had created.

Let your child create his own solutions for compensating. Generally, he is best suited to figuring out what will work for him, although you might help him think of ideas.

Reducing writing

If your child doesn't write well, increase the amount of time he can spend on math by using numbers and symbols written on cards. He can set out the numbers instead of writing them. If he can't line up numbers in multi-digit problems, give him graph paper with large squares. (You may be able to make these on your computer.) Let him place each digit in a square. Some children also turn their lined paper sideways and use the lines for columns. Drill work can be done on a computer. Many computer programs allow children to drill, eliminating the need to write. Your child does not have to do an entire worksheet just because that was the way it was printed. Cut it up, or draw a line after ten problems. Have your child do as many as he can comfortably do, and then gradually increase the amount of time he's able to work.

Dealing with dawdling

Because reviewing is so dull, many children dawdle when they do their work. If your child is getting into the habit of taking longer than you know he needs, take early steps to break his bad habits. You will have to figure out how long he really needs to do his work. Ask him to do a worksheet while you sit beside him and time him. Tell him he mustn't ask questions or talk because this is a timed test. Be sure he knows how to do the work well before you begin.

Later, divide the number of problems by the number of minutes he took to do the work. This will tell you the average number of minutes he needs to do one problem he knows how to do well. You will have to add a little extra time for newer types of math and for longer problems, but this gives you a general starting point. Add some extra minutes just to be nice and then put a timer at your child's workspace. Tell him you are setting the timer and you' are going to see if he can beat the clock. If you need a reward, keep it simple, like a sticker on a chart. Set the timer and put him to work. When he finishes, grade the paper and add one minute for each mistake. Record the final score on a chart. Record it in blue if he beats the baseline score and red if he is too slow. You needn't make a fuss either way. Just record it and congratulate him if he is on schedule. If he was too slow, tell him you're sure he will get faster soon.

Based on how your child is performing, you may need to adapt the baseline occasionally. If you see he is really trying, you may want to give him bonus points (or in this case, take minutes off his score) so he meets the timeline. If he goofs off and still beats the timeline, you may want to tighten it somewhat. Eventually, this may train your child to stay on task. Once he begins making his goal regularly, change your pattern so that you use this technique only occasionally. That way it won't lose its effectiveness. Any reward or game that is overdone stops working.

Teaching math to older students

As your child becomes a more experienced homeschooler, teach him to be more independent in his math studies. As he works, go into another room for a few minutes. Gradually increase the amount of time you are away until you are only checking on him occasionally. Teach him to read directions without help. As he gains confidence, encourage him to figure out how to solve a new math problem without help. When you start a new section, ask him to read the instructional materials in the textbook to you. Have him work the sample problems as he reads the instructions. Then suggest he try to work a few problems on his own. Don't step in until he has given it a fair chance on his own. In time, he should learn to teach himself math. This will keep you from having to learn calculus if you don't want to.

Look for old math textbooks in thrift stores and find

math sites on the Internet. Sometimes a book does a poor job of explaining a particular problem. When this happens, pull out additional books and find out how they explain the problem. One of them might make sense. When all else fails, learn what math classes teens in your neighborhood or church are taking. You may find a sympathetic teen willing to explain a particularly challenging concept. The first choice, however, is always to let your teen solve the problem himself in order to improve his ability to be an independent scholar. This concept is discussed in more detail in Chapter 24.

More Resources

➤ *Shoe Box Math Learning Centers* by Jacqueline Clarke
ISBN: 0439205743

Although the projects described in Jacqueline's book are designed for classrooms, they make great additions to your homeschool as well. Each of the forty kits described in the book is stored in a shoe box and can be pulled out at a moment's notice. These are excellent for crisis days or to take along to a doctor's appointment. They are also helpful when you discover you have fifteen extra minutes to fill or a lesson plan that falls apart.

➤ *Teacher2Teacher (T2T®)*
"Ask Dr. Math"
MathForum.org/t2t

The most commonly answered math questions are on this website from Drexel, but if you are really stuck, you can e-mail your question. We've used this site successfully many times. There is also a teachers' area where you can ask questions about teaching math.

➤ *Math Solutions*
MathSolutions.com/index.cfm?page=wp10&crid=3

One day, while at a seminar for middle school girls, I overheard some preteens trying to guess which of the women on the stand was the keynote speaker, mathematician Marilyn Burns. A girl made a guess and her friend said, "That can't be a math teacher. She's beautiful!" But it was the mathematician. Later, I watched Ms. Burns hold a room full of girls spellbound as she taught them complicated math lessons through games and activities. This Web page offers sample lesson plans from the publications that Math Solutions offers. These are unique in that they are offered in story form—a record of what happened when she and other gifted instructors taught real children. This allows you to see how the lessons were approached, how the children responded, and how the teacher coped with questions. Many of the lessons come from children's books.

➤ *Family Math* by Jean Kerr Stanmark, Virginia Thompson, Ruth Cossey
ISBN: 0912511060
Math doesn't have to be worksheets—it can be games you play with your children. The games in this book are excellent for children who are far advanced in understanding higher math concepts; they are equally good for helping children who don't like math to figure out why math can be fun.

➤ *CoolMath4Kids.com*
You'll find lots of online math fun on this site. Lesson plans that are simple, visual, and fun are being added as well. Please type the URL carefully and then bookmark it for your children. Unscrupulous people have purchased similar domain names, hoping children will mistype the URL. Mistyping leads to pornographic sites. The webmaster has no control over this problem (which is common on the Internet as a way to lure children into places they don't belong).

Chapter 17

Reading, Sight-Reading, Phonics, and Other Scary Words

THERE IS NOTHING MORE rewarding than to see your child lost in a book and to know you gave her that gift. I treasure reading lessons above all the other lessons I've taught my children.

Books about teaching a child to read make the process seem frightening and complicated. It's very difficult to teach a large class of children within the confines of a school day, but it's not especially difficult to teach most children to read at home. Some children will refuse to learn on the traditional schedule and some will struggle with learning disabilities, but most children want to learn to read and do so in spite of the methods we choose.

You can prepare your child to be a good reader. Most of the skills your child needs should be started when he or she is small, but it's never too late. If you are not already doing these things, start today.

Loving books
As we discussed in Chapter 11, the love of reading must come first. Read to your child every day. Make sure this reading is memorable and special by thinking about the word cozy. A small child can sit in your lap. Older children will pile on

the sofa, curl up under blankets, or sprawl on the lawn as you read. Don't stop reading when your child learns to read for herself. You can read books your children might find too difficult on their own. You can also improve their listening skills by continuing to read to them, which is essential to a good education.

There's one more good reason for reading aloud to your children. You're creating a shared family culture. Periodically, someone in our family will say something that sends everyone into giggles. Outsiders stare at us in confusion. The sentence that sets us off is an inside joke, a line from a book we read together. Inside jokes build a family bond that tells our children no one outside our family can understand us the way we do. When faced with a challenge, we might, as a group, draw comfort from a shared book. When Christmas comes at a financially challenging time, we can remember how thankful Laura Ingalls was to receive the simple items she found in her stocking Christmas morning. When the power is out in the middle of winter, we recall Laura's hard winter. Stories from books somehow lodge themselves more firmly into our hearts than movies do. Read to your children and create a bond resulting only from written words.

Fill your house with books. Double and triple stack them on the shelves. Leave especially good ones on the coffee table, in the bathroom, and on the kitchen table. Make sure your children have print books. E-books can't be handed down to younger siblings or your own children, and there is something magical and bonding about reading the very same copy of a book your grandmother and mother read. Make sure your children assume houses must have books. Make sure they're sorry for any child who lives without this treasure.

When my children were young, we had a little neighbor who loved books dearly. She couldn't read yet and she lived in a home where books were not valued. She hadn't a single book. My children were shocked, and began inviting her to our home each day to be read to. When we cleaned off shelves so overflowing even we couldn't manage, they gathered several boxes of outgrown picture books and asked the child's mother if she could have them. Her mother didn't care and the children lugged the boxes to her home. The little girl knelt beside the books and touched them reverently, her eyes wide, her heart too full to speak. As my children watched her touching and hugging each book, they were in awe. They spent days and days reading them to her and afterwards looked at their own overflowing shelves, so taken for granted, with new appreciation. You may not be able to find a child such as this one, but search out ways to show your children how lucky they are to be in a book-filled home.

Language skills

A child needs a good vocabulary and a good grasp of spoken language before she learns to read. You don't need formal vocabulary lessons to do this. When you talk to your child, use grammatical sentences and hard words. Avoid the temptation to imitate your child's adorable language mistakes. Don't bring your vocabulary to her level. Use good, hard words and teach her what they mean. Parents who don't think a thing of saying words like watermelon or dinosaur to a child will reduce other communication to child-level words. *Ambulate* has fewer syllables than watermelon. Try asking your child to ambulate to the kitchen one day. Tell her what it means (to walk) and then use the word repeatedly over the next several days. Soon it will become her word. Give her words to describe her feelings, her activities, and her world.

Little children love big words. So do big children because they can show off with them. Choose a new word every day and write it on a big wipe-off board, or make a sign. Call it the word of the day. Expect your children to use it as often as possible—make a game of it. As old as I am, I still remember my seventh grade English teacher, Charles Thompson, fresh from college and already smarter than most experienced teachers. He gave us vocabulary words that, he assured us, everyone said we were too young to be able to learn. He used the same technique to get us to tackle *The Iliad and The Odyssey*. We were, naturally, furious that anyone would challenge our brains, and we learned the words and read the books. Oddly enough, I still remember some of the words he taught us. I was so excited when I learned the word "introvert," because I hated being described as shy and quiet. Introverted fit me perfectly, and I liked it. He gave us an excitement for words that changed my life and helped me become a writer. When I began homeschooling, I imitated his methods and even taught many of the same vocabulary words. His methods worked. If you are excited about words, you will pass this love along to your children and they will become readers.

First reading lessons

There will come a day when your children will be ready to learn to read. If you are fortunate, they will come to you and tell you it's time. If they don't, you may have to introduce the subject yourself. Children do not get ready to do things at the same ages, no matter how hard traditional schools try to make them conform. Your child may decide to learn to read at age three, or she may wait until she's eight. If you decide to teach her to read before she is ready, you will need to spend more time on the lessons, but you can do that without harm if you're kind and patient. If you are required to be evaluated, you probably will have to teach on schedule. Take it step-by-step and document what you do. If your child isn't up to grade level, you will be able to show you did a good job of presenting the material.

You'll probably start with the alphabet. Chapter 21 has information on teaching that part of the subject. Whenever you talk about the letter, talk about the sound too. Some teachers say you shouldn't make the sound alone, because it distorts it. They suggest showing complete words. "This is a *B*. I know lots of words that start with *B*. Listen: book, baby, bear, banana . . . ." Keep it up until he starts suggesting words himself. You might want to write the words on your dry erase board and put the letter being discussed in a different color. Run your finger under the word as you say it.

When your child knows all the letters, you can begin teaching some combinations of letters. When I wrote the word *chin*, I put the CH in red, and the rest of the word in black. I talked about how the two letters were partners, and when they worked together as a team, they could make a whole new sound.

There are many ways to teach reading. Many teachers insist that phonics, the sounding out of words, is the only way to teach reading. Others say that only sight-reading should be used. Sight-reading means you memorize each word. My personal feeling is that reading should be taught in as many ways as possible. Sounding out every word takes too long and requires so much concentration that a child won't be able to think about meaning. On the other hand, a child who must memorize every word can't learn new words without a teacher. I used a combination of both methods.

My children, having our Irish gift of gab, learned to read quite early. For this reason, I began by playing with sight words. When they expressed a desire to learn to read, or began sight-reading some words on their own, I made flash cards (I must have used thousands of flash cards in my years of parenting) for the first names of each person in the family. I made five or six of each name, all identical except for the actual word. I began by showing my child her own name and telling her what it said. We talked about each of the letters, and I showed her how to sound it out. Then I put out three of the cards with her name and one of someone else's name. I asked her to find the name that wasn't hers. When she removed it, I congratulated her and told her whose name that was. When she could consistently remove the incorrect name, I began teaching her to read the names of each family member. She sorted all the names into piles first. Then I asked her to gather a specific name. When she seemed proficient, I used the cards more traditionally. I set them on the floor (we played on the floor so it seemed like a game) and asked her to read each card.

We also played games with the names. When the family was gathered together, the new reader was given the cards and asked to distribute them to the correct person. When no one else was around, she matched them to pictures.

Next, she learned her entire name and was soon able to put her first, middle, and last names into the correct order. By this time, she was getting the hang of reading. It was time for the first sentences. "My name is Jennifer." "My name is not Nicholas." Each word was placed on a card of its own. We talked about each word and the letters and sounds. (This taught phonics casually.) I also had a card for a period and a card with the word *my* all in lowercase. We talked about how sentences started with the capital letter. We also discussed the period, which tells the reader to stop, because the sentence is done. Then I set out the cards in order to make the sentence and read it to her, pointing to each word. Next, she took a turn. After a few tries, I mixed up the cards and let her practice putting them back in order. This is more fun than workbooks or even reading books. It looks like a game and because she had my undivided attention, it was also a way to get time with me.

Over time, I added new cards and we made sentences. By

the time this was too impractical, due to the number of cards needed, we were ready for books. I used old pre-primers from the 1950s and was fortunate enough to find a teacher's edition. Pre-primers are somewhat out of style, but my little ones liked them and they didn't teach too many words. Once you are ready for a reading book, choose any one you are comfortable using. Go slowly, and teach sounds as you teach memorization of words.

The real secret to reading isn't the method—it's the fun. As I described earlier, reading should be a great joy to a child. When you start using reading books, don't sit at the desk or table. Sit in a big cozy chair side by side or with your child in your lap. Don't answer your telephone and let your other children entertain themselves. This is your time with this child. These reading lessons should be associated with love, laughter, and words. Don't work at it for hours. Most of our reading lessons lasted only fifteen minutes.

One step most textbooks neglect is the art of reading with expression. Your child should gradually learn to read smoothly and expressively. You need to teach this as a separate skill. (Somehow, this caused my children to take up theater, so it may have unexpected side effects.) This process can begin in the pre-primer stage, after your child has some reading experience and a grasp of sight words.

Select a story your child can already read well, perhaps one he read a month ago. Ask him to read it to you. Then ask him to listen as you read it. Have him notice how you blend the words together, rather than reading one word at a time. Also talk about reading with expression, the way people talk. Read one sentence to him and have him repeat it with expression. After you have played with this—and do keep it light and fun—let him try reading the story again. Praise what he did correctly.

You might want to put a little drama into your curriculum. This will improve his reading skills. Write a very basic sentence, such as, "Here I am." Ask your child to pretend he is very scared. How would he say the sentence? What expression would he have on his face? What would his body do? How would his voice sound? As you act out sentences, stories, and plays, your child will begin to think about how people talk. When he reads with expression, he improves his comprehension and sounds like a better reader.

If your child continues to read one word at a time, robotic style, teach him familiar word combinations. Try setting out two words and having him read just those words. When he can read two-word combinations well, try three. Continue to work on this skill so he sounds like a competent reader.

Comprehension is an essential part of reading. As your child reads, ask him to tell you the story in his own words. Ask him questions to find out what he knows. What sort of person is Jimmy? Do you think Susan likes dogs? Why did Amy do that? What do you think will happen next? As the two of you discuss what he reads, he will understand the purpose of reading. Just as he was hearing a real story when you read to him, he is now reading a real story for himself.

After the beginning

Once your child understands what reading is all about and knows most of his sounds and a good number of words, it's time to put reading into the real world. When we finished the primer level, I stopped using textbooks and introduced real books to the children. This is easier now that many companies produce books for early readers marked by grade level. You can use these books just as you did the reading books, but the stories are better.

Whenever possible, let your child select his own reading material. Just as you did when he was first learning to read, listen to him in a cozy setting. Put a notepad nearby and jot down words your child cannot read by sight and those he has trouble sounding out. Later, look at this list. The words he had trouble sounding out will tell you what phonics skills he needs to learn. Create lesson plans to teach those skills. Now review the sight word list. Some of the words are not important enough to learn to sight-read. The name of a rare animal may never be encountered again. Choose only those words you consider important for him to be able to read from memory and teach those. You can use old-fashioned flash cards and create sentences that use the word. Most of the techniques you use to teach spelling will also help you teach sight words. In fact, learning to write and spell a word is an excellent way to teach a child to read it.

Chapter books

This is the time to introduce your child to chapter books. Each night, after reading a picture book or two, read a chapter from a novel. Your child may not understand it and he may not pay attention, but read anyway. If he is already tucked into bed, he may fall asleep as he listens. But you might be surprised at how much he actually grasps. When my two youngest were very small, I read them each a picture book and then read a chapter to my oldest child. One day, I suggested she draw a picture of the Black Thing from the book *Wrinkle in Time*, which we were reading together. My preschool age daughter glanced up from her toys and asked if she could do it too. She and her little brother both drew their interpretations and explained them to me. I realized they had been listening as they played quietly in the room. If you're reading during the day, allow the younger children to play if they choose, but instruct them to be very quiet.

Children need to listen to many books before they can read them. Telling your children stories from memory and reading chapter books will prepare them for the difficult task of reading books without pictures. Take the books slowly and talk about them as you read. Begin with the short chapter books written at a second grade level and work up to longer chapter books that appeal to little children, such as the books by Beverly Cleary.

The other stuff

If your child must take standardized tests each year, buy comprehension workbooks so your children can practice. You can find books that offer small selections similar to those on tests and also books based entirely on a well-known novel. If you choose not to use those books, spend time talking about the books and bringing the books to life. Make johnnycakes after reading *Little House on the Prairie*, build a castle after reading *A Knight's Tale*, and locate England on a map when you read about Paddington. The more fun you have with each book, the more your child will love to read. If a book discusses a social issue that interests you, consider volunteering to help the cause. Let your children discover that books can change lives.

Nonfiction books require different skills from fiction. Use good trade books to supplement your history and science. When your child asks a question, help him find a book that has the answer instead of answering the question yourself. Reading should never be just a school subject for your child—it should be a way of life.

More Resources

➤ *Dolch Word Lists*

JanBrett.com/games/jan_brett_dolch_word_list_main.htm

Dolch's word list is a list of the 220 most important words for children to know how to read from memory. Children's author Jan Brett has created some elegant versions of this list with illustrations from her books. While in the site, look around. There is nearly enough on her site to create a complete kindergarten or first grade curriculum.

➤ *The Harry Potter Lexicon*
   HP-Lexicon.org
   While admittedly not your ordinary reading site, this page offers suggestions for teaching this series. It includes in-depth analysis of the books, information about the series, and explanations of British English. Even the most reluctant reader seems willing to study Harry Potter.

➤ *Phonics Learning Games Kids Can't Resist* by Michelle Ramsey
   ISBN: 0439107962
   The games in this book require materials you probably already own or can purchase inexpensively, or they are reproducible items found in book.

Chapter 18

History: Time Machines for Homeschoolers

YOU MAY REMEMBER HISTORY as dull names, dates, and statistics and for that reason, dread having to teach it to your children. Teaching history can, if you are building your own curriculum, require a fair amount of research on your part. But you may be surprised to discover how much fun you're having as you prepare. Done correctly, history can be the highlight of your school. If you're using thematic units, you can build your entire curriculum around this subject which, when properly taught, includes music, art, math, science, literature, and every other subject you're required to teach. You can spend your entire day exploring a moment from the past and have so much fun your children won't want to stop when the unit is over. (Every day won't be this much fun, but some days will be.)

Teaching history geographically
There are two ways (at least) to teach history. Let's begin with the way it's normally taught in public schools in the United States. History is taught geographically in most public schools, rather than chronologically. This means the program begins with a child's own home and community and gradually works outward to other countries. Little children

normally learn something closer to civics, studying the duties of police officers and firefighters, learning what happens in a grocery store, or finding out how their school operates. They are introduced to history through the holidays. They learn about George Washington, Abraham Lincoln, and Martin Luther King on their birthdays. They reenact (usually incorrectly) the first Thanksgiving each November. Sometimes they will also celebrate a historic event in Mexico as part of their multicultural education.

History is not formally introduced until about fourth grade when children are usually taught the history of their own state. In fifth grade, they learn about American history, normally stopping after the Civil War. Sixth grade is devoted to some aspect of world history: usually Mexico, Canada, or ancient history. In seventh grade, more world history is taught. U.S. history and government are again taught in eighth grade. Once again, they usually end with the Civil War.

The textbooks used in these classes are usually alarmingly inaccurate, filled with myths passed along through the generations. If you choose to use textbooks, you will need to research each event to learn how accurately it's being described. If your children are older, they can do the research themselves. Encourage middle school and high school students to read real historians and find out what the textbooks got wrong.

You may wonder why the schools are using inaccurate books. Most schools do not teach history because they think children need to know history per se. History is often a chance for the government to teach children whatever it currently wants children to believe about government and the past. History books frequently teach whatever reflects the current standards for political correctness. Few textbooks written for elementary and high school students strive for balance or encourage children to decide for themselves how to view complicated events and people. Thomas Jefferson, for example, is usually portrayed as either an evil slaveholder or a great statesman, and seldom as a complex person who deserves a balanced presentation. As a parent, you're free to accept or reject whatever the current fad in history instruction is and to present a balanced approach if you choose to do so. There are good books that teach history from every possible point of view, so do your homework and choose the book that appeals to you.

Teaching history chronologically

The method I used is more complicated because at the time, I was unable to find a prepared history designed to teach history chronologically. When I taught my first child, I tried to continue the pattern set by the schools. But I found myself regularly having to explain the background. It's difficult to understand why Columbus set sail unless you know something about the events of Europe during his time. The miracle of our constitution is easier to understand if you are familiar with other forms of government. When I began homeschooling my younger children, I decided to start at the beginning.

This method has drawbacks. You can't cover all places in the world. I was going to lead up to an understanding of United States history, so I focused on Europe. This is a method of education that is losing favor in a multicultural world. I did try to do some units on China and Egypt, using a textbook, but the children became confused as we moved back through times we'd already covered. We moved so rapidly they didn't understand the issues correctly. I soon returned to my politically incorrect Eurocentric history. You will have time later, when the children are older, to return to other countries, or you can create a social studies elective about the cultures of other countries in which you include the historical highlights. Museum trips, educational videos, and good children's books can also teach world history informally. If your family has a connection to a particular part of the world, you may want to move through time in a different path. It's your curriculum, so follow the timeline in any direction you choose.

You may choose to wait until first grade to begin your time machine journey. During the kindergarten year, prepare your child to understand the world existed long before he was born. Tell stories about your childhood and begin them by saying, "Once upon a time, long, long ago, before you were born, Mommy was a little girl. One day, when she was just your age, she had an adventure." Then move even further back to tell stories of the child's grandparents. Read books about the history of holidays and read stories that take place in the past. Always make it clear to your child these events happened before he was born. Many children are surprised to find out the world existed before their birth. Some, in fact, find this information insulting, not wanting to believe the world had a right to exist without them. (You'll have to get them over that.)

The first year you can begin with prehistory. The way you approach this will depend on the pattern you plan to use throughout your school. If you are a religious family, you may want to begin with the stories in your scriptures about the creation and the first generations. Both those who want to include religion and those who do not can take a more traditional approach and learn about the earliest men, or combine both methods.

Often the best way to introduce early history is to begin with a career unit on archaeology and paleontology. Little children love these careers. When my oldest first learned about paleontology at a children's museum, her eyes widened and she asked in astonishment, "You mean someone would pay me to play in the dirt? Wow!" Find some children's books on the subject and read them to your child. Then plan some activities to let children test out the careers. Purchase dinosaur models and bury them in the sand for your children to dig up. Set out a pile of mystery items and ask your children to guess what they represent. The prehistory unit can include discussions about living without technology, and science studies can include dinosaurs.

Later in the year, you can introduce time lines. We drew pictures to represent each stage of the development of man as taught by science. On a long strip of butcher.paper, we marked off time periods and glued the pictures we made onto the correct spots.

This unit may bring about some questions from religious children. They may wonder where these primitive people fit into the Bible. Before you begin to teach, decide how you intend to answer these questions. If you have already played at being archaeologists, your children probably made incorrect guesses. You can use this experience to show them that sometimes we have to make guesses, and our guesses are not always right. You may also have other explanations for this information or your children may have their own ideas. Interestingly, many children will not be puzzled by the conflict at this age. They simply accept all knowledge as presented.

Your older children are the ones who might choose to ask. Use this as an opportunity to discuss the correct attitude toward conflicts between religion and science. Most children believe whatever they hear first, and your explanation is likely to be the one they adopt for themselves.

Presenting this information to them now will allow you to get to their hearts before they encounter the information in a college classroom when you are not available to offer input. When we discussed creation and evolution, I simply told my children, "Some people believe this and others believe that. Here is what I believe, and this is why I believe it." They already understood that many people believe differently than they do in areas of religion, morality, and education. This was not a problem for them.

The second year you can introduce ancient history to your children, or it can be the second semester of your first year. Many children find this time period quite interesting. My younger children studied mythology that year as our literature program, and both children still enjoy this study. We learned about ancient Egypt, Israel, Greece, and Rome. When we studied Israel, we switched from mythology to the Old Testament.

Research the inventions each civilization created. It's important for children to know the world has not always been the way it is now. Older children may be surprised at the sophisticated civilizations that existed in this time period. If you study Israel, consider contacting a synagogue and asking permission to visit. We planned our Israel unit to coincide with Hanukkah and carried out some celebrations of the holiday.

The next year is the very best of all. This is the year we studied the Middle Ages. Can you think of a better unit for second or third graders than to learn about castles, knights, and dragons? There are wonderful materials for young children to help you with this unit study. I had intended to teach this unit half a year, but we were having so much fun we continued it through the entire year. Build a castle, find out what the people ate (some of it sounds rather disgusting in our time, but children love disgusting) and how they ate. Learn what the lives of children were like at each level of society. Follow the path to knighthood. Learn about some real princesses. Attend a medieval reenactment. Read fairy tales and modern adaptations for literature. This is a unit that can be nearly all play.

You may have noticed that we are not discussing traditional history for our little children. Little time is spent on battles or even famous leaders, although I did introduce the lives of the great people of each time. The history you are teaching your little ones is called social history. Social history examines the way people lived. This brings the time period to life and makes it accessible to little children. Later, when you return to each time, your children will have a feel for the culture and this will make it easier to understand the more serious history. Your children will also think of history as fun and exciting, and when the history gets less playful, they will be interested enough to stay with it.

Teaching older children

As your children get older, you will naturally choose harder books for them. If you are choosing trade books instead of textbooks, the books will begin to evaluate the people, the events, and the issues in more depth as the reading level increases. The earliest history lessons are playful. Over time, the children will play less and spend more time reading, writing, and discussing the history.

When the children are in high school, give them books written by real historians. This will prepare them for college history. You might also want to select textbooks from a college bookstore, since college textbooks are more accurate. When your children are in middle school, you can read the college textbooks yourself and paraphrase them. Every day, give them a few sections from this book to read themselves and give them selections and quotes from historians. Their reading level will increase and they will be prepared to handle college level reading earlier if they read well already.

By the fourth grade, children should learn to analyze history. Develop the habit of asking why. "Why do you think the colonists decided to turn against their own country to form a new one?" "Why do you think the pioneers went west?" "Why didn't the men want the women to vote? Why did some women think they shouldn't be allowed to vote?" You don't have to know the answers to your own questions. The family search for the answers can provide a memorable experience for all of you. Encourage your children to ask their own questions. If they read something that doesn't seem right, encourage them to research. History is not all settled and done. Every day we re-evaluate and reinterpret. New discoveries are made. If your children don't like the explanations they receive, send them to look for another possibility. Ask them to write papers evaluating the issue they're studying and the validity of their sources so they can reach their own conclusions.

Your children should learn which historians are considered valid. When they receive a new book, they should always read the author's biography and look for biases. An author who is related to Thomas Jefferson may have access to material not widely available, but he may also want to show his ancestor as a perfect person rather than a balanced one. Someone who left a religion may slant his book to show the religion's history in a bad light. Ask your teenager to decide if this author has any reason to tell anything but the truth. What are the author's credentials? What sources did the author consult? What topics does he usually write on? Encourage your teenager to decide which historians he most enjoys and to build a collection of books by these authors.

Whenever possible, send teenagers to the original documents. It's much more important for them to read the Declaration of Independence than to read a book about it, although both may be helpful. If they're confused about the sort of person Christopher Columbus was, let them read the explorer's own journals. Encourage your teenagers to think for themselves rather than to believe all authors without question.

History is filled with real people

The key to outstanding homeschool history is to bring the past to life. That's why I referred to a time machine in the title. The past seems imaginary to children and teens, but it's filled with very real people. Every person who participated in the American Civil War was a real person who had family, friends, beliefs, motives, and fears. Even though a war was going on, children still played games and went to school. People married, moved, celebrated, and grieved. Help your children find out who some of those people were and to think about them. Encourage your children to write stories, draw pictures, put on plays, and imagine what the people in their books were like. Your book might say that some of the people in the town you are reading about hid slaves. Which people? Can you find the names of some of them? Can you imagine what type of person might hide a slave, and what he thought about before he fell asleep on the days someone hid in his home? If you can, and if your children can, you can make history real, exciting, and challenging.

One way to make history more personal is to do genealogy with your children. Start researching now and as soon as some of your ancestors turn up during important historical moments, write them into your lesson. Stories of the Civil War are more real and more meaningful when your own relatives were there. In my family, a woman whose kin fought for the north married a man who fought for the south. Which side did she take? How did she feel about this problem? How did it affect her relationships with various people? I don't know, but I wonder about these things when I read about the war. Ask your children to think about these relatives and to understand how their lives and choices affected your own.

Imagine a relative in Ireland during the famine. Will she stay and wait it out, or will she come to the United States? If she stays, she is likely to die. Many did. How would that have changed your life? If she stayed and lived, you might be in Ireland instead of in Kentucky. Even if you don't know much about the relative, you can research the time and place in which she lived and make some guesses about her life. History is never quite the same after you really understand how much it affected your life.

Play "what if" games as you study the history of your country or state. What if the British had won the Revolutionary War? Would your life be different today? What if there had never been a California gold rush? What if Abraham Lincoln had not been killed? This is called alternative history, and your children might like to write papers imagining what life would be like today if something had changed historically.

History is so much more than statistics. History is people and stories and imagination and analysis. Bring all of that into your lessons and try living some aspects of the lives of the people you study. If your children are little, let them build a time machine out of a refrigerator box and climb in each day before starting your history lesson. When they "arrive," they can don simple costumes, try the food, play the games, and investigate their new world. History is fun, and it's your duty and your privilege to show your children the wonders of their past.

More Resources
➤ *Teachers*

"Jean Fritz"

Scholastic.com/teachers/contributor/jean-fritz

Jean Fritz is my favorite children's author for the teaching of American history. Her picture books are historically accurate, well researched, and are fascinating enough to interest both your little children and your older ones. This site lists author resources and lesson plans based on some of her books. Ms. Fritz lived in China as the child of missionaries until the revolution, and her life story is as interesting as those lives she writes about.

➤ *MrDonn.org*

Mr. Donn is a teacher and his site is probably the most extensive for children and teachers on social studies. Choose a time period or location and quickly locate lesson plans, activities, and exciting Web pages. The site also has history clip art, timelines, and other tools to help you teach.

➤ *A History of US* (Ten Volume Set) by Joy Hakim
ISBN: 0195152603

This is a very kid-friendly series on American history that is considered by most to be politically correct. It teaches a well-rounded variation of histories, including social history, current events, geography, and even trivia and jokes. Books can also be purchased separately. Many parents supplement this to get other points of view.

➤ *Magic Tree House* by Mary Pope Osborne
ISBN: 9780375844058, et. al.

This series of books has made history and science fashionable. Two children, a boy and a girl, travel through time and space in a magic tree house, fulfilling quests. Many of the books are accompanied by research guides written at the same grade levels. They are ideal homeschooling tools. These can be given to children reading at a second grade level to read alone or they can be read as a family, and they are so well-written everyone in the family will enjoy them, even if the individuals are too old or too young for the books. Be sure to check out the companion website.

➤ *The American Primary Sources Challenge*
AmericanPrimarySource.blogspot.com
Help your older children learn history as it was written during the events of the time. Primary sources mean original documents, not someone else's retelling. This site has historical letters and other documents to help you see history through the eyes of the participants.

➤ *The Well-Trained Mind*
WellTrainedMind.com/the-story-of-the-world-history-for-the-classical-child
Susan Wise Bauer has created a history program based on the classical method of education that teaches history chronologically. This is a popular series for homeschoolers.

Chapter 19

Science: You Mean I Have to Touch That?

WHEN IT'S TAUGHT WELL, most children love science. They're interested in the world and curious about everything. They want to take things apart, touch, taste, smell, and mix. Science comes naturally to children. It does not, however, always come naturally to parents. The idea of handling a frog, mixing a nasty-smelling chemical, or looking at insects under a microscope just doesn't appeal to some of us.

However, we love our children and will do anything—well, almost anything—to educate them well. We are going to find ourselves doing some disgusting things. Later in the chapter, however, we'll learn how to avoid the very worst parts of teaching science.

But first, let's talk about the *teaching* of science. Regardless of your feelings about frogs, you may need to rethink science. Forget the weeks of memorizing the periodic table of elements, although you may do some of that. Think of it not as a school subject, but as a quest to satisfy curiosity. There is an amazing world out there, and children want to know how it works. As you help them find out, you may realize this is more exciting than you imagined.

The good part of science is that there is more flexibility in this subject, at least in elementary school, than there is in most other subjects. We move around a lot, and we've learned every state teaches it differently. Your children do need to learn about plants, space, molecules, and other basic things. You should teach them the scientific process. At the younger grades, everything else is a matter of preference.

The scientific process

The scientific process tells children how to set up their own science experiments. You will want to do many experiments, and sometimes your children will want to answer their questions by creating their own experiments, so they will need to understand this process.

First, they need to decide what they want to find out. They should ask a question: What do flies eat? Can daisies grow without sunlight? Does hot water freeze faster than cold water?

Next, they need to form their hypothesis. A hypothesis is an educated guess. This means they have to decide what they think the answer to the question is, but they should do some research first rather than make wild guesses. They should put their hypothesis in writing. Remind them that if their hypothesis turns out to be wrong, they have not failed the experiment. The purpose of an experiment should be to find the truth, not to prove something right or wrong. A wrong hypothesis is just as valuable as a correct one. Don't let insecure children become intimidated by the need to guess.

Third, they should think of a way to prove their hypothesis right or wrong. This means creating an experiment. If a child wants to know if daisies can grow in the dark, she needs to prove whatever theory she chooses. This will involve growing two sets of daisies, one in the dark and one in the light. The daisy grown in the sun is the control—the daisy that grows the usual way. That daisy helps to prove the results of growing a daisy in the dark. However, she must be very careful to make sure everything about the daisies is exactly the same except for the amount of light they receive. She needs to put them in identical pots and give them exactly the same amount of water and food. If anything other than the amount of light is different, she will not be able to tell if it was the light or some other change that caused the results.

The fourth step is to carry out the experiment. She should keep a journal every day, detailing exactly what she does and what she observes. In this case, she may want to take photos of the daisies each day.

Finally, she must evaluate the experiment. What happened to each daisy? Was the hypothesis correct or incorrect? After doing the experiment, she may realize she made a mistake and will need to start over. If her hypothesis is wrong, she may want to test again or she may accept what she has learned. She may also realize the question cannot really be answered, at least not by the methods she is able to use. Whatever the results, she is learning new ways to evaluate her world.

Elementary school science
Our school district was on a year-round schedule, and I adopted that for our homeschool. We had school for three months and took one month off. This made science easy to plan. We had three sessions, so we taught three units. Each of the two younger children chose one and I chose one. I chose the order, because I looked for topics that matched our history lessons. The first year we studied dinosaurs, which fit into our study of prehistory and the beginnings of the world. We also studied space, the human body, and rocks. The rocks also fit into our prehistory unit, since we were covering the Stone Age. (Well, that was a stretch, but they were little and you didn't have to try hard to convince them of a good match.)

Perhaps the best way to demonstrate the possibilities for

elementary science is to show you what we did, and what I would do today. (I was teaching before the Internet.) We'll begin by looking at the subject of the human body. Children are naturally curious about their bodies and they find it interesting to see how they look inside.

We made giant paper dolls of each of my two children by tracing their bodies on butcher paper. We then made models of the essential organs and, as we learned about them, we glued them onto the body in the proper location. We also made giant paper doll clothes so the dolls would be modestly dressed during the day. These giant dolls hung in the hallway when not in use, and doubled as toys for my daughter. This was more memorable than looking at charts.

When we learned about bones (at Halloween, naturally), I bought a skeleton poster and we sang the old spiritual, "Dem Bones," but used the real names of the bones as I pointed to them on the chart. After a month of this, I was thoroughly sick of the song, but the children were not. Every time they got hurt, I was told exactly which bone they had injured. They considered it a great thrill when one of them wound up with a broken bone and the doctor showed them a real x-ray. This was not part of my planned curriculum (even I won't go that far to educate my children), but homeschoolers take advantage of every odd educational opportunity. We also did more traditional activities such as watching educational cartoons about the body, reading books, and doing worksheets. As often as possible, however, I involved hands-on learning.

Space was an easier subject for me since my oldest child went through an astronaut phase. We had some educational materials I had obtained from NASA. I purchased cutouts of the planets and we chanted their names daily. My daughter could still do when she graduated. The cutouts were placed in order at the correct, but scaled down, distance apart. We learned just the highlights of each planet and, as I pointed to a planet, the children gave me its name and the essential facts. I really wasn't worried about creating astronomers, but I did want them reasonably familiar with their universe.

We watched videos and read books, the traditional activities, but we also wrote fantasy stories about space travel and life on other planets. We studied the stars through a telescope. We found out about astronauts as part of the required career education, and stayed up late to identify star constellations. The children's bedrooms were decorated with glow-in-the-dark stars they could arrange in constellations. We made models of the constellations and ate *astronaut* ice cream. We visited a planetarium. We acted out the rotation of the earth, the moon, and the sun, each of us pretending to be one of these orbs as we moved around, spinning, and pretending to collapse from dizziness.

Today, the Internet opens up new avenues for exploration. Many of the astronomy organizations and magazines have websites with dazzling pictures and special features for children. Computer games let children soar through space as if they were really there. We now realize that children can absorb far more information than previously imagined and as a consequence, materials have become more sophisticated.

As you teach your children, notice what excites them and focus on those aspects of the subject. Try to stop just before your child becomes bored, a skill that takes practice. Your primary purpose is to help your children become excited about their world, so just have fun.

The science some parents hate

Now for the *icky* stuff. For instance, one subject that soon becomes an issue is dissection. Many parents are opposed to dissection by those who are not going to be doctors or scientists. Others aren't opposed to it, but they don't want to do it. Today, Internet sites and computer programs allow children to dissect virtually. They can still see what is inside, but they don't have to kill an animal to do it.

If you have older children, they may be willing to conduct the parts of science you don't want to deal with. Older children frequently enjoy doing things their parents consider disgusting. You might even be able to convince a teenager to do it for you, although you may have to pay her. Finally, you can try to avoid any subjects that involve whatever you object to—but limit that to those activities you *really* can't tolerate. It probably won't be as painful as you think to look at a dead fly under a microscope, especially if someone else puts it there. You can buy premade slides to help with this problem, but most children are thrilled to do this for you.

Science for older students

Older children will have to spend more time on traditional activities. To keep science alive, introduce them to science that hasn't been resolved yet. Encourage them to research these issues and come to their own conclusions. This keeps their brains functioning and makes science controversial and challenging. Purchase good science magazines instead of, or in addition to, textbooks so they can read more interesting and up-to-date material.

Science textbooks at the high school level and below suffer the same problem as history textbooks: they are filled with inaccuracies. Use college textbooks or trade books and, if you must use an elementary school text, either look for reviews of the book or learn enough to identify inaccuracies yourself. Have your children supplement with real world materials and assign them to keep a chart of the mistakes they find in their textbooks. Then invite them write a letter to the publisher pointing out the mistakes. This will teach letter writing and a tame form of activism.

Give your children biographies of scientists. Your entire

science course can be taught by studying the science of scientists who worked in whatever time period you are studying in history. When we learned about Benjamin Franklin, we also studied electricity. Studying the subject in the context of a person made it more interesting. Find out what was believed before he made his discoveries and how he changed science. Then find out what research is being done today on the same subject.

Older students do have to memorize some of the dull things. Tell them it's better to learn it now, when they have the time, than to struggle with it in college when they are so much busier. Post the periodic table of elements in the restroom and over the sink. Break the task into small portions. The more experience a student has with a topic the easier it is to memorize the details.

If you're not already excited by science, you may be surprised in a few years to find yourself picking up your child's science magazines and reading them. Science is unexpectedly contagious when it's taught well.

More Resources

➤ *SpaceKids.hq.nasa.gov*
NASA has a site for children with a regularly changing assortment of news, information, and activities. Keep up with current events in space, enter contests, learn about astronomy, or just enjoy the out-of-this-world scenery.

➤ *Bill Nye the Science Guy's Consider the Following: A Way Cool Set of Science Questions, Answers, and Ideas to Ponder* by Bill Nye, Ian Saunders
ISBN: 0786814438
This book is for children in the fourth to eighth grades. Nye answers questions in the same way he does on the show, in a breezy, friendly manner. He explains terms and concepts and

offers experiments. My children loved Nye's books, videos and television program when they were young, telling people he was their science teacher.

Chapter 20

Writing Things Down: Stories, Reports, and Compositions

THE WRITTEN LANGUAGE IS essential to an effective home-school and to most careers and adult lives. Those who write well are seen as more intelligent and better educated than are those who have poor grammar and writing skills. This may not be fair, but it's the way the world operates. Spend a great deal of time developing your child's writing skills.

First, teach yourself

Many parents who decide to homeschool are very nervous about their own writing and language skills. Language arts is one of the few subjects you really do need to be able to do before you begin teaching your children. You can learn math problems with your child, but your child needs someone to read her papers and tell her how to improve them. If you aren't a writer, don't panic. Instead, use what you have discovered about teaching and learning and create a training program for yourself.

Older English textbooks are generally superior to newer ones, because students were once expected to learn English very well. Modern adult grammar books, like the ones recommended in the additional resources, will help you learn current trends. Go to a thrift store and buy a stack of used English books at various grade levels. Begin working through them on your own, before you need to teach your children if possible. Then write articles, poems, stories, or whatever else you'd like to write. The more you write and edit yourself, the better your writing will become.

I freelanced for many years as a writer. When my family needs became more demanding, I decided to take a break, continuing only the two columns I wrote for Internet publications. One day, I was reading through my earliest columns and was surprised by how bad they were. They had been my best effort when I wrote them, but several years of writing two thousand edited words each week had improved my skills. Writers are told they won't get published until they've written their first one million words. If you aren't striving for publication you may be able to get by on fewer words, but you still need to write a lot of words.

If you are uncomfortable with writing, purchase an inexpensive journal and begin writing in it each day. Don't worry about grammar or style in this book. Don't write a list of what you did all day, either. Write about the aspects of your world that matter to you. Explore how you feel about your family or town. Discuss a current political issues. Describe your fears and successes as a homeschooler. Explain what your neighborhood looks like or how you feel when you accomplish something frightening. Your purpose is to become comfortable putting your thoughts and ideas on paper.

As this becomes less stressful, try writing formal papers. Learn to type and to use a word processing program. These come with grammar checkers and will help you learn about your writing. The grammar check is only a machine, however. It doesn't really speak English and you must still learn enough to decide if it's correct. For example, I could write, "I have a stake in this," which means that I am affected by the issue, and my grammar check accepts the sentence. However, I could be talking about something holding up my tomatoes. The computer doesn't know. It also accepts the other spelling of stake for this particular sentence, because "I have a steak in this," could refer to having meat in my ice chest. Only you can tell which sentence is accurate.

Many English books offer suggestions for papers, and you should try to write one or two every week. You can use the suggestions given or think of your own. Choose topics in which you explain how to do something, why you believe something, or what something is all about. You can also write inspirational articles. Read your favorite magazines and examine the articles you find in them. Select an article on a topic you know something about and write your own article on the same subject. You won't be writing what the author wrote because this article will contain what *you* think people should know about the topic.

When you are comfortable with writing, ask someone who writes well to read your work and make suggestions. Explain that you aren't trying to publish, but want to improve your writing so you can help your children learn to write well. This will tell your friend how to grade the paper. Be very careful when you select the person who will help you. If you choose someone who is harsh and critical, you will become more afraid to write. You want someone who can show you a few types of mistakes at a time and help you fix them, but who will also applaud your efforts and show you what you've done well. Friends who really know writing are great choices. They have your best interests at heart and want to help. They also know just how much criticism you can handle and how to offer it to you. Of course, this person must also be comfortable telling you changes are needed.

Journaling with little children
Your children can and should become *writers* before they

learn to put words on paper. From the time they can speak in sentences, or as soon as you read this, help them keep journals of their own. Let them tell you what to write. When they are finished, they can illustrate the entry. Encourage them to write about their day, their toys, their family, their friends, and anything else that interests them. When you introduce the journal, tell them it's a special book. Let them look through it. If they tell you there are no words, tell them the lack of words is what makes the book special. *They* are going to decide what words go into the book. Each day or week, they will tell you what they want to write about and you will put the words they say into the book. Share with them how much fun they will have someday reading what they were like as little children, and tell them that when they grow up, their own children might want to read the book, too. If you are keeping a journal, you might share an entry with them so they understand how much fun it is to hear the entries read.

If your children are not used to dictating stories, you may have to help them at first. Here is a sample conversation you might hold with a young child who is just starting to dictate:

Mom: "What would you like to write about in your journal today?"

Jason: "I don't know."

Mom: "Well, you went to Grandma's house this week, and you played with your blocks. Would you like to write about one of those things?"

Jason: "Okay."

Mom: "Which one did you want to write about? Going to Grandma's?" (Your child will usually choose the first one you offer, so start with the one you like best.)

Jason: "Grandma and me planted flowers."

Mom: "You want to write about how you planted flow-

ers? We'll write that down. 'Grandma and me planted flowers.' What kinds of flowers did you plant?"

Jason: "Purple ones and red ones and blue ones."

Mom: "Can you give me a sentence about that?"

Jason: (Silence, because he doesn't know what that means.)

Mom: "'We planted purple ones and red ones and blue
ones.' Is that what you want me to write?"

Jason: "Yeah, purple. And we made cookies."

Mom: "After you planted flowers you made cookies? Let's
make a sentence. What should I write?"

You will guide your child through his first journal entries,
but over time, he will become more and more independent
about it. Don't worry about correcting grammar or spelling in the journal. It's likely some of his entries will be a
bit imaginative, or even a lot imaginative. There is really
nothing wrong with that, although you can make a comment about how much fun it is to pretend, if you'd like. Real
or imaginary, though, he's learning to communicate his
thoughts in writing.

Nonfiction

Once a child is writing reasonably well, perhaps by second
grade, he can begin to write his own reports and composi-
tions. You won't be getting publishable material, but you will
be teaching your child to improve his writing skills, do research, organize information, and communicate ideas. Those
are substantial benefits from one assignment.

When I've volunteered in elementary school classrooms,
I've noticed that most children simply copy the information
they need from an encyclopedia, draw a picture, and call it a
report. (Today, they copy Wikipedia.) I've even had teachers
tell me that was acceptable in the lower grades. It isn't. You
will never be able to convince a child this is plagiarism—and

therefore dishonest—if you allow it in the earliest stages. *Plagiarism is stealing the words of others and pretending they are your own.*

Because children don't understand how to use the research of others, you must guide them through their first reports. Begin by helping them choose their topics. This is actually very difficult. Most children will say, "I want to do a report on China." That's a good idea, but China is too big a subject for a book, much less a child's report. Children need to learn to narrow the topic to something manageable. A report on Chinese elementary schools might be small enough for a child. A report on why panda bears are endangered is also small enough. To help your child narrow his focus, instruct him to create a specific question he would like to answer. From these questions, a topic should emerge. Following are some questions a second grader might be able to answer in a report:

- How did pioneer children live while crossing the Plains?

- How did a young man become a knight during the Middle Ages?

- What is it like on Mars?

- Who invented telephones?

- What does the president do all day?

- Why can birds fly when I can't?

- How did Beverly Cleary become a writer?

- How do you take care of puppies?

- How did we get the flag we have today?

- What happens to the garbage after we put it on the curb?

For the first report, choose a topic you and your child are both very interested in and already have some materials on. Then go to the library to get a few more sources. Plan to use five books for the initial report, which can be picture books at this age. As your child becomes more skilled, select harder books and use more of them.

First graders and second graders who are writing their first reports can use a very simple format and create a report of only one hundred to three hundred words. The question to be answered must be very basic for a tiny report and the method used to create it can be simple. With a very young child, you can read the books to him several times and let him tell you the information back as you write it down. Then the two of you can check in the books to be sure you are right. Later, he can make a list of facts he remembers or facts he finds in books, and you can teach him how to organize them. Put each fact on a card and spread the cards out on the floor. Pick up two cards and ask him which one should go first. Set the two cards in order. Add a third card and let him decide where it goes. Each time, read the report as it currently stands. He may begin selecting cards he wants in a certain spot. Continue until all the cards have been placed and then read the "report" to see if it makes sense. Type the report and print it for your child.

If your child finds this difficult, you may want to stay at this stage for some time. Create your own body of ten or more facts and let him organize them in a way that makes sense. You can store various facts on file cards bundled by topic and let him play with them. When he is doing that comfortably, return to learning to write reports.

When the child is writing more than a few paragraphs, you will need to teach him to make an outline. Each major point to be discussed should be in the outline. For example, a report on education during a period of history might have these topics: age school starts, education of boys, education of girls, education of poor children, or education of wealthy children. Place these topics on larger index cards than you use for the facts, or on cards of a different color. First, have the child organize these cards; then let him sort out his fact cards, placing each under the correct topic. If he has cards that don't fit under any topic heading, he should either create a new heading or decide not to use the card. Learning to make this choice will improve his reports. Finally, have him organize the facts under each heading. He now has a detailed outline of his report which he should type and keep in his notebook.

He can't simply type up the list of headings and facts, however, and call it a report. The facts need to be put into his own words, and they need to have connecting sentences. His report should sound more like the books he has been reading than like a list of facts. This will take some discussion and a great deal of practice. If an older child struggles with this, have him write out the individual facts from a few pages of one of his books and then see what the author added to create a more readable manuscript. Monitor his work to be sure he is using his own words. Be sure he knows the meaning of the word *plagiarism*. You may need to practice turning a paragraph into original material, but finding information in a number of sources is a good way to avoid copying.

Computers are the perfect tools for creating reports. It's very easy to move material around and to make corrections. The child will be more inclined to edit his work if he does not have to copy it over and over. He can even write a sentence three ways, placing them in red to remind him to choose, and then decide later which one to keep. Word processing is an essential skill your child will be expected to master as a college student or as an employee, and it's easier for a young child to learn this than for an adult.

Crediting information is a tricky skill, but even little children should learn to write a bibliography (a list of sources) and, since computers make it so easy, to use footnotes or endnotes. Any time he uses ideas that are not his own, or words that are not his own, he must give the author credit. The only exception is common knowledge. For instance, a child in the United States would not be expected to explain where he learned that George Washington was the first president, because nearly everyone knows that.

To teach children to evaluate and credit sources, plan an activity with all your children who are young enough to need the lesson. When we did our first report, done as a family, we chose dinosaurs as a project. This would not normally be a good topic for a report, but I was more interested in teaching source evaluation and we had ten picture books on the subject. We assigned each book a number, taping the number onto the book and displaying the books as we worked. On a large chalkboard, we wrote the number of each book across the top. We wrote the facts down the left side. We gathered the facts by reading the first book together and writing each fact on the board as we found it. We then put a checkmark under the number of the book, along with the page number, to show where we found it. When we read the second book, we found it contained a number of facts already on the board. We placed a checkmark in the column for that book, again with the page number. If two facts contradicted each other, we drew a sad face in the square instead of a check mark by the opposing fact from the other book. In other words, if book one said dinosaurs were blue and book two said they were yellow, we would put sad faces in the columns for these books with a page number to show where the books disagreed. Soon we noticed a pattern. One of the books had a large number of conflicting facts. We checked some adult sources, decided this book was inaccurate, and threw it away. As a consequence, the children learned not to trust everything they read without finding other sources to back up the information. When they grew older they learned better ways to evaluate sources, but this was a start.

They used this list to make a bibliography. The standard formats for bibliographies are found in most English books, and children should learn to do them correctly from the start. They should learn to apply footnotes whenever they have a fact that is not commonly known.

Over time, require your children to write more formally and to write longer papers. By the time they finish high school, they should be able to produce a term paper that is five to ten pages long, typed, double-spaced, and properly documented. This paper should sound reasonably scholarly and be on a serious topic. With these skills under control, your children will easily cope with college work.

Fiction

Even if your child never intends to become a professional writer, he needs to experiment with fictional writing. This builds imagination, but it also helps students understand the fiction they read.

Little children can be turned loose to write whatever appeals to them. If their first stories sound suspiciously like the television programs and books they enjoy, gradually guide them to create their own characters and plots.

Children might first be taught to think of ideas for their stories. Let them decorate a box and use it to store ideas and story starters. They can use a small index card box and place each idea on a card, or they can put them on strips of paper and draw a random idea from the box when they need one. Story starters can be purchased commercially at school supply stores and lists of story ideas can be found online on many websites for English teachers, but it's better if your children create their own. Asking "what if" allows children to use their imaginations to create situations they haven't seen on television. What if a turtle was elected president? What if the house next door was haunted? What if a girl found a journal—and discovered it was written by her two months from now? What if a boy moved to a new town and was the only child who lived there? What if a group of girls formed a club and decided no one could join until they'd made fun of a new girl who was disabled?

Your family will want to spend a few weeks making up ideas for their story-starter boxes. Children may want to have a family story-starter box as well as one of their own for their favorite ideas. They should only use the story-starter boxes when they can't think of anything to write about on their own.

Once a child has an idea, she has to put people into the story. Let's examine the story idea about the girls who start a club. The first challenge your child has is to figure out who is in this story. She needs the girls who decide to have the club and the girl who gets teased. The story can be told from the point of view of one of the club girls, or it can be told from the point of view of the disabled child. Let's suppose she decides she wants to use one of the club girls to be the main character. Which one?

Every story needs conflict. Too many children write stories that are a list of events. "Three girls decided to have a club. They decided you had to pick on Angela if you wanted to be in the club. It was Cassie's idea to do that, and the other girls liked it. They thought Angela was stupid because she had trouble walking. They picked on Angela and they all got to be in the club. The end."

What's wrong with this story? It has no plot. No one had a problem to solve. Angela did, of course, but it wasn't her story and the author didn't say how Angela felt or what she did about the bullying. A better idea would be to have one

of the girls feel uncomfortable about the bullying requirement. Let's name her Hannah. So now all the girls have
names and personalities except one. Cassie is the leader and
the one who thinks up the bullying. She probably started
the club. Let's make the remaining girl a follower, someone
who always does whatever Cassie says. Her name can be
Robin. The story now has four people: a leader, a follower,
a doubter, and a victim. The people are different enough to
make a good story.

Your child needs to know more about these people. Make
questionnaires about people and let her fill them out. She
should decide what they look like, how they talk, how old
they are, what grade they are in, how good they are in school,
and any other information that will tell her about them. She
should describe their personalities, and their personalities
should be useful to the story.

Now that there are people in her story, she can think
about what could happen to them. If the main character
is Hannah, then Hannah needs to have a problem, and she
needs to solve it herself using her own brainpower. The problem and its resolution are the plot. It's usually a good idea to
make the solution hard and to have the main character make
a mistake or two along the way to add excitement.

My website offers a very simple story plotter for children. After they have a little experience it will be too basic
for them, but it's a good starting point:

TerrieBittner.com/language_arts/storyplotter.html

Your child may not grasp all these concepts right at first,
but they are goals to work toward.

There are other ways to create a story. Your child could
start with the plot and decide on the people later, or she
could begin with an interesting person and decide what sort

of problem that person might have. If she spends enough time writing, your child will soon learn what works best for her. Have her study her favorite books and magazines to see how the authors carry out the stories they write. She should learn from good authors.

When your children are preteens and teens, give them writing magazines and books meant for professional authors. Most textbooks cover the basics, but materials for professionals will offer in-depth information on plotting, outlining structure, and other writing skills. If they show an interest in writing for publication, search for magazines that accept student writing. Having their work read by others is a powerful motivator for students to learn to write well.

Teach your children to write well, but also teach them to love writing so they will choose to do it often. While reading is the most important skill children must master to be successful in college and in adult life, writing is nearly as important to their future.

More Resources
➤ *BBC Education: Learning Schools*
BBC.co.uk/schools
This site changes often, but it always has various activities for children to help them learn to be better writers.

➤ *EDSITEment*
EDSITEment.neh.gov/subject/literature-language-arts
The National Endowment for the Humanities has a page of lesson plans for English and a few for history. Most of the plans are literary analysis—good for older students—but there are also lessons on *Alice in Wonderland* and other children's books. These will improve your child's ability to write about literature. He should be able to write on the concepts discussed in these lessons.

➤ *English for the Thoughtful Child* by Mary Hyde
ISBN: 1882514076
This English book isn't for every family. It was first
published in 1903, and uses an unusual "natural learning"
approach centered on narration (made popular by Charlotte
Mason for homeschoolers), creative writing, and literature. It
requires one-on-one time with a parent, and the topics to be
written on often require scientific research. Its gentle, varied
approach, however, makes it fun for many children and for
parents who want a team effort approach to English.

➤ *Word Smart Junior: Build a Straight "A" Vocabulary, 2nd
Edition* by C. L. Brantley
➤ *Word Smart Junior II: More Straight "A" Vocabulary, 2nd
Edition* by C. L. Brantley
➤ *Writing Smart Junior: The Art and Craft of Writing, 2nd
Edition* by C. L. Brantley
ISBNs: 0375762574, 0375762582, and 0375762612
I found these books a bit brash for my tastes, but my children loved them and eagerly dug into them each day. They
were learning and having fun, so I continued to purchase
them. The lessons are taught through a continuing storyline
that is entirely improbable to anyone but the nine- to twelve-
year-olds the books are written for. However, they are quite
memorable, and the stories never become so distracting that
the lesson is lost. Princeton Review offers these books for a
variety of subjects.

➤ *ScribblersRetreat.com*
My writer's website has a small section for children who
write. Teens can use the adult sections as well.

Chapter 21

Values, Religion, Electives, and other Treasures

WHEW! YOU'VE WORKED OUT math, science, reading, and writing. Those are the hard subjects, and they weren't so bad, were they? Now we can finally start planning the fun stuff: the electives, religion or values, and anything you want to teach that isn't on the official list your state requires you to teach.

Electives

Depending on your mood, your time, and your energy you can either plan formal electives or just let life happen and record it in your records later. There are so many wonderful subjects to study, and too many of them don't really fit into all the required subjects. There are some things we do just for joy, and that's why schools invented electives. We don't want to avoid those parts of traditional schooling, even though we may not do them the traditional way.

You might want to have two electives, just as most schools do. Let each of your children choose one for themselves— something they love and want to spend extra time doing. You can pick the other one because it lets you sneak in something you want your children to do that they might never choose for themselves. After all, it's your school! You should get to have some fun too.

Electives can be anything at all. If you and your children pick something odd, just give it a respectable name and list it as an elective. Whether you study puppetry, genealogy, cooking, or novels featuring cats, you are learning one of the most important lessons of homeschooling: Learning is fun.

If you want a formal elective, consider letting your children help plan the electives they chose. This will give them training in course planning which they will need later as they become more independent. Ask them what they want to learn and then suggest they make a list of things to do and ways to learn. Go over the list with them and help them see which ideas are actually practical. If you feel their plan is too flaky, reserve the right to add to it. Then put everything in order and create a loose schedule. Congratulate them on planning a wonderful class. As they carry out their plan, help them make adaptations as needed.

When planning your own elective, try to tie it into other subjects whenever possible. Genealogy can be tied to your history class, and cooking can be tied to a nutrition course. Although you will probably use art in most of your classes, you might want to try a few art electives, such as pottery or a course in famous artists. You can teach one subject all semester or do mini-units that last as long as you're all interested. You can do them at a set time each day or you can just play it by ear, figuring out later how to list it on your time sheets. Sometimes a group of things can be lumped together so you can spend less time on them, but still look organized on paper. For instance, you might do creative writing, public speaking, cartooning, and art and call it all Communications.

Another good way to cover the electives is to use an organized youth program. If your church has a structured youth program, you might be able to use that if the activities are educational. Many homeschooling parents use Scouting or 4-H to teach some of their homeschooling subjects. If you dislike organized programs, try creating your own badges with your children and have a family club. If you invite a friend or two, you've created a new club without the costs and regulations of the established ones.

Religion and values

For some parents, a desire to tailor their child's education to their religion is a primary reason for homeschooling. Others homeschool for academic or social reasons or to strengthen their families, but still want to teach special principles. Because homeschooling is so entwined into the heart of family life, it's natural to include religion and values in your educational day just as you do in your everyday life, even if it isn't the focus of your school.

One of the criticisms frequently hurled at homeschoolers is that their children will only learn one point of view. As with every other accusation, this is a stereotype. There are so many homeschoolers and so many ways to homeschool that it's impossible to throw any single label onto them.

There is nothing wrong with teaching your children your beliefs, whether they are spiritual, political, moral, or social. In fact, it's impossible to spend time with a child and not share values. When my children were in public school, they learned a great deal about the values of their teachers—from their opinions on war to their attitudes about religion. Often they tried to adopt these values, only to change again the next year when they had a new teacher. Parents who homeschool can provide a much more stable value system to children who may not yet be mature enough to make an informed decision.

We don't have to have a religion class or a political science class to pass along our beliefs during school hours. Many homeschool families begin with a prayer and include scripture reading as part of their day. If they are homeschooling where this cannot be listed on the official forms, they simply give it a new name. Most scriptures are classic literature and can be listed as such. The Old Testament can also be a history of Israel and its people. History offers extensive opportunities to teach our children our values. As we teach the history of our country, we can share our thoughts on the events that occurred, encourage patriotism, point out the ways our country improved because someone dared to take an unpopular stand, or even show the evils of greed and dishonesty. We can point out those who struggled to free slaves and improve hospitals. We can tell the stories of people who took a stand and discuss how we feel about that stand.

We can choose stories and books in our literature courses that portray challenging choices and talk to our children about these choices, helping our students apply them to their own lives. We can ask children to write stories about people facing moral dilemmas. We will want to teach our children to read the language of our scriptures and to know about the history of their faith. It's largely through our conversations about the things we learn that we will pass along our values, but we can also take educational opportunities to put them into action.

Volunteer work

Some states now require a number of hours in *service learning* to graduate from public school. This means students must put in hours as a volunteer, usually as part of a social studies course. This is an outstanding way to teach values and to show children how to act on their values. Volunteerism has always been an essential part of most homeschools. As our children serve, they learn to reach outside themselves and notice the needs of others. They experiment with careers and become a valued part of their community. The community sees these children hard at work and looks at homeschooling in a more positive light.

Don't choose your volunteer work lightly. There may be programs you will serve in together, particularly when your children are young. Later, they may select their own. As you help your children select projects, consider those issues that matter to you and work in those fields. We have spent time working with disability organizations, volunteering in public schools, participating in a reader's theater program that taught literature to children, and working in community food banks. These projects helped my children to know that education, literacy, poverty assistance, and disability issues were values our family considered important. I wanted them to believe they must act on those issues that matter to them. A few hours in a food bank teaches them more about serving the poor than hours of preaching.

Learning other points of view

There will be times when your textbooks and trade books teach something you do not believe. You may find they speak negatively about your religion, praise or criticize a political leader you have strong opinions about, or take a different approach to science than you do. This is your opportunity to show your children how to cope with differing beliefs.

I noticed my children tended to believe whatever they learned first. If they read a book and then saw the movie, they considered the book to be the "real" version and the movie to be the medium that must live up to the book. I realized it was best to expose my children to opposing viewpoints at home, where I could control how they were presented and could explain our family's beliefs. Once I'd given them a firm foundation in my own beliefs, they were not troubled by the discovery that others think differently.

In the last chapter, I discussed how we realized that one of our dinosaur books was filled with false information. The children learned that books don't always tell the truth. This discovery was easily applied to all other subjects they studied over the years. When it was time to teach creation and evolution, I began by telling them all the choices and which one I believed. We read material on all sides, but I was the teacher and I showed them how to evaluate the arguments they were reading. We looked for holes in the arguments as well. When we finished, the children agreed with me and with what they had been taught all their lives. Had they received the information in a public school, they would not have been told there were options.

If they had not heard of evolution until college, they might have felt I was lying to them or hiding something. I saw this happen often when I was in college, and many students who had attended private religious schools lost their faith. If they had learned the arguments when they were still so young that they believed everything they were told, they would have been trained to withstand what they were learning in college. Sending your child to a religious college will not prevent this problem, because they are still, at some point in life, going to find out there are other viewpoints out there besides their own or their parent's. They need to learn at a young age that some people believe in creation, some believe in evolution, and some believe in a combination of the two.

When books present falsehoods about your religious or personal beliefs, help your children learn why this happens. What causes people to lie about a religion or to speak negatively of ideals you hold close to your heart? This is a good time to discuss the Bill of Rights and issues involving freedom of speech. It's a chance to tell children about agency, and the rights of others to choose what they want to believe. This same discussion can open communication on how your family prefers to handle those who oppose your beliefs, and how to show respect for the beliefs of others. Finally, teach them where you want them to seek their truths. Whether it's from scriptures, science, or logic, you need to guide them to the sources you trust. Help them understand that they can know something exists without choosing to be part of it.

One of the advantages of homeschooling is the opportunity to share the world in all its varieties and complexities with your children. This includes letting them know there are many ways to view all aspects of the world, and that even though some people believe differently than they do about certain things, they don't have to follow those paths. You are the primary role model for your children; you are the person they will look to for clues about how to live their lives. Your example will matter more than the words of any stranger.

Chapter 22

Opening Your School

YOU DID IT! YOU convinced everyone to let you homeschool, tracked down the applicable laws, and organized your supplies and your day. This was the worst part of the process because it was boring and did not actually involve teaching your children—which is the part you've been waiting for. You are finally ready to open your school, and most of it will be fun. In this chapter, you will learn how to set up kindergarten, how to remove a child from public school, and how to help your older child recover from the negative lessons he learned in public school.

Getting started with your kindergartner

If you are teaching a kindergartner, you get to skip the next intimidating part and just get to work planning. In many states, kindergarten is optional. If this first year is not mandatory, and you are not required to notify anyone that you are homeschooling, don't. Never report until you have to. If you are not "officially" homeschooling, you are not subject to rules of any kind and you can experiment or start slowly. If your child is not ready to read and write, you don't have to teach those things yet. If you only want to teach for an hour or two a day at first, you can.

This means you are free to run your school any way you

want the first year. If you have not done any homeschooling or structured learning before this year, and your child has not gone to preschool or a structured church class, you may want to move slowly into the schedule.

Make a list of all the educational things you already do. Some of these will become part of your school day. Now make a list of all the subjects taught in your neighborhood kindergarten. You can get this list from neighbors or you can visit the school and ask them for information on what is taught. You don't have to tell them you are planning to home-school. Just act like a parent who wants to know what her child will be learning this year, which is exactly what you are.

Another source of information is the education website for your state board of education. Once again, the Internet can lead you to this information. First, type the name of your state, followed by "department of education" or "board of education." If this doesn't lead you to facts about what children are supposed to learn in each grade, type the name of your state followed by the words "scope and sequence." You are searching for the state standards for each grade. These tell you what your state requires the schools to teach at each level. If your state requires you to teach a curriculum that is comparable to that of the public schools, use these guidelines to help you. If it does not require this, use it to give you ideas.

Find out if your local school teaches formal academics in kindergarten. It's important to have a general idea of whether or not your child is at the same level as other children their age, even if you intentionally choose a different pace. If, for any reason, you have to put your child back into school, you'll want to know if he's going to be ahead or behind. And if you have to report to someone, you'll know what they are expecting. Knowing where your child is in comparison to others helps you to make decisions.

This is all the information you need to get started. Whatever you want to do now is up to you. You can do fun readiness activities all day or you can mix those activities with academics. You can start with only one hour of formal school and work your way up to a full kindergarten day, or you can jump right in and do the entire day. You can teach whatever you want, however you want.

Since your child is probably not used to school, he has no preconceived ideas of what should happen. This is a real advantage since you will not be compared to his last teacher. If he did go to preschool, you may choose to mimic the preschool for awhile so you are both comfortable. Then gradually introduce your own style.

The best parts of kindergarten don't happen at a desk. Let your school be filled with fun and activity. Draw, use clay, paint, make giant drawings with sidewalk chalk, and create masterpieces from a box of junk. Put on some classical music and invite your child to dance or to draw what the music makes him feel. Make instruments out of whatever junk you have in the house. (Your definition of junk will change dramatically when you homeschool. So much that seemed like junk will soon look like treasures.) Play a video of an orchestra and pretend to conduct it. Write songs together and record them. In other words, have fun!

Science, to a young child, is discovery of the world. Spend long hours following an ant trail or spying on the birds that visit your homemade bird feeder. Peer deep into the nearest pond. Plant a garden. Buy an annual pass to the zoo and become personally acquainted with one animal. Read books and watch videos. Sit under the stars and talk about them. If your child likes worksheets, use them, but spend most of your science time exploring the world you live in. This is all the science a five-year-old needs. If he fills his heart with wonder now, he will be ready for the harder learning that comes later, because he will care about the world he is studying.

Math can be taught through games and hands-on experiences. Teach children to count their own toys and to match their own socks. If Timmy has three green blocks and two blue blocks, how many blocks does he have? Timmy doesn't know? Let him set out the blocks, ring the sets (groups) with yarn and count for himself. I looked at the workbooks created for children and then invented ways to bring the learning into the real world so it looked more like play than school. Eventually, Timmy will need worksheets, but unless he loves them (and some children do), don't bother with too many. Do just enough to get him used to them for the future. There will be too many dull years ahead of sitting at a desk. This is your child's time to play. Teach him the point of all this learning by letting him put his hands on the math he is doing.

Reading begins not in a pre-primer, but in a mother's arms. When a child sits in a parent's lap and listens to a story, he begins to associate reading with comfort and pleasure. Soon, most children long to read for themselves. Not all reach this stage in kindergarten, however. Some children worry they won't be read to if they learn to read, and some prefer other types of learning. Other children just aren't quite ready. Wherever he is in his development, however, your child is becoming a better reader every time the two of you share a book. Spend as many hours as you can enjoying books and stories in every possible way.

You can introduce letters and phonics in a playful way throughout your day. Point out letters you encounter in everyday life—on cereal boxes, on signs while you wait, in the books you read. Make a giant poster of one letter, lower-case and capital, and put it on the wall of your child's room. Talk about it often. Discuss what it is called, what sounds it makes, what it looks like. Trace it with your fingers. Glue pictures onto it of words that start with that letter. By the end of the year, your child may know all or most of the letters. Invite your child to make his body into the shape of the letters. Louisa May Alcott learned her alphabet this way from her father. Draw the letter on the driveway in chalk and let your child move along the letter, walking, skipping, tiptoeing, and dancing. Let him paint it with water outside. Your child may learn to write the letter as he learns to read it.

Because kindergarten should be a time of joy, you may not want to begin formal reading lessons until your child is ready, unless you must report to someone on his progress or unless you are trying to keep up with the public schools. As he learns his letters and discovers how the letters come together to make words, reading will happen. If he asks to learn to read, teach him gently and casually. We spent less than fifteen minutes a day on formal reading lessons, and only if the child felt like doing it that day. My children curled up in my arms and no one was allowed to interrupt. Together, we discussed the pictures and the words in an ancient pre-primer and learned to read. Then we sat on the floor and played games with the words and letters to teach formal skills. If the child wasn't interested, we stopped. Reading was supposed to be fun, something you did because you wanted to do it. When your child is in kindergarten, you sometimes have that luxury.

History, in kindergarten, is often no more than what is called Holiday History. Children learn about Pilgrims on Thanksgiving and Martin Luther King on his birthday. You can choose to take a relaxed approach to this subject enjoying books and toys, or you can create a formal history curriculum. If you plan to teach history chronologically, you can introduce prehistory this year and include the study of rocks and dinosaurs in your kindergarten. Let your children try to figure out how to do things without technology. Explore books that show how early people lived and how such wonders as written language came about. If you are religious,

271

this is an excellent time to explore the books of your religious faith. Travel the days of creation by learning about each step in a unit study—a week of animals, a week of day and night, and so on. This could even be your science for the entire year.

If your child does not already know shapes and colors, kindergarten is the time to do that. Pick a color and celebrate a full day of that color. On Blue Celebration Day, eat blue oatmeal or pancakes. (This is done with food coloring.) Fill the child's room with blue balloons, perhaps stuck to the walls while he is asleep. If you rub a balloon on your hair, it will stick to the walls. (Don't leave your child alone with the balloons—if they break and he puts one in his mouth, he could choke.) Learn about the sky and make sky crafts. Of course, you will wear blue clothing and use blue soap in the tub. Finger-paint with blue paint. Go for a walk and discover how many blue things are on your street. You get the idea. After a full day of noticing blue things, your child won't need a flashcard or worksheet to recognize blue in all its shades. The same technique can be used to teach shapes, although it may take a little more imagination.

Gym class is barely necessary for most children, but give your child ample opportunities to ride bikes, run, skip, jump, and twirl. Children love to move and if you play with your kindergartner and limit television and computer time, he will be happy to stay in perpetual motion all day long.

As the year progresses, you may want to gradually increase the amount of seatwork so your child is ready for a slightly less exciting first grade. However, most of his time should be spent exploring his world with his family and friends. Save the seatwork for next year.

Removing a child from public school
If your child is already in school, you have a little more work to do before you can begin his homeschool. You have to re-

move him from his current school, and you want to do it with as little controversy as possible. This makes life easier for you and keeps the door open in case you decide to put your child back in school someday.

To prepare, look over the homeschooling laws you researched and become familiar with them. You have already done this, so this is an easy step. You are just reviewing in case someone tries to make requirements you don't really have to meet.

If your state doesn't have a form you have to submit, and doesn't specify how to remove your child, write a letter stating that you will be removing your child from the school on a certain date to homeschool him according to the laws of your state. If you want to sound extra impressive (which you usually do when you are nervous), cite the part of the law that refers to homeschooling. Keep the letter short and don't explain your reasons. You might get asked for them, but don't offer them if they aren't asked for. There is no reason to prompt an argument and there is nothing to be gained by hurting someone's feelings. You may want to be especially kind and thank the school for all it has done for your child. Schools are less inclined to resist when you are kind and if they are sure you won't call the school district and explain why you are really removing your child. If you have been fighting the school, they will be reassured by your kindness. End the letter by requesting that the school provide you with whatever you need from them, such as a final report card. If you don't need anything, simply ask them to tell you what you need to do on his last day of school.

Type the letter neatly on plain paper and use the spelling and grammar checker on your word processing program. The image you are trying to achieve is one of syrupy niceness. Even if you have never been nice to them before, you will be now, because you want to escape in peace.

Although you probably won't encounter any problems, we will discuss what to do if you should find someone wanting to make the process difficult. It's always a good idea to be prepared, just in case.

When you deliver the letter, dress in business attire. This will give you confidence and, if you find yourself being interviewed by the principal, you will feel (and therefore act) more professional. You want to fool your brain into believing you are not the least bit nervous or shy.

Most likely, no one will bother you at this time because they won't know what is in the letter. Put the name of the principal on the envelope and ask that it be delivered. The day you may run into trouble is the day you actually remove your child. You might be asked to sign something or to go into the office to explain where the records should be sent. (The school usually keeps them.) Then you will suddenly find yourself invited in to meet with the principal. You can't be forced to talk to the principal, so if you really can't handle it, tell him you have an appointment and can't stay.

If you are willing to talk, be prepared to stay calm and in control. You might want to let him know that you are not interested in discussing whether or not you should homeschool because you have researched this very carefully and have already interviewed a number of people on the subject. (You must have talked to someone!) If you know you aren't up to pressure, leave the impression that this may be a temporary action, and that you want to spend a year focusing in on a few areas where your child needs extra help. Sometimes they are less antagonistic if they think it's temporary. Assure them you will return your child if things don't go as planned. You most likely do plan to spend this year helping your child in his weakest areas, so you needn't feel guilty for saying this. And, of course, you *would* return your child to the public school if it was in his best interest. You can't foretell the future.

Often, schools are surprisingly relaxed about children leaving to homeschool. I got a little pressure the first time I pulled children out of school. Despite this, I have always pictured them having a party when we left, not because of my daughter, but because of me and my determination to get the needed accommodations. The second time, I had no trouble at all. One school didn't care in the least and the principal at the other school told me he thought it was a good move, since my children were so advanced in their work. I certainly hadn't expected to be praised for my choice. This means you don't need to go in expecting trouble. It's likely there won't be any. Schools are much more used to this sort of thing now than they were in my homeschooling days.

Bring with you the homeschooling laws to prove you can legally homeschool. You don't have to prove anything, of course, but it simplifies the discussion and makes you look professional. Place the laws in a plain manila folder. You might also want to bring a brief summary of the courses you will teach your child next year if you have prepared that. Make it sound impressive by giving classes fancy names and by listing books to be used. Drop names if you have them to drop—credentialed teachers who are ready to offer advice, professionals who will be mentoring your child, or outside courses you will send your child to. If you don't have those, don't worry. You don't need them.

Try to take control of the discussion right from the start. Begin by expressing your appreciation for all the school has done for your child and be specific. If this has been a bad year, you may have to spend a lot of time preparing for this step, but you can always find something good to say. Then, explain briefly what you hope to accomplish at home, but try to do it without accusing the school. For example:

"Kacie has made a great deal of progress this year in reading, and I feel that with some individual attention we can make even more. I've noticed how much progress she makes when she and I work alone. I know there is no way your teachers can work one-on-one with Kacie and it isn't fair to expect that. I'm sure that with a year of this sort of attention, we can get her closer to the appropriate reading level."

You have been kind, and you've demonstrated that you have not only given thought to this, but have worked successfully with your child at home during the year.

Some principals will let you go with nothing more than a half-hearted attempt. Others will attack and try to undermine your confidence. Review the answers you gave your family and friends and use these again with the principal. You might hear that you need a teaching credential to do a good job. Point out that a credential might be needed to teach thirty or more children, but you're only teaching your own and you've been teaching them ever since they were born. Parents are a child's first teacher, but science has never proven that when a child turns six, parents lose their ability to teach.

Sometimes the school officials put up a fight and often the fight becomes painful or frightening. Sometimes we are intimidated by their reaction and lose our tempers or cry. If the principal is attacking, politely excuse yourself on the pretense of an appointment. (To avoid lying, plan an appointment in advance, even if it's only an appointment to call your best friend and tell her what happened.) Thank him for his concern and tell him you will be sure to keep your child ready to return if necessary. Then firmly walk away without looking back.

Removing a special needs child

If your child has been receiving special education services from the school, you may have a few extra steps to take. Review your copies of the IEPs (individual educational plans which are designed to help a child with disabilities be more successful in school) and records of meetings you have held with the school or your child's doctors and be sure you have all of them. If not, request copies prior to letting the school know you're leaving. If possible, you may also want to request new testing. If the scores are low, you'll have additional proof you cannot possibly do worse than the school has done. You will also have those tests to help you assess your child's educational needs, although you may discover the tests are not a valid way to measure ability. Many children do much better (or much worse) in "real life" than they do on tests. However, you will at least know how well he performs on these types of tests.

If you want to continue to receive special education services after you leave, find out what the law requires and what the law allows. If the law requires the school to provide services, include a copy of the law in your written request to continue services. This can be included with your letter of departure. If the law allows the school to provide services but doesn't require them to do so, decide if it's worth the battle. If you choose to continue services, the school will monitor your child's education. Even though my children only received speech therapy, the schools always gave academic tests during the assessments. It's unlikely you can be forced to accept services, but find out by looking at the disability laws for your state. You can contact the state board of education for this information or ask the librarian to help you research it.

You may be able to receive services through your insurance if the school will not provide them, and you may also be able to find private resources or even provide services yourself. Examine your options before making the decision to remove your child. I have occasionally reminded schools that if my child is there a few hours a week, they can be sure he is okay and progressing. They seem to like having some level of supervision. This, however, can be a negative if you don't anticipate rapid improvement.

Parents of special needs children have generally spent a tremendous amount of time teaching their children at home and assisting with homework. They have participated in the IEP process and brainstormed with teachers for ideas. It's very simple for them to prove they are accustomed to teaching their child and planning his education. Use your experience, your in-depth knowledge of your child's strengths and weaknesses, and your training in handling his disability as proof you can succeed.

If it didn't go well

The most important thing to remember as you remove your child from school is that you have made this decision very carefully and thought through all the issues. You've already made a great many plans and done some very difficult preparatory work. You've shown your commitment and your skill. You don't need the school's approval. If you made mistakes, don't dwell on them. (I know this is easier to say than do.) You did the best you could, and you have much less practice at this than the school officials do.

When my oldest child was small and I was scolding her for everything, trying to be the perfect parent, someone asked me if a specific offense would matter in ten years. I realized it wouldn't since I was pretty sure she wouldn't be dumping her milk over her food by then. Since that time, this has seemed like a good question to ask in most situations.

The first time I attended an IEP meeting, I burst into tears. I was shy and afraid of conflict and I was attacked verbally. I was humiliated by my loss of dignity, even though it gained me the sympathy of the officials. This was many years ago, and I realize now that what seemed like a terrible crisis at the time has not made any real difference in my life. It was a starting place, and over the years I became better at attending those meetings. Whenever you remove your child from school, you will be less affected by what happens on that particular day. With any luck, you will never return to deal with those officials again.

If you sense you're not being treated with respect, leave. If you want to strike back instead of using an appointment as an excuse, gently say, "I want my children to be taught by people who are open-minded and considerate. The way I'm being treated today tells me this is not that sort of place, and I prefer not to leave my children here." Then walk away. If you are crying when you leave, don't be embarrassed. You may soften their hearts so they will treat the next parent with more consideration.

Some school officials will take your decision as a personal criticism, but *you* know it's just a good parenting decision. Don't let anyone take away what you've worked so hard to create. You know you are doing what is best for your child.

Take your child home. It's time for school.

Transitioning from public and private school

If your child started in a formal school, you may need some transition time. The time this will take and the steps you will choose depend on how long your child was in school and how it affected him. Consider some of the challenges your child may need to overcome as he becomes a homeschooler:

The purpose of learning: Little children learn for the joy of learning. They can spend hours watching a bird in flight, studying pictures of a far-away land, or learning to tie a shoe. When they go to school, a new element is introduced to the educational process: rewards.

The first day of homeschool, my two youngest children eagerly presented me with their completed math assignments. "Here's my work. What do I get?" I stared at them, puzzled. Were these the same children who once happily tackled grocery store workbooks just for fun? They weren't. "When we do our work, you have to give us candy," my child explained. I shook my head. No candy. "Then you have to give us a star." No star. "An *A*?" my child sighed. Not even an *A*. Instead, I explained, we were going to go over the paper together and make a little mark wherever we saw a mistake. Then the children would go back and correct those problems after we had discussed them. When the paper was perfect, the assignment would be complete. My child stared at me as if I had lost my mind. "If there isn't candy or stickers or grades, why do we have to do this?"

Why indeed? Only a few years ago, none of my children would have asked such a question. School had changed the way they viewed learning. Even a kindergartner knows children don't get paid to do fun things. We don't pay our children to eat chocolate cake, play with their friends, or watch television. We pay them for doing things that are good for them, but that they would never want to do otherwise. When they go to school and start receiving candy, stickers, and grades for their work, they realize that learning was not meant to be fun. It was meant to be something that was good for them, but that they would never do otherwise. The joy with which they once tackled learning disappears and it just becomes work. They also discover they have to do this work whether they feel like it or not. Writing was fun for me when I just wrote to relax. Now I have deadlines and a certain amount of writing that must be done, and it isn't as exciting anymore. Writing is a job. It's a job I enjoy, but it's a job all the same, and that changes my attitude.

Learning has become work, and it isn't supposed to be work. It's supposed to be wonderful, something you do to explore the world, improve your skills, and make life more rewarding. Admittedly, some of it will be dull, but most of it can be exciting. It will be your task as a parent to help your children rediscover the joy. It will be your children's job to keep you from doing this—after all, they want the candy and stickers. This is one of your first battles on the homeschool front, and for homeschooling to work its magic, it's one you have to win. Joy is one of the primary secrets to the success of homeschooling.

Stand firm on the rule of no rewards for awhile. When the children are retrained, you can offer a few rewards, but not so many you take them right back into danger. For now, let the time you spend with each child serve as the reward. When you go over the work, try to smile and relax. Even if the work is awful, be pleasant. Don't let your children get away with shabby work, but search out what is good and reward them with a smile and a compliment. Then gently suggest changes. The smile and compliment are enough of a reward at first. Later, your children will even learn to work without that. (You will smile and compliment, but not every time, because they will someday take charge of their own education.) Your children love being with you. They want your attention and your praise. Give them lots of this and they will eventually learn the real joy of knowledge.

Learning forever: You will help your children discover joy by modeling the correct attitude. Your children learn best by watching you. What are you learning? How are you tackling the material you have to learn in order to teach your children? If you grumble over the math you're reviewing, forget to plan history because you didn't want to do the research, or say you can't do something without taking a class, you send a message to your children that learning is drudgery. If, on the other hand, you are excited about the discovery of a new dinosaur, pick up a book and read more about the Civil War because it's so interesting, and chatter about Shakespeare, you are also sending a message. This time you are telling your children that learning is exciting.

When people insist parents must know everything to teach everything, they are trying to take away an important benefit of homeschooling. I once heard a young adult who had been homeschooled tell of seeing his mother studying science books on her own. He noticed how hard she studied so she could teach her children and he realized how important science must be to her. He also learned how important he was. We don't want our children to think you learn everything there is to know while you're in school, and then stop learning. How does it help our children if we leave the impression we already know everything? As you help your children recover from school, show them the teacher is the person who learns the most, and that lifelong learning is a desirable way of life.

Self-esteem: Some children who are brought home from public or private school have suffered from cruelty, failure, and loneliness. A child with a learning disability is too often the subject of teasing or contempt from peers. Some teachers have difficulty understanding a child's disability or even believing there is one. By the time the child leaves the school system, he may believe he is stupid or unlikable. Many children have become shy with peers and afraid of adults. Some have given up on themselves and learning. One of your first tasks may be to help the child learn to believe in himself again and to feel accepted in the world.

If your child is battered, you may want to take a short break, or plan a simplified curriculum for a little while. Time spent talking about what happened in traditional school and what you and your child want to have happen in their homeschool will be as valuable as a math lesson. Plan something fun and teach entirely to your child's strengths. If he cares about space, buy a telescope, make star charts, read books, take field trips, and watch videos. Let him enjoy learning without the pressure of tests and assignments. Treat this thematic unit study more like a family activity than a class. You want him to experience success in learning just to show him it's possible. That doesn't mean teaching down; it just means teaching the way he learns.

When you're ready to teach something in a formal way, start with your child's most upsetting subject. If your child can't read, this is the very first problem you must fix. Without reading, education and life are very difficult. Spend as much time each day working on reading as possible.

Do you know *why* your child can't read? Study reports and tests from the school for clues. When did the problem begin? Does your child understand phonics? Can he sight-read? Spend time working on the very basic skills and don't worry about what is appropriate for his age. Go all the way back to the beginning if necessary. In fact, when my children struggled, it helped to go so far back the work was too easy. This gave them confidence, and then we eased our way forward to harder material.

Try to teach the basic academics through topics your child loves. The astronomer can learn to read books on astronomy and the chef can read recipes. Right at first, it doesn't matter what a child reads. Your goal is to help him believe he can learn to read, and then to teach him he wants to read. Formal instruction is far more successful after you overcome those two challenges

It's unnerving to parents when a child throws her book and screams she can't do this because she is stupid. Your first instincts are seldom the best ones in this situation. Anger frightens the child and creates a hostile environment. Children don't learn well on battlefields. Punishing her won't resolve the cause of the problem. (You don't have to accept her right to throw things, but do accept the reason she threw it.) Telling her she could do it if she would just try doesn't help either. She heard that in school year after year. As one who heard it myself for many years, I can assure you this is the worst possible answer. When my teachers told me I wasn't trying, I became resistant because I knew I was trying. Then, after thinking it over, I decided I must just be stupid. What may seem to be laziness may just be fear—a fear of trying and still being unable to do the material, leaving stupidity as the only explanation. It may also be a natural reluctance to avoid anything unsuccessful, unfulfilling, and baffling.

Try to establish honest communication about the problems your child faced in school, how they affected her, and how they affected your family. You may have been angry with her as you helped with homework because you were tired and worried about the teacher's reactions. Explain how you felt about the problems the school caused and how you are working to overcome the ways this hurt you. Ask your child to create her own solutions to the problems she sees. Does she think she can learn? What can the two of you do together to help her become a good student?

Schools often tackle self-esteem through classes and worksheets. Children can't learn self-esteem from a book. A feeling of self-worth comes from accomplishing difficult tasks and by having others believe in us. Your job is to set up an environment in which your child can achieve hard things, and to put into her life people who believe in her and praise her. The praise has to be real, though. Even children know when praise is faked. If you become ecstatic over every little achievement, your child will not only become skeptical of your sincerity, but may wonder what is wrong with her that you must get excited over stupid things. In addition, she won't know when you really are excited by an accomplishment.

Move backwards until the work is too easy. When she

completes the assignment without any real effort, don't clap and cheer. Say, "I knew this was something you could handle. I don't see any reason to spend more time on something that's so easy for you. Let's try something harder." You've acknowledged her success and shown you considered her capable of doing this task. You've also shown your faith in her ability to handle the next step. If the next assignment is also too easy, say, "At this rate, we'll be caught up in no time. I know we can find something that will challenge your brain!" When you finally reach a step she can't do, you've prepared her to have the proper attitude. You've suggested that you were only searching for a starting point, not testing her. You've shown her how much she really knows, even if it was below grade level.

"Finally! You found something for me to teach you! Now comes the fun part. I wonder how fast we'll master this one? It looks a little tricky, but from what we've seen in the other assignments, I know you can learn it. Look at all the things you've already learned." You may want to remind her that since you are new to teaching, you may have to try several different methods before you figure out the best way to teach this subject. Invite her to make suggestions as well since she may very well know just how she learns best.

Spend lots of time on activities in which she excels and treat her like an expert in these areas. Ask her to explain them to you, or to tell you how she learned the skills she demonstrates. In addition, let her be the teacher sometimes. Have her teach you something she knows well. She will feel important and smart as she teaches you, and may also develop more patience for your own efforts as a teacher.

Social skills

We often struggle with people who think homeschoolers won't develop social skills. My children went to school confident and outgoing, but came back home shy and insecure. Whatever they were learning at school wasn't socialization, and this is particularly true for children with disabilities or shyness. You may need to make socialization an actual subject in your school.

If a child has had negative experiences with teachers and other adults at school, you will need to help her learn that most adults are kind and good. Helping children notice the kind adults in their world is a good way to help children learn the unkind teacher who hurt them was the exception, not the standard. If possible, help your child get to know some schoolteachers on a social level, perhaps through your church or in your neighborhood. Let him enroll in outside classes only after researching the teachers to find the kindest one.

Make sure he has access to many adults. If he is afraid of them or is shy, assign him to call museums to learn their hours of operation, return things to a store, or ask a librarian for assistance.

Overcoming socialization issues involving peers may be a greater challenge. If your child didn't have friends in school, simply continuing those friendships is not an option. Instead, you will have to help your child find new friends. Select a church with an active youth program. Enroll your child in an activity class she is especially interested in. Find a club. You cannot drag a child into the house and beg her to play with your child, but you can place your child in the path of other children. If your child is shy, she may have difficulty initiating friendships. Help her to become involved in projects that involve working with someone else. A sympathetic leader can pick out a likely friend and ask the two children to work together on something important.

If your shy child would like to have a party, select a format that will not leave her standing on the sidelines. My children enjoyed craft parties. Since all the girls were at a table making crafts, no one was really left out; yet they all had something to do, so the party didn't lag. You might also select a service project and invite a group of children to assist. Even fairly young children can tie quilts, plant a garden for an elderly person, or stuff rag dolls.

Chapter 23

So, Did They Learn Anything?

"How do you know if they are learning?" I'm often asked about testing when I talk to those who don't homeschool. Because I'm with my children while they work, and because I'm listening, watching, and asking questions, I know exactly what they know. However, we sometimes have to prove what they are learning to others and prepare our children to be tested in college (or in school, should they return). Even when we're certain we know how much they know, we should do some formal evaluations of their skills every now and then.

Tests

Tests are not good indicators of learning because they're artificial. The teacher chooses what she considers important and the student, who studies by guessing what the teacher will ask, hopes he is studying the right material. On the other hand, students and even employees are tested, so it becomes important to learn how to take tests and how to conform your learning to the tastes of others. You can periodically give your child tests so he becomes familiar with the format and develops test-taking skills. Try to vary the focus so he learns how to study different types of materials. When I tested, I focused on vocabulary and big concepts, not details; but when my children went to college, they had teachers who cared more about details. They had to learn to conform to the testing styles of four or more teachers at the same time. Note, however, that even though I made a mistake in not preparing them for this, they're still doing very well in school. Mistakes are seldom fatal in homeschooling, because what they did learn was more important than what they did not learn. All the same, it's a good idea to give a variety of tests.

To show you how to create a test, we will use Chapter 10 in this book. This chapter is called, "How Am I Going to Teach? How Are They Going to Learn?" I'll create test questions based on the information in this chapter to show you how to build your own tests. Feel free to cheat and look up the answers. (A test that allows a student to look up the answers is called an open book test.)

Multiple Choice Tests

This type of test offers several answers to choose from. The question may be an actual question, or it may be a sentence with a blank to be filled in from the choices. Most tests have four to six choices. These can be easy questions requiring some knowledge but not extensive study. They can also be tricky, with some answers included that are almost right, but not quite. A question is harder if the choices include, "None of the above," or "All of the Above," because a student can't just recognize the answer when she sees it. Try answering these questions about Chapter 10:

1. What is a curriculum?

a) A package purchased to teach children.

b) A collection of subjects you are teaching.

c) What the public schools teach.

d) A method of teaching that requires a degree.

2. **What are some of the benefits of purchasing a curriculum?**

   a) It usually takes less of your time.

   b) It allows you to learn how to work with your children before you create your own materials.

   c) It builds confidence in newcomers.

   d) It is always less expensive.

   e) All of the above except for (d).

3. **What are some factors to consider when choosing a purchased curriculum?**

   a) Cost

   b) Ability to mix grade levels

   c) Location of vendor

   d) Your child's learning style

   e) A, B and C

   f) A, B, and D

Now let's go back and look at each question. The first question evaluates the student's ability to define a word. The first and third answers are only partially correct. You can purchase a curriculum, but you don't have to. You can make your own. A public school does use a curriculum, but so do other types of schools. The last answer is completely wrong. The second choice was almost word-for-word from the chapter and is correct. I chose the question because a student must know the answer to that question to understand the chapter, so it's a very important issue.

The second question is based on my own opinions. There are times when you will want your children to be able to identify what the author of a story or article believes. They should be able to read a document and tell you the beliefs the author holds about a subject. The last choice is the correct one. Children should be told to watch for the words *always* and *never*. Authors seldom use such strong language. It would be impossible for me to say that a purchased curriculum is always less expensive than making one, because I don't know what every person in the world spends, nor do I know what every curriculum costs. Even if I did, that information is likely to change.

The next question is also based on my opinion, but it's essential to my instructions for choosing a curriculum. Students should be able to identify the factors an author outlines as part of his instructions or his arguments. The one choice that was not correct, "location of vendor," might be a factor for some people, but my chapter does not mention that. Tests are based on the material presented in class, and our own opinions are not to be considered unless the question specifically asks for an opinion. The student should note that I asked for factors, a plural word. That means more than one answer had to be correct. Knowing that, the student knows the correct answer isn't any of the first four choices. That leaves him with only two to choose from and he has a fifty percent chance of being correct. Students should be taught to look for clues in the question, and even in other questions where the answer is sometimes revealed.

True/False

Another common type of test question is the true-false question. Take the questions I asked above and turn them into true-false questions yourself. In these types of questions, the entire statement may be false, or it can be completely true except for one word. These are much more difficult, but are common in tests for older students.

Example: A curriculum is a collection of subjects and topics taught to students in traditional schools.

To a limited extent, this would be true, but it's not a complete definition because curricula are also used in non-traditional schools, including homeschools. Most teachers would expect this question to be considered false. If it's not entirely true, it's false. Teach your child to do this by playing games. Give him something to read and let him answer the questions with the material right in front of him. Tell him you will try to trick him, so he must be very careful. Then let him try to trick you. Both of you can create questions based on the same material and try to trick each other. If he learns to think of tests as games, he may find them less frightening.

Fill in the blanks

In this type of question, the teacher writes a sentence, but leaves out one or more important words. For instance: *A _____ is a collection of subjects and topics used to teach children.* The student must add the missing words. Sometimes students are given a list of words to choose from, but other times the student must come up with these words from memory. These questions are very difficult for students with word-recall disabilities and should be practiced often before they go to college. Let them work with you to figure out strategies for themselves. I often go through the alphabet to find the missing word. I have no idea why that helps, but it does. If the child is visual, another possibility is to create pictures that will bring the word to mind. The missing words are usually vocabulary words or names, so make sure your student drills those items and can bring them to mind with ease.

Short answer

These are very short essays. Usually a teacher wants the five most important facts about a topic. A typical question might be: *What factors should a parent consider before purchasing a curriculum?* If this were an essay, a teacher would want details; but in short answers, the response will be little more than a list. Sometimes these are called identifications, and they test a student's recognition of vocabulary or names. Typical identification terms might be: Charlemagne, conspicuous consumption, gravity, *King Lear*. The student should not tell everything she knows.

For whatever reason, in college, five has been the magic number with every teacher I've taken classes from. Teachers want the five *most* important facts. This means the student must be able to think about everything she has learned on the subject she's taking and figure out which five are the most important. Often, the teacher allows a word count of one hundred to three hundred words for an answer. The student can then list more than five facts, but should be sure the five most important are there. In this instance, write the answer in paragraph form, not as a list.

Essay

Because I'm a writer, this is my favorite type of test, but most people don't like essay tests at all. Since they're going to be a major factor in college, it's important you teach your child to write this sort of test. The most important way to prepare is to have your child do a great deal of writing in your school. Have him write a short essay every week and turn in research papers regularly. At the end of each chapter, assign an essay based on a question in the chapter. The question should be one that requires analysis. Ask why? Why did Columbus set out on his journey? Why did the colonists rebel against England? Why did the Native Americans lose to the early settlers and explorers? Why did Rome fall?

Your child should be able to figure out why things happened and explain the events that caused them to happen. He should be able to put those facts into an order that makes sense and be able to help the reader see things the way he does. When your child can do this comfortably using the book, he should practice answering the questions from memory. Let him answer a question from what he knows, and then go back and answer it again with the book open so he can decide what he left out. Help him figure out what he should have studied to be able to answer that question well. Ask him to evaluate his arguments to make sure they make sense and are based on facts, not emotions. No matter who he thinks should have won the Civil war, he should be able to explain why the North won and what the South might have done differently. When students take essay tests in school, grammar, spelling, and penmanship count. If your child is disabled, he will be able to receive accommodations; but all other children need to be able to write an essay test within the allowed time frame, and write so the teacher can read it (they might need to print). The grammar and spelling should be reasonably accurate.

Learning to test

Begin teaching your child how to take a test by giving these tests as worksheets. He will be able to practice without pressure. You can even let him use his book at first. When he is comfortable with each type of test, have him try to do the worksheet without his books. By the time he is in second or third grade, he should be taking tests.

Standardized tests are required by some states. There are many books designed to help parents teach standardized testing skills to children. Because tests change often, use a current testing book. Follow the same pattern of first doing them as worksheets and then as tests. When your child is comfortable, give a simulated test with time limits. Be sure to teach him to fill in the bubbles on standardized tests. Many children, especially those with poor motor skills, find them hard to fill correctly. Test preparation books often have pages of these bubble forms you can photocopy. You might have your child practice filling them in accurately and quickly without actually answering any questions. Give him the sheet and tell him to fill in one row of bubbles each day. This is really boring, so ask him to think of a way to make it more interesting, or at least follow it up with something fun.

Nontraditional ways to evaluate learning

Testing is only one way to find out what your children know. It's incomplete at best, so although you should teach testing, you want to use a variety of methods to find out how your children are doing.

One of the best ways to evaluate learning is to talk to your children. As they do math problems, ask them to explain what they are doing and why. When you read about the Civil War, ask questions. *Why do you think the war was fought? How do you feel about the decisions Lincoln made? Would you have been willing to hide a runaway slave? Why or why not? What did people who had a chance to do that have to think about before making the decision?* Asking questions that require thought allow children and teens to show you the depth of their understanding and their ability to explain what they know and what they believe. These discussions can be held in school, but they can also be held at the dinner table, in the car, or in the grocery store.

Quiz games are an easy way to test. When I was a child, we all worked on our chores at the same time and in the same part of the house. As we worked, my mother called out questions from history, science, and current events. I always assumed she was distracting us from the unpleasantness of work until I grew up and had children of my own. Only then did I realize how much we learned in those games. She also called out the first line of a poem, and we had to name the poet and recite as much of the poem as we could remember. She gave us the next line and moved on, but returned often until we had the poem memorized. She told us memorized poems could keep us company when we were alone.

Projects are another good way to monitor learning. When a child builds a diorama of a Greek home, you will soon know if he really understands what it looked like. If he adds computers and telephones, you've forgotten to explain a few things. From third grade on, most children should be able to create a science experiment based on the science learned. Asking children to write a script about an historical event helps you find out how they view the event. The best way to monitor learning is to watch your child at work. The less help he needs, the more often he solves his own problems; the more he enjoys what he does, the better he is at learning. Watch, ask questions, listen, and explore. You'll know.

More Resources
➤ *McGraw-Hill Education*
  MHEonline.com
  McGraw-Hill is a well-known publisher of public school textbooks and they have added a department for homeschoolers. This page displays their lines of homeschool books. McGraw-Hill is my favorite publisher for workbooks. The stories in the literature books are so interesting I found myself reading them just for pleasure. Spectrum, one of their product lines, is especially interesting. Spectrum has a series of preparation workbooks for standardized testing, valuable for those children who must be tested.

Chapter 24

Homeschooling until High School Graduation

MANY PEOPLE WHO FEEL comfortable homeschooling a young child for a few years aren't sure they can continue the challenge for the long run. As children get older and become more experienced with homeschooling, their needs change. Although their needs will change, you will grow right along with your children. When they're older, you'll already know what works and you will know how they learn. You will gradually make changes in how you work. The first few years, I prepared fancy lessons and taught just like a public school teacher. I gradually gave my children more independence and eventually taught them to teach themselves. When I started, I didn't know how I would do all that, or even that I would do it. It just happened little by little.

When your child reaches middle school, buy a homeschooling book specifically for parents of high school students. You will want to prepare him for college, but there is far too much information available on that topic to cover completely in this book. However, if your child is going to a community college, you need only be sure he reads and writes well and has reasonable math skills. If he is going to a university, he will need more.

In this chapter, we'll discuss issues you'll be dealing with over the years: creating independent learners so you won't have to teach physics; surviving really bad days; homeschooling when your life is falling apart; returning your child to public school; and finally, getting into college. This last section will only be touched on lightly since it's worth a book all by itself. The list of resources at the end of this chapter will suggest books you can read if you would like to know more about this subject.

Creating independent learners

Teaching your children to be lifelong, independent scholars is one of the most valuable gifts you can give them. It's a skill they are unlikely to learn in a traditional school. Traditionally-educated children who are able to do this either learn it at home or are personally motivated.

The reason a less-educated but motivated parent can teach her children is because she can teach herself the material. When she learns to teach herself, she can pass that skill on to her children. This skill is very important for the homeschooling parent to master, because homeschooling looks a lot less scary if we know our children can teach themselves what we don't know, and perhaps don't want to know.

In the early days of homeschooling, let your children help plan your curriculum. Ask them what they'd like to study in science and then include some of those topics in your plan for the year. When your children ask a question you can't answer, offer to help them find the answer. Ask them how they think they could find out and then go with them to see if their ideas work. If the idea doesn't work, suggest other places, but also continue to ask them what else they want to try. Even a first grader might suggest going to the library if that is part of her experience.

Introduce your child to the librarian. Instead of approaching the librarian yourself, have your child do it. (If your child is shy, practice at home and then go with her in case she panics.) Even though I knew how to look up material, I told the librarian I wanted my children to be comfortable asking her for help, so I would be sending them to her sometimes instead of showing them myself.

Bookstores are another good source of information. In addition, we became familiar with local museums and the experts in our own church. When my children had a question, I asked, "Where can we find your answer?" I presented the task of seeking information as a treasure hunt and we enjoyed searching our resources and gathering clues. We learned to check more than one source in order to see if they agreed, to see if there was more information available, and to evaluate the quality of the source. When your children read a book, teach them to check the author's qualifications and her sources.

Once your children are good at finding answers to their questions, they need to learn how to create entire courses. Suppose you ask your child what he'd like to learn about in science and he suggests astronomy. Ask, "Okay, how shall we do that? I don't know very much about it, so you'll have to help me plan the class and then we'll learn together. What should we do in this class?" If he doesn't know, ask if he thinks you should get some books. If he agrees, ask him where you can find books. (If he doesn't want books, convince him he does.) Then ask if there are any field trips you could go on. Are there any activities you could do together? Would he be interested in videos or computer programs? You may need to visit the library and bookstores together to gather your information. Always reserve the right to make the final choices. If his choices are too expensive, say so. He needs to work within a budget when he wants to learn. If he selects a method that is too time-consuming, let him know. (If he offers to make more time, perhaps by taking over some of your chores, negotiate.)

Once you've gathered all the materials, teach him how to put this class together. Share with him all you've learned about teaching, learning, and lesson planning. You can list this under career exploration (teaching) if you want credit for it. Make this class a true team effort.

When that becomes comfortable, around middle school or high school, consider allowing your child to create his own class without help, but make it clear you have to approve the plan. My teens liked reading and writing, so they chose a few books and then built a course around the books. They brought the final plan to me and I made suggestions or approved it as it was. They carried it out, reporting to me first on a daily basis, and then, when I was sure they were ready, on a weekly basis.

By the time your child is in high school, he should be in charge of his education. Give him the list of classes he has to take to graduate, including electives, and let him choose what to study. You may want to use the same list of classes your school district requires. You always have the right to override a decision, however, and you should make that clear in advance. Help him learn to balance his choices so he doesn't start with fun classes and leave all the less interesting ones to be done at the same time. He needs self-control to balance the fun courses with the required ones and to take enough classes to be sure he gets into the college he chooses. I insisted on English every year, with one semester being writing and one being literature, although they were allowed to turn it into a one year combined course if they prefer. Their reading material had to include at least one of Shakespeare's works and a good number of classics. I encouraged them to include material related to their history class. (If you don't start Shakespeare until high school, you might want to includc two plays instead of one.) We've been doing him since second grade, starting with children's versions, and my children like him. (I don't, but they do, so you can see that your limitations needn't interfere with your child's education.)

That's all there is to it. Teach your children to read, write, and research and they can learn without help. By the time they're in high school, you'll have free time on your hands because your children will study alone most of the time. Your job will be to listen at the dinner table as they discuss Einstein's theory or the cause of the French Revolution. If you haven't any idea what they're talking about, make them put it in terms you can understand. This forces them to understand it more clearly.

Or you can just tune them out.

Surviving really bad days

We're not talking about ordinary bad days here. We're talking about the terrible days when the baby has a high fever, your in-laws are coming for dinner, and you're having the world's worst headache. These are the days you can't remember why you started homeschooling. They might even be the days you can't remember why you had children. What do you do on a day when you just don't have the time or the patience or the will to be a teacher?

One solution is to call in a substitute. If you know another homeschooling parent who admits to having these kinds of days, agree to take each other's children one day a month on a moment's notice. If the end of the month comes along and one of you hasn't needed the break, take it the last day (or last two if you both have a day coming). You will both need to plan ahead in order to take extra children without notice, so discuss how you will do it. Will you plan a special one-day unit study that is ready to go at a moment's notice? Will it be field trip day?

If you have cooperative grandparents, they might be willing to take the children for the day as long as you don't abuse the privilege. Send the children with something to do while they are there, including as much of their homeschool work as possible.

A third option is to plan an emergency lesson plan kit. This is a one-day thematic unit study that can be done with little or no help on your part. Include everything you need to teach the class in the box or bag and write out detailed instructions. It should be simple enough to be followed on a moment's notice. If you have to bring in a babysitter, she should be able to do it for you. (Knowing an older homeschooler is helpful because she will understand homeschooling.) A kit on castle life might include a book to read or look at, a kit for building a castle, a medieval snack, medieval paper dolls, and instructions for writing a story. The castle kit can just be blocks—you don't have to be fancy. The emergency kit need not take the entire day, just enough so you feel like you did something and enough to keep the kids busy while you cope.

Or, if none of the above ideas work for you and you're feeling really stressed or burned out, just take the day off. Go on a field trip or declare a school holiday. As long as you don't do it too often, it won't hurt anything. Make up the lost hours by taking a Saturday field trip later. Some days we stopped after our hour of math. I could often manage an hour, even on a really bad day.

Don't teach when you're in a bad mood. If you find yourself getting out of control, tell the children you're putting yourself in time out and ask them to work or play quietly for a little while. Then go to your room if you can safely leave the children. If you can't, do whatever will help you unwind but make it clear to the children that when you are in time out, you must not be disturbed except in an emergency. Read a book for fifteen minutes, take a walk around your backyard, or take the kids on a walk around the block. Call a friend. When you are ready, thank your children for being patient and apologize if you behaved in a way you weren't happy with before the time out. You will teach your children a lesson far more valuable than the one you interrupted when you show them how you manage your anger appropriately.

These bad days are going to happen. Few parents get through parenthood without losing their tempers, getting too sick to teach, or feeling completely overwhelmed. But bad days don't mean you can't homeschool, they are just a part of life, so forgive yourself and move on. Give yourself permission to be less than perfect.

Homeschooling in crisis mode

There are times in our lives that go beyond a bad day. I have homeschooled through unemployment, my father's death, and serious challenges in our family. When we reach these times, we may want to return our children to school. If this is your solution, accept it. You have not failed. Homeschooling takes tremendous emotional energy and sometimes, particularly when our children are younger, we have to ration our emotional demands. You may return to homeschooling later on, but if you don't, you've had a wonderful experience together.

If you choose to remain a homeschooler, allow yourself to take a break. If the family is grieving, give yourself a few weeks to just feel sad, cope with the challenges of the event, and do whatever makes you peaceful. After a few weeks, your heart may long for normalcy and you will return to your schedule. However, grief can return without warning, even when you think it's over. When my father died, an out-of-state friend, LuAnn Lawhon, who shared with us information on teaching a child who is behind in reading, sent me some money and asked me to hang on to it until unexpected grief created the need to order in a meal. Friends brought in food at first, but many months later I was suddenly overwhelmed by grief. By then, of course, the helpers had gone back to their own lives. I wanted my children close by me rather desperately, and because they were teens, I knew they'd rather spend their free day goofing off. I used LuAnn's gift to bribe them with food, and they went out with me for the day.

Prepare yourself for days like these when you're *not* in crisis. Have a general idea of where your curriculum is headed and give thought to how it could be adapted if your world falls apart. Make sure your children have as many independent learning skills as possible so you can let your older children teach themselves for awhile. (You learned how to do this in a previous section of this chapter.) Lessons can be fun and interesting even without your participation, particularly if you have more than one child. (Older children can read to their younger siblings and share their science experiments with them.)

If you have younger children, try to keep up with their math and reading; these are essentials you don't want to get behind in (but only math has to be formally taught as long as your child is reading at a second grade level or higher). You can then let your children learn by exploring their world, reading books, testing ideas, and doing whatever else looks reasonably educational. Crafts can be simple and done from a child's imagination and videos are an easy way to teach. Think about simple teaching methods to get you through the bad times. This might even be a time to test unschooling.

If your children are already advanced, you can allow them to study whatever they like for a few weeks without your help, perhaps by reading or by doing a long-term project. A family can learn quite a lot when the children work together to build a model of a Hebrew town for several weeks without help from adults. You can often take several days or even weeks off, filling in the missing hours later with field trips and week-end projects. You may even want to indulge in a tutor if you can afford it. (A homeschooled teenager or a college student might be less expensive.) Check your homeschooling laws, but it's likely to be acceptable as long as you're listed as the teacher and continue to oversee the program.

In any event, when needful, give yourself permission to cancel school and just do whatever you need to do to get through the day. Whatever you do is okay as long as it is safe and more important than the missed math lesson. Naturally, if you miss too many days you will need to decide how to make sure your children receive an education while you are unable to teach, such as asking a relative to help. You might also decide to make up the lost days during the summer.

One year, my husband was laid off without warning. We had never been through this and I was overwhelmed for a time by fear. I really neglected school for several months as I learned to adapt our budget, help my husband search for work, and cope with the emotional challenges the entire family faced. The school year came to a close before the challenge ended. The following fall, my two younger children decided to try the public school part-time. In the admission interview, the counselor asked them what they had learned the previous year. I caught my breath and considered making something up. To my surprise, they gave wonderful answers. Later, when I asked them about their answers, my daughter said, "Since you stopped teaching us, we could study anything we wanted, so that's what we did." One child had spent the year studying the Civil War and another explored science. They both kept up their math on their own, and since they were already avid readers, they read many books.

Returning children to public school

For many children, homeschooling is a temporary option. A

child who has fallen behind or who has a particularly bad teacher may homeschool for a year or two and then return, stronger, and ready to face the world again. Some parents only plan to homeschool for a few grades, long enough to give the child a powerful start. Other children return unexpectedly when parents divorce or a family situation changes.

And sometimes, homeschooling just doesn't quite work out; the parents realize they don't enjoy teaching or the child never adapts. A demanding or severely disabled child may be so challenging the parents realize they need the break a school provides.

Some homeschools have revolving doors. I homeschooled my first child for a year and a half due to school challenges. When we realized our personalities were clashing too much, she went back to school and we were both relieved. I couldn't figure out how to work with her and I didn't know anyone I could ask. However, after a half year of sixth grade and only a few weeks of seventh, she decided she'd had enough. She wasn't learning enough to suit her. When she asked to return home, her siblings asked to be homeschooled as well. When there were three children home, my energies were spread out and the personality clash wasn't as big an issue.

Returning a child to a traditional school is not an admission of failure—it's just a change. Your children need an education, and the solution that provides the best education this year may not be the solution that is best next year.

When you chose to bring your child home to school, you made a very difficult and unselfish decision. You gave up a lot, and you worked hard to learn what you needed to know. For whatever time your child was home, you gave him the very best you had to offer and did the very best you could. You sacrificed to meet his needs. However long that time lasted, it was a precious gift to your child and you can be proud you gave it. He will return to school with something of value, whether it's the knowledge that he was worth the sacrifice, some newly acquired academic skills, or just having had more time with his family.

Please don't tell the school homeschooling didn't work out. You will make the path harder for those families who still want to teach their children at home. Just say you've achieved what you took your child home to do and are now ready to return him. If a crisis is the cause of your decision, explain that changes in your life make it necessary to send your child to school.

Before returning your child to school, make sure he is ready. Teach him to work in a noisy, busy environment if he's never been to school. Tell him what to expect and take him to visit the school. Ask the school to carefully select his teacher to help him with his transition. If he is behind in his skills, have him tested and meet with the school to create a plan. (The school can offer an Individualized Educational Plan, known as an IEP that will outline the services and accommodations he will receive.)

Talk to your child about homeschooling. Discuss what went well and what went badly. Grieve if you want to, but also celebrate what was good. Tell your child how much you valued this time with him and thank him for letting you be his teacher for awhile. Discuss his feelings about returning to school and show faith in his ability to succeed. If the return was your idea, reassure him that he is not being sent to school due to his failures. Talk about how you will be able to continue what he liked best about homeschooling.

The first day back, take him to dinner or for ice cream and talk about the experience. Be prepared to help him understand his challenges and to celebrate what went well. Most children who return to school go through an adjustment period, but eventually they do quite well.

Getting into college

Many people who consider homeschooling worry about college. If your child is young, this is really not an issue. You could homeschool through eighth grade, return your child to school, and never have to deal with the problem. However, homeschooling is so common today that there is no reason to worry about college.

When my oldest daughter started high school, we attended several college fairs. As my daughter checked out schools without me, I wandered around chatting with representatives from each school about their attitude towards homeschoolers. Even though this was many years ago, every school official but one could instantly tell me how homeschoolers could be accepted into their schools and even how many homeschoolers were there and how they were doing. Today, most schools have policies in place for homeschoolers and many have improved their methods of evaluating them.

You need to check with the specific schools you are interested in for the details since they vary. However, most schools expect the student to take the same classes they would have taken in a public high school, and the classes need to be as difficult. I was advised to keep good records of the books my child read, the projects she completed, and samples of the papers she wrote. If I gave grades, I was to keep those as well. In addition, I needed to show I had obeyed the homeschooling laws for our state. SAT scores were considered more important for homeschoolers than for others, because they were considered impartial. Finally, I was advised to have her take classes from people not related to her, at a community college if possible, and to get letters of recommendation saying she had been a good, capable student with reasonable social skills. They advised us to show a history of outside activities and service that could be verified. I was also told to be sure my child went to interviews with a representative of the school without me and could competently describe her homeschooling years and studies. She needed to show she had helped plan her curriculum and had taken an active role in her own education since in the minds of college officials, this is considered one of the important benefits of homeschooling. They often see homeschoolers as motivated learners, but they want to make sure they aren't overly dependent on their parents.

We have talked about all these factors throughout the book. If you have an interesting, demanding homeschooling program, your child will be welcome in college. In each child's freshman year of high school, I asked my children to select four colleges they might like to attend. We also added the state school nearest our home. We looked at the entrance requirements for each one and used these to help us decide what classes to offer in our school. We wanted to be sure our children would be accepted at any of these schools, and felt secure that even if they changed their minds later, they would be close to the requirements for most of them. Since they all chose to attend community colleges first, this really wasn't an issue, but they began community college well prepared for whatever classes they chose to take. There were some adjustments in learning to work with other teachers, but they have gotten good grades whenever they've attended public schools at any level.

If your child is young, you only need to be sure he is learning to read, write, and calculate well and that he spends time in the outside world. You have many years before college is really a challenge for you. If your child is older, have your teenager contact several colleges to learn what they require. You should not do this for him because they want to know your child can function alone.

Don't worry too much about this issue before middle school. The world changes, and when the time comes it will be an easy process to go online and find out what sort of high school you have to run.

She will get into college—but will she succeed?

To answer this question, I turned to Rebecca Auerbach, a young woman who lives in California. She was unschooled, and then attended Napa Valley College (a community college), Sonoma State University, and Dominican University of California. Rebecca has a wonderful home page on homeschooling and is writing a book on unschooling. I was so impressed by her that I asked her to answer some questions about her life since graduating from homeschool, and about homeschooling in general:

Rebecca: "I was homeschooled, unschooling style, from first grade through high school. In college, I took an unschooling approach: following my own course of study instead of pursuing a degree, focusing on true learning rather than grades and credits, and finding my studies to be a joy instead of a chore. I have been out of school for two years, presently working as an inspector for the Agriculture Department, with a long-term goal of becoming a land surveyor. I am working on a book about unschooling."

Terrie: "How did homeschooling make you different from other teenagers?"

Rebecca: "As a teenager, I felt little interest in or connection with the mainstream youth culture with its popular music and movies, its fashion obsession, and its general priorities and lifestyle. I was passionately interested in intellectual and artistic pursuits, tending to devote myself to one or two interests at a time with intense enthusiasm (for awhile, I recall, my particular passions were politics and canine psychology). I loved spending contemplative time in nature. Life seemed a profoundly beautiful and fascinating thing that I was eager to explore, experience, and comprehend. I was very introspective and very spiritual. I watched little T.V. I was never bored. (Sad? Angry? Frustrated? Yes. But not bored). The people I found the most connection to were other homeschoolers and older people; a number of my friends were in their 40s and 50s."

Terrie: "What was the biggest surprise about college?"

Rebecca: "My biggest surprise in college was how few people were interested in learning for its own sake. I had expected that since college (unlike high school) was voluntary, students would be there because they enjoyed studying and would approach their coursework as free adults pursuing knowledge and understanding. Instead, I found the majority attended because of family and societal expectations or degree requirements for careers. They saw their studies as a chore and had little interest in discussion and exploration beyond, 'What do I have to do to get a good grade?' It was not the intellectual community I had hoped for. I was very passionate about my studies and did not often find other students I could share this with (though I made many friends in college with whom I shared other things)."

Terrie: "What do you want new homeschooling parents to know or to think about as they start their homeschools?"

Rebecca: "I would advise homeschooling parents to very carefully question conventional assumptions and their own automatic responses whenever they make a decision about their children's upbringing and education. Is there really any reason your child needs to follow that curriculum/do that assignment/know that fact? Don't stop with, 'Well, everybody needs to know.' Why does everybody need to know it? Why should they learn it this way and not another? Why can't they learn it five years from now instead of today? What will I accomplish if I take this particular approach, and what harm might I do?

"So much of what is taken for granted as educationally necessary is only necessary in schools where education must be standardized and scheduled, where children all learn the same things at the same times so they can keep moving through the system. Some homeschooling children don't learn to read until they're ten years old, but by age twelve they read at college level, perhaps with very little formal teaching. Homeschoolers have the freedom to learn what they truly want or need to learn, when they want and need to, and in the ways that will best allow each child to truly learn and understand. Take advantage of this freedom."

Terrie: "Do you plan to homeschool your own children if you become a parent?"

Rebecca: "I plan to have children and will definitely homeschool them with an unschooling approach. (No way in heck will I marry a man who does not support this; it's nonnegotiable!)"[†]

Aren't you excited to see the type of adults we are raising when we homeschool our children? Rebecca gives me great

---

†   Rebecca Auerbach, personal correspondence with the author.

hope for the future of our world as homeschooling continues to grow in popularity.

Her comment on the disappointment of discovering the other college students weren't particularly interested in learning was mirrored by my own children. They didn't find college difficult, but they did sometimes find it annoying or disappointing.

How do we know when we're done?

This seems like an odd question, but the first time I was asked it I realized I wasn't really sure. How did I know when I was done? There are several ways to make the decision.

First, of course, you can simply graduate your students whenever their peers are graduating. However, some homeschoolers aren't ready for college or have a few more subjects to study, and you may put in an extra year. Other homeschoolers are ready to move on before the traditional graduation date, and many homeschoolers begin attending community college early. Some homeschoolers bypass college or delay it while they go to work for awhile whenever their state allows them to do so.

In other words, there's not a specific time to be finished. Your state may have compulsory attendance laws and these will keep your child homeschooling or attending college until the required age. Beyond that, your child will graduate whenever he is ready to move to the next level. Naturally, you don't want him to continue homeschooling forever, but a year or two either direction won't hurt anything if you feel it's in your child's best interest. It's up to you and your child.

Whenever your child is finished, have him create a diploma on the computer and fill it out with a school name he has chosen. For his official records, it should be something that sounds like a real school; for unofficial purposes, he can choose any name he wants. When a college or employer asks the child if he graduated from high school, he can truthfully say he did and even present a diploma if asked. If homeschooling is legal, the diploma you sign is also legal. He will need to explain to a college that he homeschooled, but it's unlikely he will ever need to explain it to an employer unless he chooses to do so.

Many homeschooling organizations now sponsor proms and graduations if your children are interested. I rather wish I'd taken that path for my children. I didn't because I didn't do either when I was in high school by my own choice and didn't consider it important. However, some students will care, so ask them what they like.

More Resources
➤ *Homeschooling High School: Planning Ahead for College Admission* by Jeanne Gowen Dennis
ISBN: 1883002699
This is an outstanding resource for learning how to get your child into college. The author interviewed large numbers of college admissions officials to find out exactly what they wanted. Her book includes forms to keep accurate, professional records and even has a professional transcript that will look as if it came from a public or private school. The book is written from a Christian viewpoint, but those of other faiths will be able to benefit from the book as well.

➤ *And What About College?* by Caffi Cohen
ISBN: 0913677116
Caffi Cohen is considered the expert on homeschooling teenagers. Her book shows you just what you need to do to get your teenager into an excellent college, even if you homeschool nontraditionally.

➤ *My Life as an Unschooler*
WebSpace.webring.com/people/ru/unschoolgrad
Rachael Auerbach was unschooled and is the sort of adult we all hope we are raising. Her Web page describes her experiences as a homeschooled student. My favorite part of the page is her journal, describing her first experiences in community college and her thoughts on formal education. Do you wonder if your child will be okay in college? I found Rachael's journal to be extremely reassuring and very well written. This page is a gem!

➤ *College-Prep Homeschooling: Your Complete Guide to Homeschooling through High School* by David and Chandra Byers
ISBN: 1600651003
The Byers had an unusual homeschool arrangement. David, who has a Ph.D. in education and teaches college, prepared the lessons. His wife reluctantly took on the teaching work. The book shows how their children successfully finished homeschool high school and got into college. Because David works at the college level, he is able to demonstrate how to make college look good to the universities. Chandra's "in the trenches" commentaries, sprinkled throughout the book, are an honest and charming look at one mom's journey from reluctant to enthusiastic homeschooling. This book focuses on the high school years.

Chapter 25

Stupid Questions and How to Answer Them

ONE OF THE HARDEST parts of homeschooling really isn't the lesson planning, the teaching, or the discipline. It's answering all the dumb questions you will get asked. We've covered some of this in the first chapters, but now that you know more about homeschooling, you're ready to revisit these issues and learn how to answer them. (Some of these are a bit tongue-in-cheek and not really recommended as a regular answer; at this point you're ready to relax a little, though.) After you read my answers, head over to my blog† and offer up your own answers to the following questions. Let's begin with the *big question* and get it over with.

What about socialization?

You are going to get really tired of this question. Everyone, absolutely everyone, asks you about what we fondly call the "S-word." School, naturally, is the only place we can send our children to get socialized. Right? Everyone knows that only people who go to school have friends and learn how to interact with others. Right?

Did you go to school? If not, do you have friends? If you

---

† TerrieLynnBittner.com/?p=45

did go to school, is that the only place you met people? Do your preschoolers have friends even if they don't go to pre-school? Children traditionally hang out with the children in their neighborhood, and if you're lucky, there will *be* children in your neighborhood. If not, you'll take them someplace where there are children.

Since you're going to be asked this question more times than your best math student can count, you might as well write out an answer and memorize it. One answer will be plenty at first. Later, you will probably develop a number of answers and give the one that suits your mood:

Scholarly answer: "Recent studies done on homeschool-ers show that when observers are asked to watch a group of children play together and choose the homeschoolers, they are unable to do so." (There is always a study to prove every-thing. I'm sure you'll find one that suits your mood.)

Clueless answer: "Socialization? Oh yes, that's one of the main reasons we want to homeschool. You're right, what children learn in schools from other children these days is just awful, isn't it?"

Sarcastic answer: "Oh, I know, I'm depriving him of the chance to be so bullied and of the chance to make fun of peo-ple and to learn thirty-seven insults to use on his siblings. If his academics weren't so important, I wouldn't dream of de-priving him of such glorious opportunities."

"Let's get this over with" answer: "We don't believe that a fifth grade boy is the best person to teach social skills to a fifth grade boy. It's as unnatural for a child to spend his entire day with only thirty-seven children who are the same age, and mostly the same race and economic status, as it would be for you to only spend your time with people your own age. We feel the best way to teach our child socialization is to expose him to a wide range of people in a wide range of situations." (This is the usual answer.)

Doesn't it worry you that your sister's children read better than yours?

Naturally, when we were children, we were competitive with our siblings. But we should try to move beyond that now. At any rate, that isn't what this question means. It could be a veiled suggestion that you aren't doing a good job. Or it could be sincere concern. Either way, the approach is to focus the questioner on the individuality of children and of the benefits of self-paced education.

In other words, children should be allowed to learn at their own pace. Some children learn to read when they're two and others when they're nine. As long as they do learn to read, the actual age at which it happens isn't really important. Explain that your children will learn to read hard books when they're ready. Then point out all the wonderful things your child is doing and learning. Some of them will be things your sister's child is not doing. Naturally, you're too polite to point that out, but with any luck your listener will figure that out on her own.

What about college?

"What *about* it?" is the answer you may be tempted to give, but you probably won't. (Well, in a few years you might. Answering the same question a thousand times does something to your manners.) Instead, tell those who ask that nearly every college accepts homeschoolers, usually based on SAT scores and your own transcripts. Homeschoolers are doing very well in college and are even attending Ivy League schools. Not only that, they also get higher SAT and ACT scores overall than traditionally-schooled children do, so you are not at all worried. If they are worried, suggest they call a few colleges and ask if homeschoolers are accepted. It's unlikely they will call.

How can you teach algebra— you flunked it three times!

When we discussed this earlier, I said it's usually our own parents who hurl this question at us. When it's asked by others (assuming you aren't having a chat with your former math teacher) they are usually curious about the level of education a teacher needs. They assume teachers know everything they teach in advance. We already know, of course, that we can learn this material *with* our children. People who have never tried to teach themselves something, though, may not believe this is possible. You have to keep that in mind when you're choosing your answer to these types of questions.

Smart-aleck answer: "Oh, I won't even try. I have someone all lined up to teach that for me—assuming she doesn't die before my five-year-old is ready for algebra."

Concerned parent answer: "As soon as we're settled, I'm hiring a private tutor to teach me algebra so I'll be ready. I'm sure that even I can learn it in seven years."

"Ever the teacher" answer: "One of the abiding principles of homeschooling is that students learn best when they are self-taught. As I train my children to teach themselves, I will set the example by learning algebra and other subjects without the aid of an instructor. We intend to use Abraham Lincoln as our role model. He was, as you know, largely self-taught."

"Historian" answer: "You know, both Thomas Edison and Albert Einstein were homeschooled for many years. I'm certain their mothers weren't scientists, and yet, somehow they managed to train their sons well enough to become great scientists. Just as they did, I will find the resources my children need and the people who can help them if they are unable to help themselves."

How can you stand being with your children all day?

My children always got upset when they heard people ask this question. They believed the children of the questioners were probably hurt too. They thought this comment suggested that they were unloved and unwanted. When I thought about it, I realized this was indeed an insulting question. We never ask how a parent can stand being with his or her friends or coworkers all day. We do, however, ask this about children and husbands. Your reaction to this question can appropriately be surprise.

Many parents really don't enjoy spending extended amounts of time with their children. Some parents of traditionally schooled children love every moment they have with their little ones; but many, even those who love their children dearly, can't imagine spending so much time with them. So here are some suggested answers to this question:

Sarcastic answer: "I raised my children to be the sort of people I like to be around—didn't you?" (I've never given this answer, but I've always wanted to.)

Gentle answer: "I guess I'm one of those people who loves to be with children. You know me, just one overgrown child!"

Professional answer: "Public school teachers enjoy being with their students. I'm a teacher, and I'm looking forward to spending my days teaching *my* students."

"Mother of the Year" answer: "I feel it is my responsibility as a parent to give of myself as much as possible. I'm looking forward to contributing to their well-being and furthering their education." (I think you're supposed to be wearing a bathing suit, a sash, and a tiara when you give this answer.)

"Mother of challenging children" answer: "I feel I'm providing a valuable service to the public school teachers of America by making sure they never have to teach my children."

Are you ever planning to do the laundry again?

There's an easy enough answer to this one: "Nope, my kids only wear pajamas all day anyway, so why bother?"

What makes you think you know more than a trained teacher?

If a credentialed teacher is asking the question, she's probably offended. She spent a fortune going to school and learning how to teach and now parents around the world are teaching their children and doing a good job *without* that expensive education.

To be fair, what this teacher has accomplished, and what she is giving our nation, is vital. Give her the respect she wants and deserves. Good public school teachers are changing the world, and we need them. I have battled with teachers and I chose to homeschool—and yet I have a tremendous admiration for any man or woman who can stand before thirty or more children (who may have backgrounds, languages and disabilities he or she does not have personal experience with) and teach them well. Without training, I would not dare.

If you're responding to a teacher, acknowledge the difference between teaching your own children and teaching the children of others. You would probably want training before taking on her job. Teaching your own children, though, is not entirely different from helping them with their homework, particularly if your child often doesn't understand the homework. If you know her well, ask if she would be willing to give you advice when you need it. I've used many teachers as advisors and found them tremendously helpful. This also allows you to acknowledge their training.

If the person asking is not a teacher, you can give a similar answer; but you don't have to worry about hurting anyone's feelings. You can discuss whatever you've learned about professional teaching methods. Toss in a few fancy terms and they will assume you know what you're talking about. Mention that the classical system is gaining in popularity, and you've been researching that as well as studying

Montessori's methods. Pretty soon they'll probably get bored and go away. Boredom is my favorite line of defense.

How will they experience the real world stuck at home with you all day?

I always have to answer this question with another question: "What is the real world?" Do you wonder what they're picturing the so-called real world to be like? Or for that matter, what they are picturing your home life to be like? I presume, because I like to think nice things about people, that those who ask this question believe our children are living in a warm, loving environment, and that the real world involves coping with people who don't love them and don't care about their well-being.

There seems to be a general attitude that little children have to be exposed to the harsh world as soon as possible, and for as many hours a day as we can manage. (Really? They need exposure to someone teasing them and fighting with them? They need to be in competition with people who will do anything to look better than them? They need exposure to people who view the world differently than they do? This is why we give them siblings!

Can any playground crowd give a child more challenges than a sibling? Home is a great training ground for the real world. No matter how much siblings love each other, they are together a lot and they will fight, compete, and share disparate views of the world. In addition, they will be exposed to different ideologies and personalities when they go on field trips, take enrichment classes, and participate in activities with other homeschoolers. They won't be "stuck at home" all day.

I remember when I was in school our teachers always told us we'd be in trouble when we got into the real world—they obviously knew school wasn't it.

Don't you think your children ought to get exposed to a wider range of ideas than just yours?

Your answer to this will depend on whether you think they *do* need a wider range of ideas. Little children don't need a wide range of ideas because they aren't old enough to evaluate them. Once a child is old enough to be exposed to new ideas, you might want to clarify how you plan to introduce and explain these ideas. (Well, you don't have to, of course. You don't have to explain anything to anyone outside your family, but it's easier to just give an explanation and get on with your life.)

The standard belief is that school children will be exposed to a wide range of beliefs and ideas. I'm not sure where this belief comes from. Most teachers share their own beliefs—or avoid beliefs altogether. Textbooks are chosen to reflect the beliefs of the government, and teachers are usually restricted in what personal beliefs they're allowed to offer. So, children are not presented with twenty ways to view an issue. They're often told what they're supposed to believe—then they're even tested on it. Court challenges to such issues as creationism vs. evolution, for example, are usually won by the evolutionists. Children are seldom told there are a number of possibilities for how the world was created. When war broke out while my children were in school, they were instructed on how to view the war. They were not given the issues and told to decide for themselves.

At home, we're in charge. We can offer only our own beliefs, or we can say there are three popular views of this subject and here is what they are. We can tell them what we want them to believe or we can let them decide for themselves, but there won't be any laws or policies we're required to follow in making that decision.

The other side of this question seems to indicate that parents don't have the right to tell their children what to believe, or that there's something wrong with wanting their children to see the world as they do. While many parents do want to let their children make their own choices, others are pleased with the choices *they've* made and hope their children will make the same choices—or at least avoid making the bad ones.

Actually, it is impossible for parents to avoid showing their children what the parents believe or to avoid influencing their thoughts. When we take them to clean up a park, we tell them how we feel about litter. If we make a rule about how our children must treat each other, we pass along beliefs about family. If children are raised without any moral foundation, they may never develop one. At any rate, if anyone has the right to tell a child what to believe, it is the parent, not the government.

Ask your questioner how he thinks a child ought to learn about the choices available to him. If he says the child should be given many ideas and then be allowed to make his own choice ask, "And he should make this choice based on his own value system?" If the questioner says yes, remind him that the child will need to *have* a value system before he can evaluate anything by it. Then remind him that public schools are really government schools, so they have a certain agenda to carry out. The child is no more likely to get a variety of opinions there than he is anywhere else, and your opinions are just as valid as his teachers' are. Therefore, if you plan to introduce many choices, say so. If not, leave the conversation where it is.

What about the prom, grad night, graduation . . .
I have trouble worrying about these things because even though I went to public school, I didn't go through any of them. The prom was boycotted the year I was a junior and almost no one went. It was the beginning of the over-priced

proms and we didn't like it. I passed the high school proficiency test that year, which allowed high school students to graduate without finishing their educations, so I escaped an unchallenging school in my junior year. By law, I was allowed to return for all those senior things, but I didn't bother. I was busy with my new college life.

Today, many homeschooling organizations offer those types of activities for children who care about them. Find one when your children are teens and get involved. If those things aren't important to you, find out if they're important to your children. If they aren't, don't worry about them. It just doesn't make sense to send your child to high school—if that is *not* the best educational option—just so he can go to the prom and have a graduation. Where are our priorities?

Chapter 26

The Bad Stuff No One Tells You

AS I MENTIONED IN the introduction, we tend to put a good face on homeschooling. We are, after all, missionaries for a new way of life and we consider the bad stuff to be saved for the converted. Others may already think badly of our decision and we don't want to give them any more ammunition. However, there are both good and bad aspects to homeschooling that seldom get discussed. This chapter lets you in on some of the secrets.

Your children might hate homeschooling— at least sometimes

If your children started in traditional schools, they probably loved school some days and hated it on others. Homeschooling is no different. We have days when we are great teachers and our kids are having a wonderful time. Then we have days when we're cranky or bored or boring, and our kids wish they were back in school. They wish this because they have selective memories about what school was like (if they went to a traditional school) and fantasies about what school *would* be like if they did not.

Early in our homeschool days, my children used to want to go back to school every Friday. Friday was Disney movie day at their school. In our homeschool, Disney movies were not considered educational, so at the beginning we worked on Fridays. Later, it became our day off. Somehow, in their minds, public school became a place where they did practically nothing but watch movies, have recess, and enjoy parties and field trips. Since my memory was much better than theirs, I remembered the days they came home overloaded with homework after a long and tiring day and were too busy to play and be children. I remembered stressful days before tests, playground fights, and days when their teacher hurt their feelings. There were wonderful days filled with joyful learning in their schools, but there were plenty of days that were not.

When your children tell you public school was more fun, don't take it personally. They've just forgotten. We all do. I was certain my eighth grade year of school was exciting and fun. It was the year I was in a major play, won the journalism award, and worked on a marine research ship for a day. One day, when my oldest child was that age, I pulled out my journal to try to remember what eighth grade was like. I was surprised to realize how difficult that year had seemed when I was living through it. The memories I had of friends, successes, and trips were all there; but there was also my first experience with racism that targeted a friend, a teacher who didn't understand my learning challenges, friendship worries, struggles with big decisions, and periodic boredom. I had pushed those memories aside and retained only the good parts of the year. Your children will do the same thing. It isn't about you or how great your homeschool is. It's just that children have selective memories.

If your children have never been to school, they may have unrealistic expectations of what happens in a school. Their ideas are based on television programs where most of the action happens at lunchtime, or on what their friends tell them which naturally hits the highlights. Who dwells on a dull hour of science lectures? My son was sure he was missing something by not going to school, having left at the age of six or so. When he went back part-time in the fifth grade, he had been thoroughly indoctrinated by my views of education and was shocked by what he encountered. Although he enjoyed meeting new students and being the "smart" kid in class, he was upset to find out that his computer class was a typing class. (He thought they would build, repair, and program computers.) He was furious to learn that the exciting astronomy class covered material we had studied when he was a second grader, and that the teacher wasn't going to find him something harder just because he already knew the material. He was used to a personalized curriculum. He watched children manipulate the time to get out of learning, saw the way they treated each other, and was disturbed by the lack of excitement over learning. He dropped back out of school.

His sisters, on the other hand, enjoyed their part-time experiences and often took a class or two. However, when my middle child was invited to spend a day at a high school, she received royal treatment from her friend's teachers who were told a homeschooler was visiting and might be persuaded to go to school. One teacher, after expressing his admiration for her writing skills, asked her if she was enjoying her school experience. She said, "Well, yes, but I'm having fun because I know it's just a visit." She was pleasantly surprised to discover the work she observed was generally too easy for her.

Parents get to choose how their children are educated and it really doesn't matter if the children like it or not. Most children think whatever life they *aren't* living must be superior to the one they *are* living. It's part of childhood. However, their education isn't necessarily up to them. They will most likely survive whichever method you happen to choose.

Your house might not be tidy
Okay, for some of us this is no big deal because our houses

weren't tidy to begin with. Few homes with creative, busy children are perfect every moment. Perfect homes often have toys containing only one tidy piece, such as a pretty doll or a truck. Child-oriented homes tend to have messy toys—dolls with a million accessories that magically multiply each time you clean the bedroom, tiny plastic building blocks that escape from their boxes and position themselves where bare feet will step on them during the night, and enough craft supplies to stock a good-sized public school.

Sometimes the children have a tent set up in the living room where they're having fun "camping," or they may have a strange array of strings strung around the room that are going to prove something really exciting—just as soon as they can think of what it is. Then there are the parts of a complicated craft project they left on a table to be finished the following day. The mess gets cleaned up, but visitors are sometimes going to show up in the middle of a very exciting day and may get to experience the temporary messiness of creativity.

We've talked about this in previous chapters. It is, I'm sure, possible to homeschool and have a perfectly tidy house all the time. I couldn't do it, though, and many homeschoolers consider it their biggest challenge. It helps if you change your mindset from full-time homemaker to full-time homeschooler. You now have a job, and that means you have to run your house differently than you did before. School is your full-time job, and everyone pitches in when both parents are employed. If you aren't sure what to do, ask the moms you know who work outside their homes how they manage. Of course, they probably have some advantages over you in that often, everyone is out of the house all day so it stays clean. Still, they usually know how to delegate and they know shortcuts, and that's what you want to learn.

In the meantime, just do the best you can. Set your priorities. Decide the most important thing to get done and do that. I try to make sure that no matter how chaotic life gets, I don't get behind with the dishes. Once that happens, I'm doomed. Even worse, I feel doomed and out of control. So the first chance I get, I do dishes. Then I run around the kitchen and put things away, since we tend to be absent-minded daydreamers at our house. I not only have to put things away, I have to make sure the ice cream didn't get put in the cupboard!

Start with whatever bothers you the most. When it's done, use your next free moment to do the second thing on the list. Sometimes it helps to make a list of chores and put a checkmark on the day you do them. Then you can just look to see what hasn't been done recently. When you're feeling frazzled, that's easier than trying to remember how long it's been since you mopped the dining room. Make your family help and don't invite friends over who can't take your house-keeping. Encourage people to call before coming over. Hand your spouse a broom.

Finally, don't obsess over it. The kids will grow up, the house will get cleaned up and stay that way—and you'll be lonely for the messy old days.

Some days you won't be a good teacher

You didn't want to know that, did you? You wanted to believe you would be a miracle worker every single day. You won't be. Believe it or not, you probably don't want to be, even though it will be a great many years before you understand that.

For a parent, one of the rewards of homeschooling is the opportunity to grow. We learn far more than our children do, and not just about math and science. We develop our teaching skills to a very professional level after years of working with our little lab rats . . . ummm . . . children. Freed from much of the government regulation traditional teachers face, and freed from the need to please paying parents that private school teachers face, we can experiment to our heart's content. We can try one method this week and a different one the following week. We can try ideas we've read about and ideas we've invented. This is what makes homeschooling so challenging and enriching for parents.

If you were the perfect teacher on the very first day, never needing to test new ideas and never needing to improve on yesterday's efforts, school would soon become boring. I've taught little children in church for many years. After awhile, I could glance at the lesson manual and know just what to do because I'd taught the lesson so many times. When I fell into a rut and just did what I already knew worked, I became bored and restless, ready for a challenge. When I tackled the lessons as if I'd never seen them before and tested new skills, the class became fun again.

Homeschooling is a constantly changing environment. You change, your children change, and your circumstances change. You will always be tweaking your program, seeking new methods, learning new skills. It's better that way. Some of your great ideas will be disasters you'll laugh about later or your kids will still be complaining about when they're parents, but neither their lives nor yours will be ruined because of it. If you are a bad teacher today, put it behind you and move on. You won't be a bad teacher every day. Just keep growing.

Some days you and your children will be tired of each other

Homeschooling families are together much more than other families, and the time we spend is more intense than it is in most families, too. We aren't just plopped in front of the television together. We are actually interacting with each other for a good portion of the day. As a result, we tend to get rather tired of each other.

When the children were young, one of our rules was that school ended at lunchtime. After lunch, everyone went off for unstructured time. This gave us a break from each other as we spread out in the house. The younger children often played together, but it was understood they would be playing without me. For about an hour, I took a break from them and, equally important, they took a break from me.

Family time is essential, and you need both the structured family time homeschooling offers and the unstructured playtime you have with your children later in the day. At the same time, you need time to focus on yourself. You need hobbies, time to curl up with a book, time to stare into space and dream.

You also need time to be an adult. Plan a date night with your spouse every week and get away from your beloved children. Find a sitter you trust and make sure the time your children have with her is special too. If you have one you can hire on a permanent basis, you won't be tempted to stay home because you forgot to get a sitter or because you're busy. Every Friday night, that sitter will show up at your door and will be counting on your money. Pay her well and consider it an investment in your marriage. Your marriage is worth the cost and it's the best gift you can give your children.

To make your home a favorite with your sitter, don't ask her to do chores. I asked only that I would find the house approximately as I left it. I didn't ask my sitter to cook dinner—I just bought instant food for the kids or ordered a pizza. Dishes could be piled on the counter or they could use disposable ones. I saved special games or videos just for her to use, and I paid a bonus if the children were asleep when I returned home. If I didn't order something in, I left out food for the sitter to serve the children and something for her to nibble on after the children were in bed. Food is a key to getting and keeping good sitters.

Try to spend one-on-one time with each child. When you run errands, take a child with you and talk to her in the car. Don't lecture, just talk. More importantly, listen. Schedule one hour each week with each child and do whatever he or she wants. Remind the others that they need to leave you alone during that hour because they'll want to be left alone when it's their turn. Periodically, take the child to lunch or somewhere else out of the house. You can keep your family relationship strong when you remember to treat your children as individuals and not as a unit.

Sometimes you will ditch school

Traditionally-schooled children don't go to school every single day, Monday through Friday, from September to June. Not only do they have the traditional days off, they also have short days off for teacher conferences and full days off for teacher in-service days—days when the teachers are supposed to go to class and learn new teaching methods. In some states, schools take off for snow days as well. So that means you get to take days off, too. You can plan for them when you do your calendar in September, or you can keep track of your schedule so you know when you are ahead and then plan them in the near future. You can even wake up one morning and announce you're all going on a picnic, no school books allowed, and take off without any advance planning at all.

Chapter 27

The Good Stuff Most People Won't Tell You

NOW TO THE PARTS you really wanted to know. What good things will happen to you and your family when you homeschool? Many articles and books focus on the positives, but they tend to be the same things—those benefits we think will impress the world. We'll talk about some of those, but let's also talk about the good things you might not hear about very often.

When my daughter was seventeen, she helped me with this list, and some of her answers surprised me. (Some of the items are *goofy*, but homeschooling doesn't always have to be serious.) She started homeschooling in the third grade, but went part-time in middle school. Today she is married and a mom herself.

Your kids will never have to eat a school lunch
So many jokes have been made about school lunches that I guess this needs no real explanation. Naturally, this was a teenager's suggestion. I don't really remember a lot about the taste of the food when I was in school. I'm not a picky eater. What I do remember is that I mostly ate hamburgers and pizza. When my children were in school, there was a wonderful salad bar; naturally, my children bypassed it and

went straight for the hamburgers and pizza. Even I can manage a better lunch for a child than that.

Your children will say good things about you behind your back

The same children who will gripe about the hard work and the rules and the missed parties will be quietly tell their friends things they'd never say within your hearing. You may never know what they said, unless an adult happens to hear them and tells you about it.

One day, when my children were young, a new friend reported to me that my children had been talking to her children. One of mine said, "Oh, you go to public school? Well, we're sure your mother loves you anyway, and she'd homeschool you if she could." This was naturally not the sort of thing they said when I was around, but it was apparently what they said when I wasn't listening. I kept that comment in my heart for the days I doubted myself and my decision.

Even if no one ever tells you that your children are saying nice things about you, know that they probably are. I've spent a lot of time around children and teens and I've noticed they usually speak very admirably of their parents when their parents aren't around.

Your children will know more important stuff than other kids will

Sometimes people criticize homeschool curricula because we often don't cover the range of material each year. Our science class might cover four topics instead of twenty. The difference is that we cover those topics in depth. As educating parents, we want our children to learn the important aspects of education. We aren't going for numbers; we're working for lifelong, quality education. Our children will know *how* to learn, which is more important than *what* they learn. We will teach our children to look for the values that match ours or that we want them to have or perhaps even teach them how to create a value system. Through our example, we will give our children the excitement for learning that we have.

Beyond the wonderful, educational benefits we give our children, however, we give them something that is best learned through homeschooling: we teach them that they matter. Obviously, this can be taught by parents who send their children to traditional schools and taught well, but we have an extra way to prove it. My daughter told me once that her friends were jealous that she was homeschooled. They told her that her parents must love her a lot, because their parents would never want to spend so much time with them. Is there anything in any textbook more important than this?

Your kids will avoid labeling

My teenager gave me this one. Although she has friends who attend traditional schools, she says it's easier to avoid the people who choose to hand out labels if you are home-schooled. You can choose your friends more easily. When one of my children attended school part-time, she had some friends who weren't bad, but weren't the type of friends I had expected her to choose. When she left the school, frustrated over the school's priorities, she stopped seeing those girls. When I asked about them she said, "I don't have to be friends with them anymore." At school, she needed friends to talk to at the start of class or to sit with at lunch. At home, she chose her friends for compatibility from the children at church, in her extracurricular activities, or in her neighborhood. She never felt the pressure to have friends "just to have friends." She also didn't have to spend extensive amounts of time with people who weren't nice to her. Although we required her to attend her church activities, everything else was optional. So, if she didn't like the people involved in an activity, she could sacrifice the activity to avoid their association. She was in control.

People will try to tell you that learning to cope with bullies is just part of life. So is teasing or name-calling. Think carefully about your adult life before you accept these comments as truth. Do you intentionally put yourself into situations where you will be abused? When you're an adult, there are laws that protect you from being picked on in the workforce or anywhere else. Adults aren't supposed to take it—only children are. Does that make sense? After all, school bullies are not heroes who are doing the world a service by picking on others.

There is no real way to avoid labels, but why throw our children into situations where they will hear them often— without the loving presence of an adult to help explain the labels? An older child can learn to cope with bullying and labeling, but a younger child has a right to be protected, if possible. (Children don't have to be in school to encounter bullying, though; it can happen anywhere there are people.)

Labels can be good or bad, but a child needs the maturity and the self-esteem to know if a label is valid and what to do with it if it is. Can he make the label a positive? For instance, being labeled with a learning disability just indicates that something is harder for the child, so he works harder. Being able to work hard and have courage is good, so the label can be good if an adult helps the child see it that way. At home, his learning disability may be no big deal, since you will teach to his strengths. At school, it may be a huge deal where students taunt and teachers deride.

A label based on physical appearance can be devastating to a child. If he is being teased for something he can't change, or chooses not to change, you need time to give him an internalized self-esteem which will allow him to know he is wonderful and that no outside influence can affect that. Being able to put off the label until the child is older, or until you're the one who presents the meaning of the label, is a positive of homeschooling.

Your kids won't know certain things traditionally schooled children do

This can be either good or bad, depending on whether you're asking parents or children. My children thought this was bad, but I thought it was good. It's my book, so I put it on the good list. You can put it on whichever list you like.

When one of my children was in kindergarten, she came home from public school upset. One of the girls in her class was having a party. She invited all the girls in their circle of friends except one. "You can't come. We don't let black people in our house." I struggled to talk to her about it without giving her a decision, because I really wanted her to figure this out for herself. We discussed all the issues and options and she decided, to my pleasure, not to go. Her heart was broken, though, to learn that this was how the world sometimes was. Certainly, she had to learn this lesson at some point, but five is just a little too young to understand the complex issues of racism. I didn't encounter it until junior high, and it was hard then. Imagine how much harder it is for a kindergartner! Some children are forced to confront it because of their own race; but whenever possible, I like children to have the maturity to cope with the real world before they have to do so.

Homeschooling doesn't prevent our children from learning what other kids know, especially if our children watch television or have friends who aren't homeschooled. However, we have a little more control over who they know and what they see when we homeschool. We might be able to at least stall the dirty jokes, the cruel taunts, and the bad attitudes toward learning many traditionally schooled children encounter in kindergarten—long before they're ready for them. Today, it's considered a terrible thing to shelter a child; but I believe that when we refuse to shelter our children a little, we rob them of something precious. Children have the right to be innocent and to have that innocence and goodness taken from them gradually as they gain the maturity to understand. To me, not knowing everything too soon is a positive of homeschooling. I believe children have the right to have a parent standing beside them when they face these complicated situations, not a stranger on the school playground.

Your children will grow up knowing you better than their traditionally-schooled friends know their parents

We always know best those we spend the most meaningful time with. When my children were traditionally schooled, they had a very long bus ride in each direction. By the time they got home, rested, did their homework, and completed their chores, there was barely time to play, much less have quality family time. The teachers were forever saying the parents had the responsibility to teach the child this or that because the children were with us more. In reality, this was not true. My children spent more time in school or in school-directed homework than they did at home with me doing what I wanted them to do each day.

I began to see that their teachers had more influence over their values and ideas than I did. Since I was responsible for the way they turned out, I was concerned. It wasn't a problem when I agreed with the teacher's values, as I often did. It was a tremendous challenge, however, when teachers showed immoral movies and said it was okay because all kids watched that sort of thing, tried to make my child violate a religious belief, or made fun of children who read classic literature for pleasure.

By the time my children came home from school, they were tired. They had been with other people all day long, and just wanted time alone. They didn't want to think or have serious discussions. I began to feel I was losing control of our relationship simply because we didn't have any time together.

As your children get older, they will begin to develop ideas that don't always match your own, and they will spend even more time away from you. This is natural and healthy. However, removing your influence from your child too soon can be dangerous. The popular view is that children should develop their own beliefs, and this is true—eventually. However, a child needs some sort of foundation to build his or her beliefs on. It's our right, and even our responsibility, to give our children some values to use as a base. If we've chosen well, our children might adopt our beliefs as their own, particularly if we've set a good example and didn't just preach to them. (Even then, not all children follow their parent's example, no matter how perfect.)

The best way to give a child values is to spend time with him and let him see how you live your life. You act in a way that reflects what you believe; you talk to him about things that matter; and you tell him about yourself, your life, and your choices. Your child will know you better because he has spent meaningful time with you learning, serving, and growing together. This builds a family that can last forever. That's a benefit that makes every minute worthwhile.

You are freed from arbitrary schedules for vacations, class length, and life

I love this part of homeschooling. Aren't there days when you just long to take your children and escape the world? As a homeschooler, you can do just that. As long as we were ahead in our hours, we skipped school periodically to go to Disneyland, to play together in the park, or to just hang out together. My children got the message that they mattered, and that family mattered as much as education did. They knew school mattered because I worked them hard, but they also needed to know that they mattered.

When they were in school, Saturdays were for them. But that was a day we *scheduled* for them, and sometimes they suspected we felt obligated to spend that day with them because it was "on the calendar." When, as homeschoolers, they woke up in the morning and I said, "Oh look, we're three weeks ahead in hours and in our work. What do you say we take the day off and go play together?" they understood that I loved being with them and that sometimes just wasting time together was more important than yet another page of math. Family is what matters most, and homeschooling offers so many opportunities to show your children they are loved and valued, and that they are people worth being with.

From an educational point of view, that freedom demonstrates itself in the ability to spend as much or as little time as you like on a subject. There is a real luxury in knowing you will be teaching the same children from year to year. If the Revolutionary War is really exciting, a public school teacher can't afford to stay on it as long as she likes. The rest of the country's history is still waiting. As homeschoolers, we're free to spend six months on it if we like. We'll make up the lost time when we get to something dull, or we'll just pick up where we left off next year. There is always another year (for awhile anyway).

Kids brag about learning in their jammies and having short days

It's sort of funny to find out what children like about homeschooling. While parents are interested in a more personalized education, a better moral environment, and a stronger family, the kids are focusing on what is really important—at

341

least in their eyes. I don't know what the big fascination is with going to school in your pajamas, but not only is it the part many homeschoolers like best, it's invariably what traditionally-schooled children ask me first when they want to know about homeschooling. If you want to impress an adult, tell them your child is two grades ahead. If you want to impress a child, tell them your children go to school in their pajamas.

Now let me insert a disclaimer here: all homeschoolers do not stay in their pajamas. Some get up, get dressed, comb their hair, and so on. But some kids stay in their pajamas for a few hours. When my children were younger and I gave them formal schooling, I made them get dressed. I had some idea they had to do this. At my very advanced age, of course, having become much more casual, I can't remember why this was. It had something to do with feeling in school mode.

Later, we made a rule they had to be dressed by recess. As teens, it was up to them. Whether or not your children get to stay in their pajamas is entirely up to you. They will look more like they really go to school if anyone drops by, and some children do need to get dressed to move into a learning attitude. But if they don't need to be dressed to feel alert, and if you don't care, don't worry about it.

I think this bonus is really about the ability to enjoy life. If your children are in school all day, carefully conforming to whatever rules are in style, and then come home and do homework, chores, lessons, and so on, they just don't have much time to have fun. Everyone, at any age, needs time to do nothing. We need time to pursue a hobby for fun without being on a team, in a class, or in a contest. Homeschoolers have this time. A quality elementary school program can be carried out in fifteen hours a week. The rest of the time is yours and your child's. Think how many hours your children have freed up to paint pictures, write stories, feed pigeons, or stare at a dandelion. They have enough time left over in their day to ponder where King Tut's father's grave is (a serious concern the first year we homeschooled) or to wonder what they'd like to be when they grow up. In other words, they have time to be children doing the real work of a child—discovering the world.

You don't need a back-to-school wardrobe

Naturally, my teenagers did not consider this a good thing. I did. August was as expensive as Christmas, or even more so. The children needed so many clothes and supplies. After we started homeschooling, they got annoyed that their friends were getting great new clothes and they weren't. We compromised and bought one or two new things, but I pointed out that we had to buy all our homeschool supplies that month. Of course, the next thing I saved for was Christmas, so if they didn't mind cutting into that budget, we could do clothes. They minded. We soon fell into a pattern of just buying clothes when the children needed them. It meant we didn't have to ponder the confusion of buying winter clothes in September when it was still hot. We bought what we needed to wear right now, such as back-to-school jammies.

You will educate yourself

You will, in fact, get so well-educated you will be astounded. Maybe today you don't know what a black hole is or what dinosaurs eat, but in two years you'll be able to discuss those subjects knowledgeably. Today you may stare blankly at a long division problem, but in four years you won't even need a calculator. Right now, the thought of discussing Shakespeare with a teenager terrifies you, but in about fourteen years you will have a favorite play.

Today, words like sight-reading, the Montessori Method, and classical education are a foreign language you aren't sure you can learn, but in five years you will sound as though you have a teaching degree.

Today, you are in awe of teachers. This year, you're going to become one.

**This is supposed to be fun—you
will learn to laugh at yourself**
Sometimes you'll just cry, but eventually you will learn to laugh most of the time. The "do you remember" game we like to play in our home always includes some monumental blunders, but some of them were funny. When I learned that every bad lesson wasn't proof I couldn't teach, I learned to find the humor. If I squirmed at the sight of a bug meant for the microscope or taught improper fractions incorrectly and had to re-teach it later—well, those things happen. The lesson plan that seemed so brilliant on the day you thought of it turned out to be a flop; but in a few years, it will be something to be remembered with laughter (nothing worse than the prom dress you were so proud of that your children giggle at today). Admit it, that dress looks pretty silly to you now, too, and yet it didn't ruin your life. Neither will a bad lesson plan. Homeschooling really is fun, especially in retrospect.

You are making memories to last an eternity
The child who is whining about long division will someday look back fondly on these crazy first days of homeschooling when you were extra motivated and tried extra hard. My children, now teens and adults, still play "do you remember" about the early days of homeschooling. "Do you remember that dumb song mom used to make us sing about the bones?" "Yeah, but do you remember the science experiment where we dropped things off the balcony?" "Do you remember when we celebrated Hanukkah?"

You'll play it too, but you might not remember the same

things. Do you remember the day your child read a story alone for the first time? Do you remember crying together over long division and then having cake to celebrate finally getting it? Or the day someone asked your teenager how she learned so much and she said that her mom was a hard teacher, and then when she taught herself, she was even harder on herself than her mom was? Do you remember all the things you learned about yourself, your children, and your world as you explored it together, day after challenging day?

If so, you are a homeschool parent.

You will remember this as your greatest achievement

Nothing you ever do will be more important or have more impact on the world than the time you spend parenting. Homeschooling is parenting in its highest form—an extra measure of time, study, and love. The time you give your children is time you could have spent earning money, writing a best seller, or just taking a nap. All good parents make sacrifices to raise their children; homeschooling parents make extra sacrifices because their private lives are put on hold for an extra thirteen years or more. Is it worth it?

Oh, yeah! The little things I gave up were not as important or as exciting as teaching my children to love books or listening to them debate the age of the earth. They weren't more fun than counting coins in United Cerebral Palsy's back office. They weren't nearly as exciting as seeing a cougar in the mountains. Not one of the things I gave up mattered more than putting out the word that my kids came first.

Naturally, my children won't completely appreciate any of that for many years, but I appreciate it. No matter how my accomplishments are viewed by the world, I am proud of what I did, more so because I was positive I couldn't do it. It was scary, it was hard, it made me cry, and it made me become more than I ever dreamed I could be. Yes—it was worth it!

Chapter 28

How Homeschooling Will Strengthen Your Family

I CAN'T TELL YOU THAT you now know everything there is to know about homeschooling. There is much to learn, but most of it will be learned with time and experience. However, you know enough to get started on your adventure, and an adventure is just what it is. As with any adventure, some days will be exciting, some will be frightening, and some will be ordinary. The combination of these days will be the greatest memory of your life and one that defines you in many ways. In this final chapter, I'd like to share with you some of the ways homeschooling will change you, your children, and your family forever.

The title of this book suggests that it is for those who doubt their own abilities. I was one of those people, and it's why I wanted to write this book with that emphasis. As you've read, you've confronted fears and worries, but you've also been asked to look at your strengths. If you read well enough to read this book, you read well enough to teach your children. If you love your children enough to study the best ways to homeschool, you love them enough to teach them. If you have the courage to face your fears, even a little, you are brave enough to teach your children.

Some of us approach homeschooling with low self-esteem

and fear. We aren't used to being good at things, and we wonder how we can ever succeed at the hardest thing we've tried yet. But homeschooling isn't the hardest task you'll ever approach—parenting is. If you work hard at being a good parent, you will work hard at your homeschooling because homeschooling is just really good, really intense parenting. You've been homeschooling since the day you became a parent. You've taught your little ones millions of things. Formalizing it doesn't make it harder. You've only given it a name.

You will never be the same after you become a homeschooling parent. The courage it has taken you to confront your fears and your limitations will make you stronger and braver than you've ever been before. At first, you may find yourself focusing on what you can't do: the lesson that fell apart, the day you lost your temper, the months your child didn't master long division. Taken day by day, there may be times when you think you aren't doing a good job.

Homeschooling, like parenting, isn't measured in minutes, however, it's measured in a lifetime. Mixed in with all those bad days and the lessons that didn't work will be the good days and the lessons that did work. Your child will learn things, even if she doesn't learn as fast as you hoped. Concentrate on what went right and learn from what went wrong. What seems impossibly hard today will seem easier in a few months. Over time, homeschooling will stop being too hard—it will just become a way of life. Keep a journal. Each week record all the things that went well and one thing you learned. Put this in positive terms, not in terms of a failure. Don't write: "I tried to teach long division too fast." Do write: "I discovered Jason learns best when I teach one step at a time and don't move on until he masters it."

As a homeschooling parent, you will gain a new identity. When asked what you do you will say you homeschool. You'll come to feel like part of a huge sorority of other parents who also homeschool, and meeting another homeschooler will create instant conversation and connection.

As a homeschooling parent, you will develop hundreds of new skills. You'll learn to teach, of course, but you'll also learn more about parenting, science, math, socialization, patience, and anything else you want to pull from the experience. You'll try new things in the interest of education that you might never have tried for any other reason.

If you and your spouse work together to create your school, you strengthen your partnership and work together for a common goal. You will gain new respect for each other as you each contribute your strengths to the welfare of your little school.

As a family, you will become closer than you imagined possible. Homeschooled children tend to be closer to their parents and to their siblings because they spend so much time together. You become a team, working together to discover your world. Siblings help each other gain knowledge and experience the challenges of growing up. Older children develop teaching skills and learn to interact with children younger than themselves. The bonds siblings create during this time can help them develop a friendship that will last forever.

Homeschooling isn't easy but it's worth it. You may have limitations, but none so great that you can't teach your children. When you find the courage deep within yourself and keep going no matter how frustrated you become, when you learn to reach out to others for support, and when you learn to count your successes and learn from your mistakes, you will have learned the lessons only homeschooling can teach.

Now, take a deep breath! *You can do this!*

Glossary of Common Homeschooling Terms

Accommodations   Adjustments to the way a child learns a subject or the way he demonstrates learning. These are developed to help a child with a disability study the same subjects as other students. Accommodations might include the use of Braille, untimed testing for a child who reads or writes slowly, or having a textbook read to a student who cannot read.

Afterschooler   A child who attends a traditional school but receives supplemental teaching from his parents in the evenings, on weekends, and during vacations.

Auditory learner   A child who learns best by listening.

Coordinated learning   Having each child in your family study the same subject, but at his own level. Some portions of the lesson will be done together and others will be done individually, with each child doing something appropriate for his own abilities. The children then share what they have learned.

Cross-curriculum lessons   A lesson which teaches several subjects at once. For example, a poster about a book on Mars will teach both art and science. If a brief report appears at the bottom of the poster, it may also be considered language arts; and if it's typed, it may be listed as computer skills.

Curriculum   The subjects studied in your school and the topics and skills covered throughout the year.

Eclectic learning   A combination of structured learning and unschooling. Parents select the method that best suits the subject being taught, the learning style of the child, and the needs of the family at any given time. Methods often change as the home situation changes.

Government schools   Public schools. Homeschoolers often refer to public schools as government schools to remind people that their children are being educated by the government, which has an agenda for your child that may not match yours.

Homeschooling   The education of a child by one or more members of his family.

IEP   Individual Educational Plan. Public schools write these plans to set goals and select learning methods for disabled students.

Inclusive support group   A support group that accepts all types of homeschooling families, regardless of religious preference or homeschooling method.

Kinesthetic learner   A student who learns best by touching or doing.

Nontraditional learning   Learning that is conducted in a manner other than listening to a lecture, reading a book, or completing a worksheet. Homeschool lessons often involve flying kites, serving at a soup kitchen, or keeping a life book of birds your child has seen. In other words, they learn from life.

Online support groups   Homeschooling parents who offer support and help to each other through e-mail lists or forum message boards on the Internet. They lack face-to-face contact, but are especially valuable for those who don't know other homeschoolers, for those who are shy, and for those who are on a tight schedule and don't want to get involved in a busy local group.

Part-time homeschooling Attending public or private school, but having your education supplemented by the parents.

Phonics A reading method that teaches children to sound out new words.

Portfolio A sampling of a child's schoolwork, educational activities, and accomplishments for a year. Some states allow these to be evaluated by a professional teacher instead of requiring a child to take a standardized test.

Restrictive support groups Groups that restrict membership to certain types of people. Homeschooling groups most commonly restrict membership to one type of homeschooling style or to a specific religion. Groups occasionally restrict membership to a specific race or nationality.

Scope and Sequence School districts create scope and sequence lists to show what children should learn at each grade level. These are often rather vague, but are valuable to parents as a way to prove they are teaching whatever the state thinks is important during a given year. You can use the language of your state's list to outline your course of study.

Sight-reading A reading method that requires the child to memorize each word as an entire unit. Some teachers combine sight-reading with phonics, but others use one or the other exclusively.

S-Word Socialization.

Socialization The first thing homeschoolers are asked about. A new homeschooler should memorize an explanation of how her children will learn to play with other children. This question is nearly always asked exactly this way: "But what about socialization?"

Standardized Tests Tests that are supposed to evaluate how well a child has learned a subject compared to other children in his grade or age group. Some states require such testing of homeschoolers.

Structured Learning Homeschooling that resembles a traditional public school education with lessons planned by the parent in a systematic format.

Support groups A group of homeschooling parents who meet together to offer encouragement and support for the homeschooling process. Some groups also provide training, legal advocacy, and co-op classes.

Teacher's Notebook A three-ring binder kept by the teacher that contains official school records, including attendance, lesson plans and test results.

Thematic Unit See *unit study*.

Trade Books Books you can purchase at any bookstore that are designed for the general public. Many homeschoolers use these books instead of expensive and often inaccurate textbooks.

Traditionally-educated Receiving schooling at a public or private school, rather than at home with your family.

Unit Study A series of lessons drawing from a variety of school subjects used to teach a topic in-depth. For instance, a unit study on Harry Potter might include geography lessons on England, the making of a mural of the school, a science lesson on herbs, and a history lesson on education with material for each subject relating to the book in some way. Also known as a thematic unit study.

Unschooling An informal method of education in which a child learns through his own experiences and follows a course of learning largely determined by his own interests.

Visual Learner A student who learns best by seeing the material to be learned.

Index

MORE GREAT BOOKS FROM MAPLETREE PUBLISHING COMPANY

College-Prep Homeschooling: Your Complete Guide to Homeschooling through High School

Based on experience derived from more than twenty years of homeschooling, David and Chandra Byers show parents how to successfully homeschool their children through high school—even in subjects where the parents have no expertise. College-Prep Homeschooling contains a wealth of information to guide homeschoolers through the complexities and rewards of the homeschooling process. The Byers clearly outline curricula choices, teaching methods, and activity opportunities. In addition to preparing their own children for college, the Byers have seen firsthand that most home-taught children are fully prepared for advanced education and/or life, and often outperform their traditionally-schooled contemporaries. So far, they have two college graduates to validate their claim.

Revised and Updated Second Edition
978-1-60065-013-0 • Paperback • 408pp
$11.95 • David & Chandra Beyers

The Well-Adjusted Child: The Social Benefits of Homeschooling

Socialization may well be the single most important aspect of education today. With high and rising rates of divorce, drug abuse, youth violence, alcoholism, teen promiscuity, and so forth, we cannot afford to let this issue go unexamined. Today, people feel more disconnected than ever before; but the benefits of homeschooling—including the rich, fulfilling, and healthy social life our youth need for the future—can overcome these many issues. Homeschooling offers great social benefits to kids and parents.

978-1-60065-107-6 • Paperback • 288pg
$14.95 • Rachel Gathercole

Order Now at http://www.MapletreePublishing.com